W9-BSZ-459

WITHDRAWN
NDSU

Interpretations
on Behalf of Place

SUNY Series in Environmental
and Architectural Phenomenology

David Seamon, Editor
The SUNY series in Environmental and Architectural Phenomenology presents authored and edited volumes that emphasize a
qualitative, descriptive approach to architectural and environmental experience and behavior. A key concern is scholarship,
education, planning, and design that support and enhance natural and built environments that are beautiful, alive, and humane.
A clear conceptual stance is intergral to informed research and
design, and the series gives first priority to phenomenological
ane hermeneutical approaches to the environment but also spon-
sors other styles of qualitative, interpretive research.

Volumes include:

Interpretations
on Behalf of Place

Environmental Displacements
and Alternative Responses

Robert Mugerauer

State University of New York Press

An embryonic version of chapter 2 on Derrida first appeared as "Derrida and Beyond" in Michael Benedikt, editor, *Buildings and Reality, Center,* volume 4, 1988, pp. 66–75 and is reprinted with the permission of the Center for the Study of American Architecture and Design.

The following illustrations have been provided by and reprinted with permission: Adler, Goodman, and Kalish, Airport at Managua, Nicaragua, with permission by Richard M. Adler; Sir Geoffrey Jellico, Proposed Plan for Historical Gardens, Galveston, Texas, with permission of Sir Geofrey Jellico and the Moody Gardens; Nold Egenter, Phaseological Schema of 4 Types of Architecture, with permission of Nold Egenter; Brodsky, Hopf, and Adler, Dallas-Fort Worth Airport, with permission of Richard M. Adler; Conceptual Plan of Subcore Concept for Governor's State University, Park Forest South, Illinois, by permission of Lance Tatum; Nuran, City of Illumination, Isfahan, Iran, Masterplan by the Mandala Collaborative, Nadar Ardalan, Principal-in-charge of Design, by permission of Nader Ardalan; Terry Harkness, An East Central Illinois Garden, with permission of Terry Harkness; Glenn Murcutt, Neville Frederick House, Jamberoo, with permission of Glenn Murcutt; Black and Vernooy, Municipal Office Complex, Austin, Texas, with permission of Sinclair Black; Atkinson and Associates, Project for Sierra Alta, Monterrey, Mexico, by permission of Simon Atkinson.

Published by
State University of New York Press, Albany

©1994 State University of New York

All rights reserved

Printed in the United States of America

No part of this book may be used or reproduced
in any manner whatsoever without written permission
except in the case of brief quotations embodied in
critical articles and reviews.

For information, address the State University of New York Press,
State University Plaza, Albany, NY 12246

Library of Congress Cataloging-in-Publication Data

Mugerauer, Robert.
    Interpretations on behalf of place : environmental displacements
and alternative responses / Robert Mugerauer.
        p.   cm. — (SUNY series in environmental and architectural
phenomenology)
    Includes bibliographical references and index.
    ISBN 0-7914-1943-6 (HC). — ISBN 0-7914-1944-4 (PB)
    1. Architecture—Environmental aspects. 2. Buildings-
-Environmental engineering. I. Title.   II. Series.
    NA2542.35.M84   1994
    720'.47—dc20   93-11617
                                                   CIP

10 9 8 7 6 5 4 3 2 1

For Martha and Hugo Leipziger-Pearce
Colleagues, Friends, and Neighbors

Contents

Illustrations

Acknowledgments

Special thanks are due to the R. H. Kinsey Foundation for aid in securing funds which made possible the initial year of research and travel necessary to begin this book and to the C. A. Putnam Foundation for sustained financial and moral support. Dr. Sandi Rosenbloom also contributed vitally in this regard. The University Research Institute of the University of Texas sponsored the conversion of the manuscript from one electronic format to another. Colleague J. Stryker Sessions graciously provided the illustrations for the "Engineered Room Number Systems."

The University of Texas at Austin supported this research in many ways. Dr. William S. Livingston, Vice-President and Dean of Graduate Studies, graciously appointed me a Visiting Scholar to the Graduate School, where the first year's research was done in 1984–85. Dean Hal Box's vision of the School of Architecture included developing theory, thus encouraging my research and teaching in this area. My colleagues in architecture, community and regional planning, philosophy, geography, and American studies have been stimulating and supportive. More than that, they have given me a gift for which I owe thanks beyond what I can say—a place for me to teach and work.

I especially would like to acknowledge the following scholars and friends who helpfully criticized various drafts of the manuscript: Wayne Attoe, Michael Benedikt, Robin Doughty, Ken Foote, J. B. Jackson, Roderick Lawrence, J. Gray Sweeney, and Necdet Teymur. I also appreciate my graduate students' responses when I tried out many of these ideas in seminars, especially François Levy and Christopher Tadych for their close readings and comments on several chapters.

Patrick Condon, Kimberly Dovey, and David Saile have carefully read the manuscript in the course of publication and have provided clear guidance for improvements. I hope I have met their encouraging expectations. I am grateful to Carola F. Sauter, Editor at SUNY Press, for supporting the manuscript's acceptance and for her work on the SUNY Series. Production Editor Christine M. Lynch caringly saw the work through the complex process of publication; her good judgment, complemented by Copy Editor David Hopkins' thoughtful clarifications, notably improved the final product.

I am happy to thank David Seamon, Editor of the SUNY Series in Environmental and Architectural Phenomenology, for his detailed comments, frank editing, and patience that helped transform a typically huge and unwieldy manuscript into a polished book. He consistently has encouraged my efforts to apply theory, especially phenomenology, to the built environment and has been a welcome kindred spirit on the tangled pathways of the last decade.

Introduction

This book by Robert Mugerauer is the second volume in the SUNY series *Environmental and Architectural Phenomenology*. Initiated in 1993, this series seeks to explore the multifaceted relationship between human experience and the natural and built environments. One aim is to examine ways in which the reflexive philosophies of existentialism, phenomenology, and hermeneutics might inform both theory and practice in the environmental disciplines and professions—architecture, geography, ecology, planning, landscape architecture, environmental psychology, and so forth.

In his book, Mugerauer emphasizes the interplay between European continental philosophy and North American environments and architecture. Drawing on a keen understanding of conceptual trends in both scholarship and the design professions, he clarifies various competing philosophical visions and their considerably different perspectives on environment, place and architecture.

Mugerauer argues that, most broadly, these competing visions are best identified as two: first, "poststructuralism and deconstruction," which emphasize diversity, difference, change, and multiple meanings; and second, "phenomenology and hermeneutics," which speak to commonality, continuity, pattern, and underlying order. Mugerauer demonstrates that, for both theory and praxis, the central dilemma toward which these two contrasting approaches point is "how to have plural meaning and yet a basis for saying that not just anything goes?"

An answer to this question is a major aim of Mugerauer's book. In part one, "Theoretical Possibilities," he explores the two competing visions in detail by reviewing the work of two exemplary thinkers each—Michel Foucault and Jacques Derrida as representatives of poststructuralism and deconstruction, and Mircea Eliade and Martin Heidegger as representatives of phenomenology and hermeneutics. To each of these influential twentieth-century thinkers, Mugerauer devotes a chapter that includes a discussion of how the thinker's work has bearing on environmental and architectural issues. In presenting the real-world implications of Foucault's thinking, for example, Mugerauer examines past and present room-numbering systems; he astutely demonstrates how one current scheme—the Acree Carlisle system—illustrates Foucault's presentation of a postmodern heterotopia where schema display an arbitrary and anonymous order beyond the control of specific individuals, groups, institutions, or places.

In part two, "Practical Directions," Mugerauer asks how our postmodern world might take responsibility for the technological landscape and create places that support wholeness and mutual regard as, at the same time, they allow for multiple world views, lifestyles, and meanings. He provocatively suggests that, for a better future, practical and conceptual efforts must embrace the best aspects of both poststructuralism and hermeneutic phenomenology. The result might be "a transforming combination of innovation and retrieval of tradition."

The last three chapters of the book indicate how this creative reconciliation might be expressed through architecture, landscape architecture, and environmental thinking. Mugerauer calls this encouraging possibility "fitting placement"—a style of understanding, design, and policy that respects and responds to the character of technology yet also encourages the emergence of local peoples, places, and landscapes.

To illustrate fitting placement practically, Mugerauer highlights the work of architects, landscape architects, and environmental scholars who illustrate "design on behalf of place"—for example, Christian Norberg-Schulz and Thomas Thiis-Evensen's thoughtful phenomenologies of architecture and landscape, Terry Harkness's Mid-Western garden designs that arise from a sensitivity to place and the natural environment, Glenn Murcutt's efforts to harmonize cultural and historical needs with modern technologies and materials, and Christopher Alexander's vision for making design a living process by encouraging client and user participation in planning, design, and construction.

Mugerauer then returns to his original question of how, in our complex, interdependent world, difference and commonality might be reconciled. He identifies a series of design principles that might facilitate belonging and mutual understanding—for example, finding ways to attune thinking and design to ecological rhythms and lifestyle needs, carefully adapting traditional elements, collaborating with the clients and users for whom the designer works, and seeking creative new ways to see and understand people and their worlds more sensitively and fully.

Mugerauer's book is a helpful guide to the multiple, often conflicting, philosophical conceptions that underlie and sometimes dictate contemporary theory and practice. He clarifies these conceptions and helps the reader realize their considerable impact on environmental thinking and action. At the same time, he clearly demonstrates that the relationship between theory and practice is reciprocal. He offers the hopeful conclusion that environmental research and design might spur new philosophical conceptions and help bring forth worlds and world views in which differences are held together through belonging.

David Seamon
Editor, SUNY Series in Environmental and Architectural Phenomenology

Part I
Theoretical Possibilities

1

The Dance of Disassembling and Gathering

This book explores the significance of recent continental theories for planning, architecture, and urban design. As I began this project, I realized that it would involve significant variations and disagreements. I understood that the often contentious positions led to very different practical implications for critical research and practice. Powerful thinkers such as Heidegger and Derrida would help us make sense of the realm of high technology that produces the huge landscapes of transportation systems and at the same time aspatial information networks. Foucault and Eliade would show us how to appreciate and to change or preserve the ordinary environments, both beautiful and ugly, that too often are overlooked because we take them for granted. Working out these alternative environmental interpretations by applying the theories to houses and hallways, villages and campgrounds, museums and conservatories was as lively as expected.

This subject matter is complex, to say the least. That is why we have problems. It is hard to know what you are doing or need to do. Trying to figure out what deconstruction, post-structuralism, and hermeneutics are, what difference they make, much less how to apply them or whether to approve or descry them, is in itself a big job.

As with the Berlin wall, it is hard to understand the sudden collapse of the established disciplinary boundaries, the radical subversion of what institutions had enforced for hundreds of years (of course, there is a rear guard working to repair and bolster those structures). It is hard to fathom the fascinating cross-traffic among philosophy, literary theory, history, geography, anthropology, and the professional practices of psychiatry, architecture, planning, urban design, and law. The interest in non-discursive practices intertwines with studies of discursive formations. Here emerges a new sort of cultural heterotopia, a postmodern, post-Freudian, postcolonial, and post-Marxist bazaar of exchange.

It is difficult to try to plan and design and make sense out of the environments that are emerging through new buildings with "the plumbing on the outside" or with their elements all askew, or through credit systems with, apparently, randomly shaped and located transaction machines and, somewhere, data glowing on display screens before unknown managers. Simultaneous with exploring these new technologies and ways of living there is a "counter" surge to reembrace local and regional traditions that specific cultural groups have shared. People advocate returning to buildings that have recognizable and interesting forms such as roofs that look like roofs, rooms that we can use, towns that have a balance of intelligible private and public space, and fields and gardens that are ecologically and symbolically sustainable.

Similarly, while many would privilege the house and rootedness, others are restless, seeking a nomadic, mobile form of belonging that alternates satisfying places for staying and periods of lingering with the choice and change associated with the road and open-ended identity and possibilities.[1] As Karsten Harries observes, the challenge is to critique our lives and world and "to make our building more thoughtful," which can only be done if we manage to avoid the misleading and dangerous nostalgia for what has "perished"—as opposed to what endures and "continues to speak to us with an immediacy." He argues, "The world presupposed by such [nostalgic] building not only lies behind us, but we cannot responsibly wish for its return. . . . Authenticity today demands a yes to the still uncertain promise of our future and that includes a more wholehearted yes to technology than allowed by Heidegger's own broken 'yes' and 'no'."[2]

What are the necessary critiques, justified criteria, and appropriate responses? Where are they to be found? Essaying this territory is my central task. Among the routes that weave across the emerging post-structural landscape, one that is especially interesting goes from American problems and environments over to Continental theory and then comes back to applications in the American scene. I frequent this passage way because here the major strands of my work and interests converge.[3] Passing over to and back from others' perspectives is beneficial because it dissipates smug and judgmental attitudes by promoting a new tolerance and understanding of differences as well as fresh insights into what was at home all along.

After almost thirty years of trying to learn how to do hermeneutics (which, generally, is simply called the theory and practice of interpretation), I was able to come full circle, back from the long journey of interpreting texts to interpret the natural and built world.[4] In thinking through the relationships among the natural and humanly made aspects of the world, culture, language, and texts, *the essays took up the old, previously suppressed movement of hermeneutics.* Hermeneutics not only distinguishes, it also helps join things that belong together. Accordingly, it has shuttled back and forth between texts and the world for over two thousand years.[5]

Initially, hermeneutics was a way to understand "profane" and "sacred" texts and a created world. In classical antiquity, Greek and Jewish thinkers, encountering the great myths and stories of their or each others' past, wanted to find and salvage a useful moral sense or spiritual meaning in what, though it conflicted with their beliefs, nonetheless seemed to be profound.[6] The real development of the approach, however, was for the purpose of finding a way to interpret what God had said and written in The Book. The Bible, so the account goes, was important because whereas once humans had understood directly the meaning of the world given by God when He created it, after humans sinned we lost that relation and ability. So God gave a second and indirect key for understanding or reading the world by giving us the Bible.

In contrast, the humanly acquired knowledge that philosophy and the other sciences could give us, though actual, was understood as little more than darkness. As the Franciscan St. Bonaventure said in the thirteenth century:

> Man before sin had complete knowledge of created things and by this knowledge he was led to God, to praise, adore and love Him: for this was the only purpose of creatures and thus through man they were united to God. But man fell, and having lost this knowledge, there was no one to bring things back to God. Therefore this book, the world, became incomprehensible; the key to its understanding was lost. Hence another book was necessary by which man might be enlightened to grasp the metaphorical meaning of things. This book is Sacred Scripture, which again places before our eyes the analogies and metaphorical properties of the things written in the book of the world. This book of Scripture restores to creatures, so to speak, their voice by which they might make their Lord known, praised and loved.[7]

The Bible put into human language a more or less explicit gloss on the meaning of things: how they came to be, how they are to be used, what we are to believe, and especially how we are to act and to what we may look forward. In order to live in the world in a loving way and for the sake of saving our immortal souls, humans needed to interpret the Bible and thereby the cosmos. What could matter more?[8]

While it was the philosophically and theologically sophisticated who discerned the fine-grained senses of scripture and thus creation, the basic interpretation was available to everyone since it was transmitted by ordinary language and shared symbols. Not only monastery rituals and university lectures, but sermons and morality plays and visual phenomena such as sculpture and stained-glass windows on cathedrals spread and maintained the understanding.

Then a turn occurred. Though derived from the tradition that one could fathom the meaning of things, modern science became powerful—and exclusive—by successfully contending that the real meaning of phenomena could not be found in the written or spoken *word,* but only through abstraction that reduced phenomena to univocal concepts understood *mathematically.*

In 1623, three hundred and fifty years after Bonaventure, Galileo would write,

> Philosophy is written in this grand book, the universe, which stands continually open to our gaze. But the book cannot be understood unless one first learns to comprehend the language and read the letters in which it is composed. It is written in the language of mathematics, and its characters are triangles, circles, and other geometric figures without which it is humanly impossible to understand a single word of it; without these, one wanders about in a dark labyrinth.[9]

Of course, there had been a previous mathematical tradition from the ancient East and the Greek world that had run parallel to the literary one. But, this old mathematics became as obsolete as the other kinds of texts in the era of the new mathematics and science. The new mathematics did not work with geometry toward constructed or physical bodies such as carefully drawn Euclidean figures, models of circular planetary motion, or harmoniously proportioned temples. Rather, it reduced bodies to conceptual mass points (Galileo) and operated with relational notations, as seen in the absorption of the old geometry into analytic geometry, that is, into algebra (Descartes).[10]

With the powerful gains of modern science and technology there thus was a simultaneous loss. Not everyone could understand the world through this new mathematics; even fewer could actually carry out the procedures themselves, which were much harder than using ordinary language. So, while there were specialists in both the ancient and modern traditions, in modern mathematical science one could not really translate or accurately disseminate understanding into the vernacular. Luckily, our souls did not depend on the faultless operations of the experts—though soon thereafter, large numbers of people ceased to believe in the existence of the soul. In any case, the complex, ambiguous languageful interpretation of the spiritual, literary, and human dimensions of the world went in one direction and the univocal, clear and distinct method of interpreting physical matter in another, though not without clashing. In the end, of course, the sciences eclipsed the humanities and arts; the qualitative yielded to the quantitative.

The fruit of mathematical science has been harvested in the late nineteenth and early twentieth centuries as the phenomenal heavens and earth and the modern classical conceptions of space and matter have given way to a macro and micro universe understood through non-Euclidean, n-dimensional geometry, through space-time relativity, and through incredible nuclear and electronic information technology. But, some of the harvest is bitter. Not only is the world reduced to mathematical abstractions, and substantial dimensions of "nature" lost in the process, but so too is the human sphere. Hence the acrimonious relation between the hard and soft sciences where "pretenders" such as sociology, psychology, and linguistics strive for the precision and results—*not to mention power, prestige, and funding for research*—of physics and chemistry. Hence the assumption that the scientific protagonists share: the humanities and arts are so far removed from mathematical truth as not to participate in the contest at all.

A large part of the story of the end of the last century and of most of this one has been the revolt against the dominance of absolutizing philosophies and mathematical-logical science, which were shown to be inadequately grounded and guilty of overblown claims to knowledge. In addition, great efforts have been made to recover a non-reductive, multilayered understanding of the wonderfully messy and vastly complex "natural" world and the humanly made "environments" in which we live. This resistance occurred on all fronts: by scientists such as Gödel and Heisenberg; by philosophers from Schopenhauer, Nietzsche, and Kierkegaard to Husserl, Wittgenstein, Heidegger, and Derrida; by historians and theorists of science; by literary and artistic theorists, critics, and practitioners.[11] *The shift has attempted to open us again to indeterminacy, to undecidability, to ambiguity, to polysemous meaning.*

The danger, of course, is that with so many meanings there is no way to discern one from another; we risk shifting from an overbearing dogmatism to a useless skepticism and relativism. The question, as Scheler, Frye, and MacIntyre argue, is how to have plural meaning and yet a basis for saying that not just anything goes.[12] This is a pressing issue for theory and praxis. The question is how to interpret now, for our needs and time, the philosophical, scientific, and literary texts, and through them, the natural environment and landscape, our homes and cities.[13] The way we think and understand through texts and discussions dynamically interacts with the way we interpret planning and design, the way we build physical and cultural environments, the way we open and develop our own lives and possibilities and, since the rest of the planet seems to lie within the zone of our power, those of all living beings. What could be more important? Or more interesting?

In working out the alternative hermeneutical theories and specific environmental interpretations presented in this book, I assumed that the many differences would resolve into a fundamental disagreement. For example, behind the scientific points and general tactics advanced by deconstruction, archaeology, genealogy, phenomenology, and the varieties of hermeneutics would be a quarrel over whether or not our world has some sort of "objective" meaning that we can discern and use in order to non-arbitrarily plan and build as well as we can. This basic tension between those who deconstructed and those who tried to retrieve originary meanings did emerge. Clearly, it *is crucial* to understand this difference and to choose how to proceed in regard to what is at stake. As a result and as I had hoped, after charting the relevant territory, I found that the general noise from simultaneous movements resolved into a din from the two distinct camps. Unexpectedly, the contesting sounds further resolved into something far more unified and compelling, as do complex melodies in music—and not a kind of music I might have expected.

What surprised me in passing back and forth between these differing positions and in listening to them was how syncopated the passage became. Each counterpoint displaced what the other had taken to be dominant and regular; each stressed precisely what the other had taken to be weak. As each group temporarily subordinated what the other emphasized, it became apparent that they were singing different parts in the same song. To be precise, both groups unexpectedly took up and elaborated the *alternating integrations and exclusions* that characterize much of human thought and action and the encompassing *epochal disclosures and concealments* that unfold in the history of culture. For example, it appears that, as interpreted by the best thinkers on both sides, the American story of desired belonging and individuality occurs as a localized version of an ontological *disassembling and gathering* and of archetypal *cycles of transformation* that play through human life. The same would be true of the character and our complex experiences of *loss coupled with gain* in the development of technology which changes the earth.

The differences, while substantial and critical, also finally appear as radically opposite stresses within one larger song, as countermoves to its tune. The apparent cacophony resolves into a polyphony where both sides sing together and to which they dance in their different ways. Finally, then, *the alternative environmental interpretations move within this dynamic of personal and cultural displacements and of appropriate responses that attempt to facilitate "replacements."*

The vital action is not to be missed, even by those who would rather look on than actively participate. Try to imagine the complex song that both sides are singing and to which they are dancing, in a kind of powerful, syncopated rhythm.

The Song of Displacement and Appropriate Response

Deconstruct	Reconstruct	Alterities	Same
Heidegger	Gadamer	Eliade	Jung
Nietzsche	Derrida	G. Deleuze	Sartre
Disassemble	Difference	Identity	Place
Jacques Lacan	Kristeva	Irigary	Freud
Wittgenstein	Lakatos	Feyerabend	Kuhn
Disassemble	Difference	Identity	Place
M. Foucault	DeCerteau	Benjamin	Barthes
Baudrillard	Lyotard	Habermas	Marx
Deconstruct	Reconstruct	Alterities	Same

The sounds of the chant and the moving feet echoing though our streets and off our buildings is almost primal. Mesmerizing. Intoxicating. The exotic dance winding though our academic and professional quarters, circles back on itself to gain even more energy and momentum, sweeps through the usually sober institutions so that they too sway, are spun about by the dance, lose their bearings and find not only their authority pickpocketed away, but themselves left embarassingly naked, emperors without clothes. The dance is fanning out into our ordinary residential sections and workplaces, its rhythm echoed, often distorted, in the clatter of construction. Amidst the noise, corridors are built into mazes within new, skewed buildings and entire polyglot and heterotopic cities are thrown together. Silent inscapes of cyberspace await on the other side of video display screens and through communication networks whose electronic antennas cover hundreds of square miles of remote forest floor. Deafening landscapes are aglow with exploding laser-guided missiles and the smoke of hundreds of burning oil wells. The post-structural sublime opens beyond conceptualizing reason, beyond faded beauty now trivialized before vast power.[14]

This dance is a dance of disassembly, taking apart the imposed structures and actions of taken-for-granted and thereby governing institutions and codes, sciences and technologies. It also is a dance that may promise a freer and more careful mode in which people can belong to each other and to the sustaining earth. In the energetic course of the new dance, the old conceptual and imperial categories are forcefully flung out of our grasp and the willful controls and exploitations fall away or are freely tossed aside.

Everyone, every place, everything is caught up in this dance, this engaging music and movement. What is it? Where does it come from and where does it go? Will it suddenly stop or will it become more intense and irresistible as it goes on? Shall we dance? Or not? Do we really have a choice? Shall we take up tambourines? Should we try to resist even as a potential partner pulls on our locked arm and braced body trying to drag us in against our will? Or, instead, as Odysseus, should we stuff our ears with cotton and wait patiently for our moment of deliverance? As Sampson, chained between pillars of transgressing power, should we be alert for a chance to bring it all down around us?

This dance is a dance of people in the world, of people and the world. Of their motion and rest. This dance is done in time and space. Therefore to dance the dance is move out of the past, through the present, and into the future. To think about it is to think about history and our insertion in the real environment of concrete, historical places. It is to question which of these should be demolished, which preserved, or which built.

This dance is done while singing. Therefore to dance the dance is to move within a languageful event. This dance of people and the world, in time and in space, involves movement between sayings and stories and texts as they lead in and out of our world. This dance occurs not only in the streets and the stamp of our feet, not only in our hearts and heads, but in the weaving back and forth between texts and world.

The disassembly of the previous willful and representational movement shows that *it never was a dance.* Rather, it was the *march* of reason which had triumphantly paraded, with scarcely a pause or obstacle, across the globe, down the royal road from ancient Greek logic and military formations, through modernity's renaissance and enlightenment with their scientific, mechanical, and political conquests, to today's postmodern cybernetic and logistical technology. This violent, forced march had suppressed the dance now being danced. The new dance is a revitalized form of an old rhythm, forgotten for two and a half millenniam, but going on, at least periodically, in its own hushed way, beneath, between, behind that loud sweep of progress.

An aspect of the dance, then, a crucial part of the accomplishment and play of the dance, is its movement against its opposite: against a kind of reason that sought to still it and through which it again breaks. From within the motion of this oldest and now newly danced dance, the opposite may yet be seen as a partner in passing, a partner which while trying to push the dance aside for a more pragmatic and direct stride, was (without knowing it) part of the dance, affecting the steps and changing where and how the dance might go and end. This dance is now playing out in our landscapes, buildings, and poems. It may linger a while, or soon peter out, or suddenly be stopped.

This book seeks to move along with the dance, taking up one step, then another, trying to move in the shoes of different, often tensed, dancers as they follow their own music. Of course, neither the music nor the dancing are simple, but involve an almost bewildering complexity of many strains and moves.

I try to discern and follow some of what makes up this dance so that we may be able to follow how it goes, and thus be able to choose what to do as it swirls about us.

How should we think about the dance and responsibly act as we are caught up in it, whether as willing partners, conscientious objectors, or as obliviously shuffling along to music that we only half hear and that is at once familiar and indistinct? How can we dance, or even decide if we want to, if we can't quite hold on to the old rhythm that already is beginning to slip from memory and yet can't quite make out the new one either, since we are caught in-between? These chapters try to receive and amplify the song to get a clear and steady sound, so you can make up your own mind whether you want to hear more or not. The book as a whole is a kind of guide to the latest dance steps, so that you can try out, in the privacy of your reading and reflecting, the choreography that moves the mind and body. The chapters begin to assemble a pattern book for the streets and the dance halls of yet unimagined forms appropriate for the dancing. What kind of place should we make for the dance that we now welcome, or await, or resist?

2

Foucault: Exposing the Localizations of Bio-Technio-Power

The two basic possibilities available to us today—stripping away what is misleading without rebuilding a substitute or removing obstacles in order to open up to a new positive, historical principle of organization—play out through many twentieth-century theories. The contenders variously appear as undoing versus reintegrating, radical movement versus traditional cycles of completion, surface versus depth, the clarified versus the mysterious. For example, Wittgenstein's uncompromisingly self-undermining activity vies with Jung's quest for self-transformation and wholeness.[1] Similarly, Habermas criticizes French post-structuralism and Gadamer; Rorty and MacIntyre differ; Peter Eisenman and Karsten Harries debate.[2] Though it is not clear why, the more skeptical way of coming to grips with our personal and cultural situation currently is developed most provocatively by Continental figures. Perhaps most powerfully of all, Michel Foucault and Jacques Derrida (following the clues given by Nietzsche in the nineteenth century and Heidegger in the twentieth) elaborate self-critical strategies to continue to expose cultural misunderstandings and to utilize partial views and multiple excursions without allowing these to become new foundations or grounding systems.

Dismantling comforting forms and meanings currently is the "hottest" alternative in academic research, spilling over into the popular press and impacting architecture, planning, and urban design. The latest of the latest theorists, such as Baudrillard, Deleuze, Lyotard, Irigaray, and DeCerteau, legitimately and necessarily try to move out of the shadows of Derrida and Foucault. Aided in no small part by the publishing industry intent on making the most of the postmodern, post-structuralist shift, the newest voices continue probing this line of development, this possibility of brushing away the cobwebs of illusion, even as the very motion of our hands tangles the sticky threads about our faces and as the webs are ceaselessly respun. All of these figures, and especially the seminal Foucault and Derrida, struggle with the same issues. How to arrive at who we are to be and how we are to live by differentiating ourselves from what we are not and do not desire to be? How to identify ourselves and what we would claim within the differences we construct? The problems are there for thinking, for politics and public policy, for planning and architecture.

INTERPRETATION, CULTURAL CONTEXT, AND THE PAST

Suppose, along with Foucault and Derrida, we ask about our relation to our culture, to language, to philosophy and building, but not in terms of individual self-identity. Suppose that without losing the *personal intensity* of the question, we manage to continue to shift it to the larger context, to the arena of socially constituted structures. Asking how to live then would require asking about the contexts in which we find ourselves and which substantially and covertly limit our possibilities. Insofar as we can think and build non-nostalgically, yet powerfully, we need adequate theory and practices, practices applying the theory in order to take our bearings and make our way. The first and necessary step to orient ourselves and to move is to interpret both our philosophical and physical environments because it is the interplay of these two that *locates* our placement, that specifically predicates our predicament.

But can we at all adequately interpret our inherited context? It may be impossible to inquire directly into the relation of the built environment and culture because we unavoidably ask our questions from within a historical social situation and amidst a multiplicity of languages, forms, and materials. We already are enmeshed and involved in the construction of our subject matter. Further, these networks of previous discourse and actions, within which our assumptions and tentative interpretations take place, are—at best—only partially recognized and understood. Our current attempts to live meaningfully and to design and build take place, then, in cultural spheres obscurely given.

What is more, our scientific and technological successes and failures are substantially linked to the specific attitude that Western consciousness has developed toward the past and time. Nietzsche definitively captured the tone that dominates our contemporary relationship to the past. In our self-definition as participants in, if not masters of, the willful control of the world and ourselves, we brook no obstacle to will. Just here, the past alone frustrates us, not only because it binds us, but also because we do not have the power to change the past. In willing change, we need to modify what has occurred, that is, the lingering results of what has gone before. Here, in the present, we struggle against the past. But, whatever success we have in overcoming the past to shape and design the future, the past itself escapes our power. The past is beyond the power of will (as understood in the West).[3] In short, *in order to live and to think, to design, to build, and to develop, we wrestle with the past; we will to overcome the culturally built world that we unavoidably inhabit.*

FOUCAULT'S DISASSEMBLY OF THE DISSEMBLED

Following Nietzsche's analysis of nihilism and also Heidegger's treatment of metaphysical epochs, Michel Foucault, until his untimely death, developed a procedure for the interpretation of the history of concepts and practices. The goal had been to undo the historical tradition and prior interpretations through detailed empirical investigation and imaginative cross-disciplinary juxtapositions. Foucault focused his study on the discontinuous and incommensurate structures that make up our historical, cultural environment, first taking them apart and then reconstructing them so we could see how they worked.[4] What was required was a series of localized and objective projects. Because, according to Foucault, there are no universally valid approaches, concepts, or results, the task is localized and involves undertaking numerous "detailed regional inquiries."[5] The work would be objective in that there is a non-arbitrary, internal correlation between the descriptive narrative that results from the study and the organized structures operating in the world. The latter, even though socially invented and imposed, can be located and described by the former, even though also fabricated. Of course, unavoidably, there is a "gap between theory/practice on the one hand, and what it purports to describe or explain on the other."[6]

Situation

Michel Foucault's work continues the analysis of Western culture and develops the conviction (shared by Derrida) that there is no deep ontological basis or meaning to be sought.

> The [Western] search is directed to "that which was already there," the image of a primordial truth fully adequate to its nature. . . . However, if the genealogist refuses to extend his faith in metaphysics, if he listens to history, he finds that there is "something altogether different" behind things: not a timeless and essential secret, but the secret that they have no essence or that their essence was fabricated in a piecemeal fashion from alien forms.[7]

For Foucault, any historical culture involves a sense of identity, of who "we" are, where this defining characteristic is constituted by historical choices. Specifically, there is a selection from and a rejection of alternatives. The West developed as it chose and rejected, respectively, reason vs. unreason, reality vs. dream, same vs. other, Being vs. non-being.[8] Spatial and cultural exclusions and integrations work out the choice. The selection of reason and the rejection of madness or unreason develops in our built environment, cultural attitudes, work habits, and even in the idea of history itself—since history is our "work" or product, and not anything accomplished by the mad.

In other words, by a series of exclusions put into effect, we organize the spheres of action and mould individuals. Our current constitution, begun in the seventeenth and eighteenth centuries, proceeds by way of increasing rationalization which turns people into validated subjects and compliant objects. Foucault isolates and identifies the pervasive organization of our society in 'bio-technio-power.' "Bio-power is the increasing ordering of all realms under the guise of improving the welfare of the individual and the entire population. . . . [T]his order reveals itself to be a strategy, with no one directing it and everyone increasingly enmeshed in it, whose only end is the increase of power and order itself."[9]

If there is no reality or deep meaning, hermeneutics fails. Because reason rejects unreason and never is reconciled with it, the process of historical exclusion is non-dialectical and idealism fails. Because there are no facts or factual realities, but only interpretations, positivism and materialism fail. Since all these attempts to return to a supposed historical origin or essence fail according to Foucault, he opposes them and believes a new approach is needed to understand the historical development.

Built Things

As a modern thinker, Foucault argues that it is senseless to talk of the essence of things. Everything, including all we build, already is involved in interpretation and in battles or plays of power.[10] Hence, the built and even our own bodies are products. The question is how things are constituted, developed, manipulated. But the answer to this question lies not in things, but, first of all, in language. Though, according to the early Foucault, we can do a history of things, there is little point in pursuing that course, since 'things' are not primary. Language or discourse is.[11] Later, Foucault comes to see that built things play a major role in the constitution of regimes of power and as the instruments of the bio-technologies that operate on our bodies.

Language

In interpreting language, Foucault developed through two stages with complementary views. First, he worked out the idea that discourse is not *about* objects in the sense of referring to them as actual things; rather, discourse constitutes things—all objects and meanings.[12] Systems of discourse, even if without deep or grounded meaning, are intelligible because they have systematic structures. Modes of discourse go through historical changes and, most interestingly, discontinuous transformations. He traces, for instance, how the concept of "insanity" disengaged itself from divine punishments of the wicked such as "leprosy," and from "poverty" and "indigence" in the psychiatric and social sciences.

Here, discursive formations, or what we usually call sciences, disciplines, or theories, can be understood by way of sets of statements. The meaning of a statement varies with the entire web of relations. This field of context, which both changes and has an internal "sense," constitutes meaning. Originally, then, Foucault held that discourse was autonomous.

In his later works, Foucault backed away from that position and argued that the discursive formations themselves occur within the context of *non-discursive practices.* It is the usually invisible, often undramatic set of social actions, especially the technology or action of excluding and controlling, which situates the discourse. Foucault's position partially turned from language to supplement it with the non-discursive dimensions of a culture. This shift marks a notable difference from Derrida, who continues to focus almost exclusively on language, even when treating architecture.

Culture

Culture can be understood as the historical transformations and displacements of dominion. Since, at any time, a culture consists of exclusions and integrations, the question is how power is achieved, applied, and held. Such power occurs or changes through shifts in cultural classification, that is, by way of practices and discourse or theory. Not surprisingly, there are successive regimes of transformations of power: "The fundamental codes of a culture—those governing its language, its schema of perception, its exchanges, its techniques, its values, the hierarchy of its practice—establish for every man, from the very first, the empirical orders with which will be dealing and within which he will be at home."[13]

Historical practices generate historical grids of intelligibility *(dispositif),* a diverse lot including "discourses, institutions, architectural arrangements, regulations laws, administrative measures, scientific statements, philosophical propositions, morality, philanthropy, and so on."[14] The analysis by way of such apparatus, for example, the army or sexuality, or hospitals and prisons, brings historical discourse and the non-discursive together as a key to interpretation.

Interpretation

Foucault insisted that the interflow of discourse and cultural practice into each other is all that there is. In such a situation, we have only interpretation, and there is no end to interpretation.[15]

> There is nothing absolutely primary to interpret because, when all is said and done, underneath it all everything is already interpretation.

> [Since] history is the violent and surreptitious appropriation of a system of rules, which in itself has no essential meaning, in order to impose a direction, to lend it to a new will, to force its participation in a different game, and to subject it to secondary rules, then the development of humanity is a series of interpretation, and there is no end to interpretation.[16]

Foucault 's own interpretive approach involved three phases. First, there is *the regular analysis* of, for example, the seeming intelligibility of a mode of discourse or particular science. This original analysis is what needs to be destroyed and replaced. The goal is (*a*) to destroy the traditional doctrines of truth, reference to directly available transcendent objects, and progress, and also (*b*) to unmask their development as successive strategies whereby they subjugate and dominate.[17] Accordingly, the traditional doctrines and interpretations are disposed by a further *double* substitution.

The initial interpretive substitution, which Foucault called *archaeology,* analyzes the apparent meaning of the traditional theory so as to substitute for it a second meaning, which is its place in a discursive formation. Here all subjects and objects are shown to be a function of the discursive formation and a product of identification which proceeds by exclusion. For example, we have noted how the interpretation of psychiatry is shown to involve the promotion of reason through the expulsion of its opposite, madness.

> The archaeology, in opposition to any interpretive history of the progress of reason, begins with a methodological ignorance of what *unreason* is. It goes on to show how the production of that identity with oneself known as reason involves the expulsion from the common space (and, in practice, the 'confinement' within the designated spaces) of all that refuses submission to such identity, all that is negatively denoted as difference, incoherence, and unreason. Internment and hospitalization come to have rational authority over this other reason.[18]

This move already involves the final substitution, where the discursive formations are themselves put into the context of what shapes them, that is, into the historical and political practices and roles of those sciences. This interpretation, called *genealogy,* considers the elements which condition, delimit, and organize discourse.

Specifically, Foucault's analysis focuses on the disciplinary technology which is connected with the rise in power of the human sciences. Especially important, for example, are the relation of power and the body in the human sciences and the ways in which these sciences are based in the carceral practices and mechanisms of disciplinary power that define and control our bodies and organize our society.[19] In such organization, referred to earlier as bio-power, the body becomes the locus for the specific implementation of power.

Needless to say, Foucault's analysis involves a radical critique of the social sciences. The goal is to expose the dangerous relation of knowledge and power in them, especially by tracing how the modern social sciences arose in the seventeenth century not out of ethical or prudent concerns, but within the context of administration and its mechanisms of disciplinary power. For example, workshops, barracks, prisons, hospitals, universities, and schools transform our bodily lives.[20] Foucault "argued that the fact that the human sciences [especially psychiatry] . . . have contributed little objective knowledge about human beings and yet have attained such importance and power in our civilization is precisely what has to be focused and explained."[21]

This final substitutional interpretation proceeds by way of massive documentation of discourse and social practice and is self-critically aware that all interpretation is war with other interpretations, especially traditional ones.[22] That is, interpretation is part of the struggle to transform knowledge and power. Genealogy exposes.

> The genealogist recognizes that the deep hidden meaning, the unreachable heights of truth, the murky interior of consciousness are all shams. Genealogy's coat of arms might read: Oppose depth, finality, and interiority. Its banner: Mistrust identity in history; they are only masks, appeals to unity.[23]

Specific Implications for Interpreting the Built Environment

Given Foucault's tenet that interpretation is the exposure of cultural relationships between discourse and non-discursive practices, his approach offers a great deal for the analysis of built environment and the disciplines of design and planning. His method includes concern for the ways space historically makes power manifest: once organized space showed the power of the gods, then economic and political control, and now the display of autonomous, anonymous order for its own sake.

Foucault was not himself interested in the meaning of the past since he did not believe one can discover it—there is no true history as a whole or deep picture. Rather, interest needs to be focused on a historical understanding of the present. Beginning with current concerns, the question becomes how we got here—which involves working back, undoing the ordinary understanding of history since what is dominant is unaware of its opposite and its own exclusionary strategies. Foucault can be used to explore the built environment and culture as practices.[24]

The crucial subject is neither institutions themselves as the apparatus of force nor the body as a set of biological functions, but the spaces between the two—called interstices, in which specific, local rituals of power are exercised over the body—that is, the sites where power is localized.[25]

ROOM NUMBERING SYSTEMS AS AN EXAMPLE

As an example of Foucault's approach, we can consider room-numbering systems, which apparently are intended to help users find their way and go about their business. In large private complexes, such as corporate headquarters, hospitals, and shopping malls, ease of movement would facilitate capital development, health care, and consumption. At public institutions such as universities, students, faculty, staff, and visitors need to make their way to lectures and carry out administrative and support activities. Yet it is not always easy to find one's way in such environments, despite the fact that each room is numbered. To better facilitate use, a shift is now taking place, though in many ways it is scarcely noticed or remarked upon.[26]

We are witnessing, in progress, a discontinuous transformation of built space, from the optics of surveillance of the modern world of subjectivity and objectivity to a postmodern heterotopia where schema display their anonymous order for its own sake.

At Princeton University, for instance, there is not a consistent numbering order, since buildings were erected over a long period of time. Older and simpler buildings have relatively small numbers of rooms and room numbers tend to be small. Further, each academic department makes, issues, and recalls its own keys. Here the burden of utilizing unnumbered service rooms is born by maintenance people, lock-and-key staff, and facility engineers. Even so, these old numbering orders and localized, small-scale practices do not work for recent larger, more complicated buildings. A quaint, even eccentric, localized way of doing things, almost as medieval as universities themselves, needs to yield to something more efficient.

A uniform system would make things easier for students, faculty, and visitors. This certainly is the case at the University of Texas' main campus in Austin, which has one hundred thirty-two departmental and institute building complexes, some of which have six or seven buildings. The chemistry complex referred to as Robert A. Welch Hall is comprised of three buildings connected by hallways and tunnels as well as courtyards; education is composed of three buildings not connected at any upper floor; business is a composite of old and new buildings joined in a non-continuous manner. A centralized room-numbering system also is more efficient for campus architects, centralized facilities support services, and maintenance staff. The architect in the campus engineering office summed up the situation in saying, ''The main goal is a perfectly logical system of numbering, whose purpose is ultimately to help students get around the campus.''[27]

Hence, rooms in most buildings on the Austin campus are numbered according to the Acree Carlisle room-numbering system, named several decades ago after its creator. The system is typical of the new generation systems, both in its general format and in that it is not identical, nor even interchangeable, with any other building scheme, as will become clear below.

Upon entering a building, a student walks past a door numbered 2.102 on her right, next past one on the left numbered 2.106, another on the left numbered 2.108. Turning left at the next corridor she passes 2.204 on her left and

FIGURE 2.1.
Carlisle Numbering System. Typical Floor and Room Arrangement.

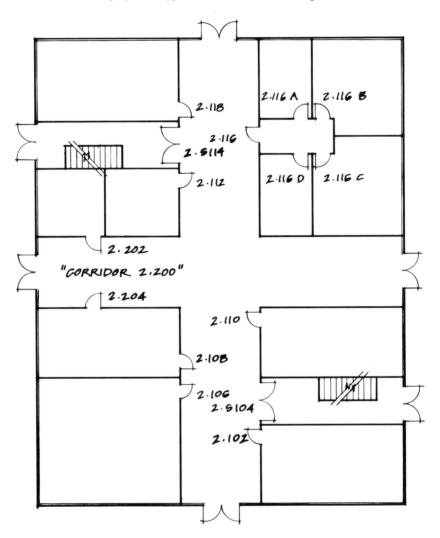

2.202 on her right. Welcome to the Acree Carlisle room-numbering system. It has its own logic. It is entirely logical. Levels are numbered beginning with the lowest level in the structure, without reference to ground or entry level. Orientation to the outside, whether to the earth's surface or to a ramp or elevator that provided access, is irrelevant. Infra-referentially, a floor number is assigned to each level; once inside the system, higher numbers simply indicate levels above and lower numbers levels below. Our student at 2.102 finds that there is one building level below her. One would not seek level 3 for an office that you "know" is three floors above the ground, if that were determined by counting up to the window through which a waiting colleague waved as you approached. If you enter and there are fifteen floors below ground, you would be on level 16 and your colleague's office on 18. Floor levels are logical, and simple.

Next in the sequence of designation, after the designated floor level, is a number indicating a hallway, or more specifically, a corridor. Each corridor on a floor is identified with a unique number. A very simple building might have a main corridor and two or three minor or "cross-corridors" labeled (for level 2) 2.*1* and then 2.*2*, 2.*3*, and 2.*4*. In the Carlisle system, corridors are those passages that open to the outside on both ends; corridor wings are closed at one end (where "closed" can denote a corridor with a fire exit at one end).

Following the floor and corridor designations are two numbers (e.g. 2.1*04*) identifying "significant" openings, a classification of *doorways* to rooms or to stairways and of *openings* to alcoves, which may, in turn, contain doors to offices, restrooms, and so on. Importantly, it is not the room that is numbered; it is the door or opening that is identified. Several doorways (2.1*08* off corridor 1 and 2.2*04* off corridor 2) may open to a given room.

An alcove has a number whether it has a door or not because it is a "significant opening" off the corridor. Any room with a door opening off a numbered alcove is then given a subnumber. That is, if an alcove on the third level, off corridor 1, is itself designated with 3.1*10,* then three doors within it would be numbered 3.110A, 3.110B, and 3.110C. Note, a small corridor wing, for example at the "end" of a building, has its own unique corridor number (e.g., 3.*5*), while an alcove, even if larger or more internally complex, is subordinated to the corridor and designated with the two numbers following the corridor number (3.1*10*).

Doors to rooms or stairways and openings to alcoves are numbered with *even* digits in *the order in which they occur in sequence* along the corridor, with no distinction between the two sides of the corridor. The intention behind the use of even numbers only is flexibility. By providing door and opening numbers that all are even, a new door or opening can be added easily in the future without reordering existing components (since there will be an odd number available).

The particular rooms and stairs are numbered, then, according to a kind of discursive structure that distinguishes and orders the spaces. The pure sequencing of logical-labeling priorities is a *discursis,* literally a "running through" main and then secondary corridors, alcoves, and doorways/openings. A key to the inner logic is that the *corridors are understood in parallel, but room designation proceeds in series*—to use the apposite terminology of electrical circuitry. That is, the arrangement of corridors is such that each of them is in effect an independent and parallel branch. In contrast, doorways and openings are numbered in strict spatial succession along their given corridor so that the numbers pass along each door or opening without branching off in differentiated or alternating left or right sides, much less down a "parallel" corridor. Diagrammatically, the corridor system is much like an electrical wiring schema as shown in figure 2.2.

This schema of heterogeneous circuitry differentiates its own elements from each other and from those of other or outside systems according to a powerful series of exclusions. Within and by means of the schema, the inner building space is distinguished from any whole or continuous system of space considered to exist outside it. Spaces outside are excluded and spaces inside are designated according to the building's infra-referential system. Centripetally discontinuous, the interior space neither is understood in terms of any encompassing spatial unity nor pretends to project any comprehensive wholeness. Organized on the basis of the mutual exclusivity of the corridors, the individual doors, openings, stairs, and rooms are collected and given their identity. They have their place and meaning insofar as they are understood as part of the corridor arrangement.

The order of the system here displays a further autonomy: its schema dematerializes and disembodies itself. The corridor and room circuits are clear

FIGURE 2.2.
Corridor System as Electrical Schema.

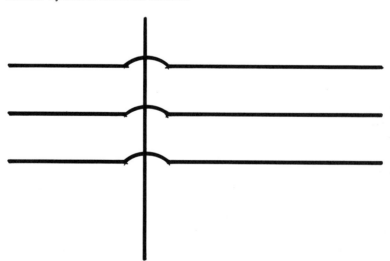

in terms of the schema, but not as materially fashioned or experienced by users. That is, the intelligible category of corridor 3.1 running from one end of the building to the other and crossed by corridor 3.2 means, in the system's terms, that 3.1 is uninterrupted while 3.2 is disjointed, stopping at and restarting after its intersection with 3.1, jumping over 3.1 at that point. It "jumps over" according to the system, in the numbering, that is, as an intelligible sequence. While the discontinuity can be understood, it cannot be seen. The intersection appears as an intersection, as a space belonging to both corridors. But, it is not. The apparent material manifestation and the human perception are incorrect or illusory, are inadequate to the system. Perception and materiality are excluded from the system of signification.

In this further exclusivity the system asserts its own identity. It not only stipulates the relations of the subelements (corridor, corridor wing, alcove, doorway, stairs, and room) as a function of its own order, independently of ordinary perceptual experience, it also asserts its power over any users. Those who enter have to make their way, which they can do only by complying to this system of signs that signifies itself. The alternative is to abandon subjective mental power, and the idea of action guided by reason, to wander more or less aimlessly, hoping to come across the desired number. The numbering system asserts itself over the user precisely at the location of the body, since it is the embodied sophomore or visitor who needs to appear at such and such an interior space within the building's schema.

Among the reported difficulties are finding rooms the first few times, or for even longer periods. College students, used to changing their classrooms every hour since elementary school, become perplexed, especially if under the pressure of time as when taking a final exam in a building where they never have had a class. Generally, people learn to use the building without understanding or learning the numbering system. Faculty and staff habitués make their way to their rooms by visual clues and mental maps: the room is two doors to the left, it is under the clock, or it is called the "green chair room." A survey of users in Sutton Hall, which houses the Graduate Program in Community and Regional Planning and School of Architecture graduate studios and offices, found that of twenty graduate students, none was conscious of the omission of odd-numbered rooms, much less the operative system itself; nor were the three staff members or three faculty who were asked.

It might be supposed that the building room-numbering system, since it simulates the building's air-circulation, plumbing, lighting, and wiring systems, is a form of power exercised over users by those who design and maintain the building and its systems. Perhaps a regrettable but necessary efficiency control led by engineers, lock-and-key staff, and maintenance and janitorial personnel? The hypothesis, old-fashionedly humanistic in its own way, fails. Service personnel either simply operate, oblivious to the system, by moving from one room to the next or, more rarely, possess the esoteric knowledge as initiates. In the Sutton Hall interviews, the janitors, who have keys to every room, did not know or care about the system; two of the three maintenance men for the building proudly announced their understanding, admitting it had been explained to them by a peer. But the higher-level service and design roles are neither free from nor exercise power over the system. To have their identity and power, they need to correspond to it. Those who "implement" the building's system are just as much disciplined and controlled by it as any other "user."

FIGURE 2.3.
Incorrect Interpretation of Carlisle Numbering System.

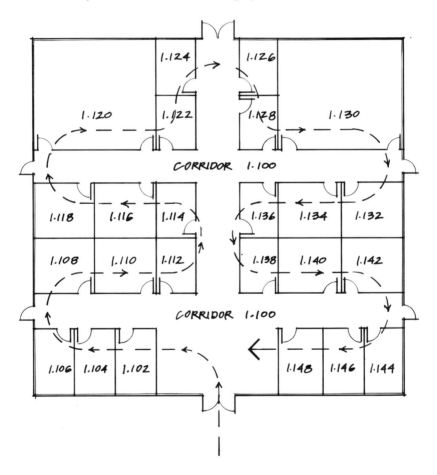

FIGURE 2.4.
Correct Interpretation of Carlisle Numbering System.

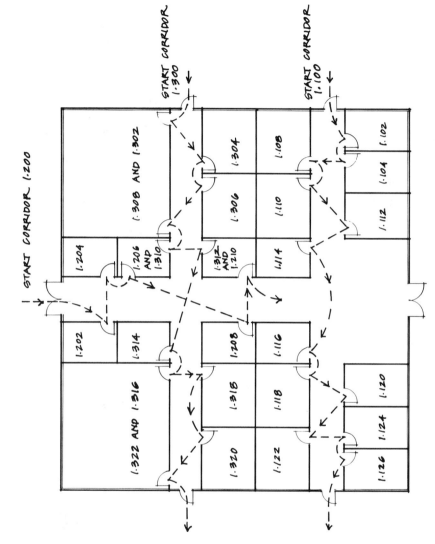

Even if we can identify Mr. Carlisle as originating the system, its application is not idiosyncratic, but must follow the system's own internal logic. As described above, the system of corridors, wings, alcoves, rooms, and so on is very complex. In the case of non-perpendicular or otherwise complex intersecting corridors, the order is very difficult to work out. Even two architects who know the system often find they have prepared different plans for the same building. The measure? The system itself; its own principle of organization. Figures 2.3 and 2.4 are both examples of the Carlisle system done by architects in the engineering office (in the lock-and-key division)—the dotted lines show the order in which the rooms are numbered. Figure 2.3, however, is considered a poor interpretation of the system and now is used as a sample of how to incorrectly interpret the rules (note the deficiency of corridor exclusions/identification in figure 2.3).

It would seem, using Foucault's ideas and the words, that such exclusions and the identity of the schema would explain the frustration and estrangement among those who can not find their way or otherwise fail to conform to the system's demands.

A Foucaultian genealogy, however, would need to go on to locate engineered room-numbering systems within the larger context of historically developed systems that we use to spatially orient, organize, and discipline ourselves. It is not merely a matter of showing that one system is a means of arbitrary bio-technio-power, but that there is a series of systems displacing one another, where each is constituted and non-natural and where each generates a variety of sub-procedures and discourses.

Thus, engineered room-numbering systems, by excluding in their very format the expectations and conventions that many users take for granted, help us to see that our "ordinary and natural" previous experience which assumes that space and spatial organization as correlate is not natural at all, but a highly internalized and self-regulating construct.

What we have come to accept as natural in fact results from the intersection of several conceptual and practical systems: (1) the Enlightenment's conceptualization of space as abstract, homogeneous, isomorphic, and absolute and the ability to manipulate objects that is worked out through Newtonian physics and its technology, (2) the discourse of Cartesian analytical geometry and the practices of applying rectangular coordinates that allow subjects to locate and calculate objects' placements in an anisotropic structure as occurred in (3) the United States Land Survey of 1785. With this triple intersection of discourses and practices, the American landscape can be understood and operated on as a scale of ordered spaces: city block, quarter sections, townships (and ranges), and (out West) entire states.

On the experiential scale of everyday life, the points of juncture of concept and action are at hand in our daily movements. Just as the Land Survey of 1785 located the 0,0 point of the coordinates on the north shore of the Ohio River at the western boundary of Pennsylvania, in Chicago, the 0,0 point is located at the intersection of State and Madison, and the building numbers of East and West Madison and on North and South State simulate the Cartesian grid in local relative space, and structure our taken-for-granted wayfinding.[28]

This tradition locally applies its power and multiplies its influence over our bodies as we move along our streets, assuming that the 500 block will be further from the 0,0 than the 400 block and that buildings on one side will have even numbers and those on the other side, odd. We arrange and find rooms along buildings' corridors in just the same way.

Thus, the shock—multiple shocks really—of the Acree Carlisle numbering system and its like. We find that our traditional convention *does not work* in the new buildings. Even more disturbing, we find that our expectations and frustrations reveal that our spatial mathematical-bodily-ideological convention is *merely a convention, nothing more*. It has no objective, absolute status. It is the product of social construction through practices and discourses of the modern sciences and political regimes. Further, our convention, rooted as it is in a socially made definition of space, subjects, and objects, is itself only a matter of technique in the service of power. It has been used and favored because it allows us to define and locate ourselves as perceiving and willful subjects able to arrange, manipulate, and control all objects whatsoever.

It is not just some numbering system that now is replaced, or some spatial notion. We are displaced as subjects. We no longer operate on objects in the given spatial system, but belong to the new schema, a schema that we little understand and apparently cannot bend to our will. Whereas in the previous arrangement, if we found ourselves in the role of object, say as a body moved or limited by others within the spatial grid, we believed that we could struggle to assume the role of controlling subject ourselves in order to dispose of the others as objects.[29] No longer. As seen above, such a posture is no use. We do not define or control the system. No one does.

Still, we are required to conform or . . . Or what? We can decline to use the new buildings. Here we would drop out of an increasing sphere of the world, gradually living in the shrinking past as an old recluse in a deteriorating apartment, never venturing outside. Lost in enervating nostalgia for what we once could do, for who and where we once were. Or, we might not notice or attend to the new schema that bear on our bodies and action, doing our best to make our way by traditional visual cues and association—scarcely an authentic, self-critical, and responsible action in this scenario. We need to confront the situation and recognize that we and our traditional arrangement of space and experience are displaced by a new convention, where the new one has no more solid a foundation than the old. Indeed, it does not pretend to. It makes no grandiose claims to universality as did the Newtonian space and the Cartesian grid. And, as we have seen, the new system is problematic for its users and those who service it.

Unlike the earlier modern discourses and practices, such as the "optics of surveillance" found in Bentham's Panopticon and which contributed to the development of the social sciences and their constant gathering of information, the new building numbering-systems are not connected to learning about those using the facility. The latter are not subjects for study, not objects of scientific research, not potential data for an objective schema. Despite being derived from cybernetic systems, the new buildings have no purpose as feedback mechanisms. The system is not keyed to the users' satisfactions, nor to the convenience or efficiency of those servicing the system itself. It is there, indifferent to and untouched by the experiences of those who flow through it. The subject, and concern with it, disappears. Unlike earlier exclusionary constructions, which fundamentally differentiated a "they" from a "we" and thus simultaneously created the identity of both the former and latter, there is no identity among the group(s) using the new facility.[30] What and who flows through the system of corridors and openings has but one obligation: not to block the flow. Not to disrupt—short circuit—the circuit.

There is a strong resemblance between the building-user system and video games. We have noted how a person moves into and through a numbering-system, not able to see or understand any whole organization, but dealing (or not) with what unfolds along the corridor's circuit. Similarly, in a video game the maze to be run *(discursis,* again) displays itself on the screen, or unfolds as the game progresses in more sophisticated versions. The characters in the game pop up and move through the maze, until they are either eliminated by an undesired contact or error or reach the end of the maze and stack up. Then the next characters run the same maze. The maze stays; the characters in it come and go indifferently. The latter are expendable, not necessary to the continued display of the maze. So too with what flows through the building's numbering systems of corridors and openings.

Hence, the numbering system displays space, but not in the traditional—modern—sense of the term. Display no longer means to lay out objects for some purpose such as attracting a customer to buy. That modern sense of display was a kind of deployment or spreading out, arranging and utilizing in some sort of strategic way. But the strategy was the correlate of the willing subject. Here there no longer is a subject in control; here there is no desire or strategy, only the laying out of the system's own order, for no tactical gain.

In the figure of the system displayed on a cathode screen: the display is booted up—always booted up. It is there, whether anyone enters and flows through it or not. Simply on display. It stays on display. That is why the spatial schema is a building.

With the new numbering-system we arrive at a heterotopic space: every building has its own arrangement and our built environment is the patchwork of localized, multiple numbering systems each of which, though seemingly well-intended and consistent, appears only for its own sake, asserting its own parochial order, which confuses and disciplines users and designers alike.

The example hints at the power and usefulness of seeing our present world in terms of the ways the past has shaped us. A Foucaultian procedure and range of interest help us to become alert, in the example of the engineered room-numbering systems, to that fact that a discontinuous transformation of built space has "progressed" from the optics of surveillance of the modern world of subjectivity and objectivity to a postmodern heterotopia where schema display their anonymous order. Since Foucault's approach covers both the overall sweep of the social-spatial discourses and practices of planning and architecture, and also the local narratives and closer textures of specific heterotopias such as motels, brothels, and ships, it seems obvious that his mode of research will be increasingly important for interpreting our constituted environments.

3

Derrida: Deconstruction
and Reconstruction

Jacques Derrida also radically pursues the idea that our culturally built world is a desire which imposes itself as a false comfort and oppression. He contends that our posturing takes the forms of pretending that there is some permanent transcendental-metaphysical "reality" to be known, whereas there is not. Consequently, the traditional goal of interpretation—the recovery or retrieval of meaning—is impossible to achieve. Since we need to try to free ourselves from the tyranny of such a deception, Derrida is working out strategies to *deconstruct* our culturally built world.

DECONSTRUCTION

The Situation

According to Derrida, Western culture is built on the assumption that there are intelligible first grounds or causes. In its most powerful form, the first principle has been called presence: the enduring of what is present to us. We proceed from a series of seemingly primal dimensions which have logical and metaphysical priority: *presence* vs. absence; *Being* vs. beings; *identity* vs. difference; *truth* vs. fiction; *life* vs. death. Our culture unfolds as the development of these privileged dimensions.

Playing out the critique of the Western metaphysical tradition, to an extreme, beyond Nietzsche and Heidegger, Derrida contends that the very foundational dimensions or concepts noted above are themselves nothing more than strategies which enable us to assume and act as if the world were intelligible. The metaphysical West, by means of metaphysics, has concealed from us its own unintelligibility, its own fictive character.[1]

Derrida argues that there is no transcendental reality or meaning and thus these privileged dimensions only feign sovereignty. Though such reality and meaning—and our knowledge of them—would appear to govern our science and philosophy, our arts and technology, they are unable to provide any foundation at all. Derrida points to the rupture effected in the discourse of our time which discloses a destructive displacement:

> the structurality of structure has always been neutralized or reduced, and this by a process of giving it a center or referring it to a point of presence, a fixed origin. . . . By orienting and organizing the coherence of the system, the center of a structure permits the play of its elements inside the total form. . . . Nevertheless, the center also closes off the play which it opens up and makes possible. . . . Thus it has always been thought that the center, which is by definition unique, constituted that very thing within a structure which while governing the structure, escapes structurality. . . . The center is at the center of the totality, and yet, since the center does not belong to the totality (is not part of the totality), the totality *has its center elsewhere*. The center is not the center. . . . [It] expresses the force of a desire.[2]

In fact, our Western enterprise has no viable center, even while one is absolutely necessary. Our need and wish for objective reality has led to ''positing a metaphysical presence which abides through various fictive appellations, from subject to substance, man, or the ultimate fiction of God.''[3]

What metaphysics conceals is that it rests on a supposition; the desired objective center only is achieved insofar as a more primal situation in concealed. A more fundamental, but complex *difference* ('*differance*') is suppressed and concealed by the dominating metaphysics. Derrida holds that difference itself—the binary tensed difference or pairing of presence/absence, Being/beings, identity/difference—is what makes possible the seeming priority of only one member of each pair, of only one dimension (for example, presence, Being, or identity). This *differance* is primal, but is no ground in itself; it necessarily has no origin or end, but is just ongoing difference.[4]

'*Differance*,' as Derrida uses it, has two senses. *Differance* means differ and defer. To *differ* means to be spatially separate. Nothing, not even the present or consciousness, is self-present or identical; there is no original identity. To *defer* means to temporally separate. Nothing ever is wholly present; even the present is always delayed. Since what we take to be objective reality is fundamentally spatial and temporal—think of what we mean by the built environment—Derrida is claiming that there is no moment when anything is given as itself, in full self-present identity. There always is a gap, an absence in the heart of reality.

Metaphysics erases the primal difference in order to suppress absence, beings, death, and so on. That is, in order to provide us with a false comfort, both in the most rigorous activities of high culture such as science and in the everydayness within which we are submerged.

Derrida contends that we need to face up to the dangers of living a sham; we need to confront the unintelligibility and non-decidable nature of the world. The false comfort of the illusion of what appears to be established and unchangeable should give way to scrupulous honesty about the situation. In short, we need to be liberated. We would become free if we see that we are within *differance*. Derrida calls the freeing technique *deconstruction*, which aims to show the fictive nature of these constructs which attempt to transcend and regulate.[5] *To be liberated, we would need to deconstruct the relationships of the built environment and culture, since the built environment and culture are built things; that is, our culturally built world is a sum of social, historical embodiments of the metaphysics of presence.*

Built Things

But, if there is no objective reality, what about things and buildings? Are there no things in themselves, no primary facts which are given to be understood? Strategically, Derrida is not so much interested in the arguments as to whether objects exist independently, as he is in exploring how nothing exists as *simply and wholly* present to be understood.

We might suppose that a house or village were an objective reality which "governs" the signifying words we use to refer to them or even the whole structure of interpretive texts. But that is too simple. It is an example according to Derrida, of the metaphysical sham—supposing that a referred-to house has a metaphysical priority. Given the principle of difference, that is, that absence always comes with presence, we can see that what we conveniently call a thing is itself a sign or referent, where there is no final identity or authoritatively determining presence. What we call a house has its sense or meaning in a whole web of references. Actually, for Derrida, the entire world, including all things and buildings, is a *text:*[6]

> the world is a texture of traces which exist autonomously as 'things' only as they refer or relate to each other. They are therefore 'signs' in that, like signs, their 'being' always lies elsewhere (because a sign is always the sign of something else; it cannot not refer to something other. . . . [N]o entity . . . has a unique being . . . apart from the web of relations and forces in which it is situated. The thing itself always escapes.[7]

We suppose we understand the meaning of a picture of pyramids by visiting the pyramids themselves. But, when we do so, the pyramids are not fully present to us; we know their original meaning is lost to us, only partially guessed at. We try to recover that original meaning by referring to other artifacts or documents which tell of the originary, grounding act of the pharaoh or even the gods. But without those documents the pyramids would be monuments whose original meaning is lost.[8] *"Being would no longer be identifiable with meaning,* for there would be being that was not *for ourselves,* namely the being of that enigmatic monument as it was when it stood, in all its meaning, before those who built it.[9] But, so cut off from the present, the past would be absent—held onto only by webs of language. Any built structure is this way: in itself it is partially absent since it is kept present and meaningful only by the web of meaning or discourse we weave around it and on to which we try to hold.

Language

The question of the character of buildings and things leads, then, for Derrida, to language. To interpret things requires an interpretation of language, not only because we interpret things by using language, but because things and world are themselves webs of signs.

What is language? The tradition holds that language, or some language at least, has access to an ultimately grounding reality. This would occur in philosophy or the sciences, which in turn make engineering and architecture possible. Indeed, our Western tradition depends on this claim. But, Derrida holds that the traditional assertion—that language represents objective reality—is a problematic maneuver which itself creates the illusion that a non-linguistic objective realm is mirrored in language.

Difference in its linguistic mode would show that sign and signified always differ and involve delay. That is, the present sign is a sign of what is absent—a missing presence; the deferred is a supposed ontological ground of the sign. As noted, Derrida deconstructs this relation to point out that "there is no presence before the semiological difference or outside it."[10] A fundamental position for Derrida, then, is that sign and signified never coincide nor are they given together. Signifiers never coincide with any transcendent signified thing or concept: on principle, there are no self-identical things or concepts. This means that the difference and delay never stop. The signifiers go on in an endless chain. "Every concept is necessarily and essentially inscribed in a chain or a system, within which it refers to another and to other concepts by the systematic play of differences."[11]

Consequently, language is a closed infra-referential system of signs whose meanings are constituted by their place in historical systems of differences. Even entire systems are unstable, shifting and drifting into obscurity. According to Derrida, the basic binary character of the total web of differences is all but obscured so that, impossibly, we try to understand nature without its difference, culture, or theory separate from practice. And that is all we have to understand, interpret, and live within: an endless web of differences, of historically masked systems of signifiers.

On this basis, Derrida rejects both idealistic (or rationalistic) and materialistic (or empirical) interpretations of culture. Idealism, as the master counterfeiting, which postulates the absolute reign of reason or mind, fails because it would require clear and distinct concepts to understand the world;

but, there aren't any. Materialism also is inadequate, since it supposes we can know the world—fully present matter—without distortion through univocal language; but, matter always needs to be interpreted and we only have systems of references. Empiricism rejects the differences between fact and reason, whereas according to Derrida there are no facts. In Derrida's account, the founding principle of difference shows that the binary reason/fact is primary; in principle it is impossible to have successful interpretation of culture by forced suppression of one dimension by the other.[12]

Against the counterfeits of imperial idealistic and materialistic-empirical modes of interpretation, Derrida's deconstruction insists on a *decentering*. "[Man] discovers that where he thought he was on solid ground—whether terra firma or presuppositions or whatever you name the substratum—he is (also) on language; then, that language is not a ground but a groundless veiling of the hypothesis (itself a grounding term) of the ground."[13] We can not get outside language to establish an orderly ground or center; there is nothing outside of discourse.[14]

Culture

We might suppose that in saying that all meaning is referential and that we are inescapably within language, Derrida is claiming that all meaning is cultural and, hence, we always interpret from out of our culture—a kind of relativism. Actually, he is taking a much more radical approach. His claim is that culture itself is a posture, its authority and accomplishments all maneuvers with no basis. This is an unavoidable sham, however, because there is no alternative.

Culture sustains itself and proceeds insofar as one of the binary terms is elevated and the other suppressed. The historical process of imposition of honorific concepts in the name of presence and identity, and their subsequent substitutions, is our culture.

We can see that Derrida's project of deconstructive interpretation aims to "question systematically and rigorously the history of those binary concepts, . . . to deconstruct them,"[15] in order to show that the whole of culture is a contrivance, that is, a desired ideal brought about through the devices of particular forms of discourse and, I would add, forms of the built environment.

This also is to say that for all our grim seriousness in imposing and enforcing the dominant terms and consequential practices, culture is merely the play or non-grounded processes of all differentiated relationships. Recognition of decentered situations, then, leads to *free play*. We extend, self-consciously now, the free play of signification. As we realize how the signified is a fiction, not meaningful except as different from the sign, we can free ourselves from the illusion of objective referents and also see that the sign need not, cannot, take its place—so the signifier is not a meaningful identity in itself either: neither signified nor sign as final signification need be held on to. We are liberated into the free play of signs.

Interpretation

At this point, we can see how Derrida would claim that all we have is interpretation. We are imprisoned in vast historical systems of language and prior interpretation, such as the varieties of idealism which hold that mind is a key to interpreting built environments or the empirical and materialistic theories which contend that the physical, built world is a key to interpreting culture. Since all these illusory attempts to know objective reality need to be rejected with a disquieting honesty, we must become open to new possible references, that is, to participating self-consciously in the free play of differences. With no prospect of arriving at anything like a final, definitive, "true" interpretation, our interpretation always remains open and underway and needs to become an affirmation of the play of signification.[16]

Derrida's interpretation, then, is not a theory. Theory is pointless. Rather, it is an activity. It is a strategy meant to free us from the tyranny of traditional metaphysical interpretation and to overcome the belief in a temporal origin or original which we can recover.[17]

The tactic is to find ways into earlier and other interpretations, contexts, and concealments so as to undo the imposition and concealment, that is, to expose the differences. We can do this by finding flaws in the metaphysical construction, marginal cases, exceptions, undecided or ambiguous points in the texts or built environments.

Derrida holds that texts undercut themselves: since the imposition of the master term depends on the supposition of its binary, one would expect to find rifts and traces of what is hidden. These flaws or fissures are exploited. "[The object of deconstruction] is to show that the text itself gives rise to figural or fictive possibilities at odds with its own confessional truth-telling ethos."[18]

Derrida's deconstruction proceeds by way of *displacement,* a strategy which is a violent situating of difference. The fundamental move in displacement is to reverse the relationship of binary terms and "consists in putting into question the system in which the preceding reduction functioned."[19] For example, whereas in the West the binary pair signified/signifier has been hidden insofar as priority has been given to the signified as the objective and transcendent reality, which is followed by the subsequent and dependent signifier representing the signified, we have seen that Derrida upends the relationship of signified and signifier, explaining the signified as absent. The signified is different from the present signifier and is always delayed. More pointedly, the signified inevitably is itself a signifier. Thus, *the traditionally subservient term becomes the dominant one for interpretation of the other and differance is momentarily emphasized, even if not restored.*

Each displacement leads to others in the system. Because all meaning is infra-referential and because the fissures in a text indicate the opening of an intervening text, the displacement, once begun, spreads systematically. Since, as we have seen, the interpretation of all systems of signifiers is nothing except another system, there is inherent violence to the dominant tradition, which pretended to elucidate things with signs.[20] Derrida would interrupt that pretense.

This is a process of displacing or dislodging the culturally dominant element and, even more radically, of removing the seeming ground for traditional understanding by not recognizing the master term as such, seeing it instead as a special case of what was excluded from or outside the dominant systems.[21] The strategy is to subvert the system of sham meaning and operation, to refuse the falsely comforting reconciliations or identities by which the tradition has swallowed differance. This displacement of the metaphysics of presence is nothing less than a reversal and dislodging of these traditional hierarchies of power.

Note, however, Derrida is not claiming or attempting to *destroy* the center or dominant terms or to end the metaphysical tradition: the fiction of a center and dominance by some terms is necessary and unavoidable if we are to have or be a culture. "[Derrida] does not attempt to put an end to fiction—for he does not think that there is anything other than fictions, contingencies, alterable configurations of the code of respectability—but only to dispel the ring of illusion which we weave around them."[22] What matters is situating the binaries (e.g., consciousness and the material, nature and culture) and especially the dominance of one term in the large linguistic system, thereby allowing it to continue to function but without illusion or the attendant harm of empowerment through ethnocentrism, sexism, or totalitarianism.[23] The objection that such a view of interpretation is skeptical, if not cynical, is met with Derrida's claim that it simply is scrupulous, albeit disconcerting, honesty.

Specific Implications for Interpreting the Built Environment

To be liberated from the delusion of false comforts, we would need to deconstruct the relation of the built environment and culture since both building and culture are built things, that is, social, historical embodiments of the metaphysics of *presence*. Culture and the built environment form a fundamental binary difference, as do nature and culture. Clearly, the binary has been worked out so we understand culture as the dominant term. Culture, we hold, is what makes the built environment possible, even necessary in the first place. The built environment is but one of many aspects of culture and is meant to be of service to culture. Who would be interested in built form, for example, if not interested in culture?

To deconstruct the binary, we could explore the inversion of the terms, seeing how culture erases its difference from the built by pretending it is not itself something built; culture does this by positing itself as generative and as an autonomous transcendent object to be studied by the human sciences. But, culture can be seen as a special case of built form and environment. A deconstruction would involve exploiting the fiction that cultural presence is instantiated in building by showing how the built-up undercuts or discloses fissures in the goals of presence and identity desired by culture.

Here we need an interpretation of the built environment as a displacement of the cultural desire for presence to deconstruct the relation of built form and culture. Of course, this involves other differences: the larger scope of differences between nature and the built, and between nature and culture. If culture is a variant of the built and so the same as the built environment, both have their difference in something other—the natural. This relation also leads to the "problem" of the disadvantage of the human sciences vis-à-vis the natural sciences.[24] Or, the binary ideal/material is closely connected to culture and built form and needs to be joined in the chain of displacements.

Though Derrida's approach was not applied to the natural and built environment until considerably after he was taken up by literary criticism (and the humanities and human sciences generally), his impact is increasingly felt and surely will continue to grow as "deconstructivist" architecture is inserted into our landscape and as deconstructive architectural and planning theory and criticism develop.[25] Certainly this approach is central to understanding the rejection and reaction beyond modern and postmodern architecture and its antecedents, since as is increasingly obvious, these traditions of design are themselves a deconstruction of the tradition.[26]

FOUR ARCHITECTURAL PROJECTS AS EXAMPLES

Bernard Tschumi

Bernard Tschumi, a French-Swiss architect, developed his Cinegram Folie for Le Parc de la Villette as part of a competition held by the French government in 1982 to develop a 125-acre site in northeast Paris.[27] The desire for a masterplan for the contemporary urban park and its numerous structures and planned activities led Tschumi to collaborate with other architects, landscape architects, artists, and philosophers—especially Derrida. Because of its early use of Derrida's ideas, its prominence, and its strategies of "substitution" to produce "discontinuities," it has become known as one of the most famous deconstructivist designs.

FIGURE 3.1.
Bernard Tschumi, Le Parc De La Villette, Paris

Tschumi played upon the ideas that technology now provides the model that nature once did and that differences among designers and changes in use over time were inevitable. For those intended local interpretations, he provided an *a priori* external and independent structure: the point grid which would serve as background and mediator for the heterogeneous collection of built elements. He explicitly used the term "deconstruction" to explain that he wanted to avoid conventional principles of organization and their constraints. "Our aim was to displace the traditional opposition between program and architecture, and to extend questioning of other architectural conventions through operations of superimposition, permutation and substitution to achieve 'a reversal of the classical opposition and a general displacement of system,' as Jacques Derrida has written, in another context, in *Marges.*"[28]

To take apart traditional distinctions and procedures, Tschumi encouraged elements in the park to work against convention, against their urban context, and against each other, so that totality would be impossible, and instead, the built environment, as a text, would be something "undecidable." Instead of contextuality, where buildings fit their urban and natural surroundings, he sought intertextuality among the dislocated buildings and their dispersed meanings.

It seems fitting to begin to discuss deconstructive environments by considering such an explicitly deconstructivist and famous project, with its undeniably heterotopian areas and multiple building fragments that deny the park in traditional geometric or organic forms and that refuse the integration of built institutions in the natural context. But, in fact, in several ways the attempt fails as a deconstruction because it not only assumes, but holds on to and uses, several of the deep conventions that it would overcome.

By beginning with the point grid as the mediating structure, Tschumi thinks in a formally Enlightenment manner as much as Newton did. Without an independent, absolute ground, individual objects apparently cannot appear or be deployed. Though Tschumi would assert the crucial difference lies in his rejection of the order of modern rational science, both he and it share the unquestioned assumption that space and order are prior to objects. Tschumi's first move is nothing other that to reestablish a Kantian *a priori* possibility for the experience of difference and change.

Secondly, as feminist criticism, such as Carolyn Merchant's in *The Death of Nature,* or radical ecology would make clear, Tschumi exhibits a classic male tendency to destroy nature. He blows up—or ignores—nature with the conceptualization and his engineered environment. Of course, his project is deconstructive; but, there is more going on here since he proceeds by way of a stereotypical "male" game of power and control. He sets up the grid; he blows it up. A little boy's game made architecture. He denies nature by the grid; he denies the latter while depending upon it and willing it.

That both the uncritical modern mathematical-rationalism and the male scientific-technological moves against nature *occur together* is crucial, since Tschumi's willingness to exhibit the destructive force of the architect, instead of the integrative possibilities, shows that this deconstruction wants to retain its claim to *control*. It does not, then, pass beyond typical Western male, professional dominance and willfulness, but yields to it. It is an insistent or willful destruction, not a deconstruction.

This is all the clearer when we consider that it was *not necessary* for Tschumi to posit an abstract, fictional grid in the first place, since he could have taken the actual, existing historical context, itself already irregular and non-totalizable. Since he could have moved by way of collage without the rationalized gridding as the initial move, that modern need appears as all the more inherent in his approach, and thus telling. If he takes it for granted, he operates uncritically as a modern; if he critically reposits it when not necessary, he operates willfully in the modern and dominant manner, all over again. Either way, the very power and accomplishment of the work against nature and context show that Le Parc de la Villette does not achieve what deconstruction desires: removal of posturing traditional (male and rationalistic-scientific) power for the sake of liberation.

Peter Eisenman

Given these indications of the persistence of rationalistic grids of space and male power that need to be undone, a perhaps more deeply deconstructive approach might be found in Peter Eisenman's museum for California State University at Long Beach and his more recent Wexner Center for the Visual Arts at Ohio State University. Eisenman, as the theoretician and designer who perhaps most explicitly utilizes Derrida's approach, contends that reality is what we reassemble after disassembling the illusion of the beliefs, stories, and norms of the traditional past.[29] Eisenman has been in the avant garde pushing architectural design beyond its usual concerns with functionalism and the socially comfortable. His early and unbuilt projects aim to force us to attend to what we take for granted about the forms and uses of buildings, attacking "the traditional notion of how you occupy a house."[30] The ordinary world of Western common sense and science, for Derrida and Eisenman, is precisely the realm to be unmasked as unreality, the posturing of prior fiction as supposed reality. The only authentic gesture would be the acknowledgment and announcement of fiction.

As Eisenman explains the process, architecture proceeds by a continual set of dislocations, to produce a place that is no place, no object, no shelter, and that has no scale, no time. Construction is begun by deconstruction of superimposed texts or fictions. For the Long Beach museum, these include traces of water at the site (river, coastline, channel), traces of the faultline, traces of the first white settlement of 1849 and of the first land division in 1949. Transferring each of the tracings, or mapped fictions, to computer graphics makes possible the rotation of all superpositions, until one hits upon the "chosen" combination. In the final steps, the building is filled in, not as a mass or set of fixed, functional elements, but as a continuation of the game, until the architecture is gone.

Similarly, in his built Wexner Center for the Visual Arts at Ohio State University in Columbus, Eisenman plays with and mediates two preexisting grids in the city that meet at the campus' edge. Within the marked grid of Columbus, the campus grid is askew by twelve and a half degrees, a splay marked in the sidewalk paving patterns across the street from the Center. Using his strategy of deconstruction of superimposed traces, in addition to the two grids, the architect represents the twin towers and red brick of an armory previously located on the site, native wildgrasses (in landscaped beds between the scaffold and the outside street), the grid gone vertical in the linear scaffolding of the corridors that connect the new galleries with the two preexisting buildings, and time itself, which is told, not by a clock in a tower, but by the scaffolding itself which vibrates in a "chime-like" manner.

The interior carries out this complex superimposition of forms, spaces, and materials, not allowing resolution in an unity, but instead attempting to hold the diversity in a physical stasis—for this complexity, for this moment. Thus, the stairs down from the entrance to the galleries do not aim at formal completion or symmetry, nor are the columns meant to support or uniformly organize space. The interior and its experience attempt to "remain open" and the visitor is expected to participate in the play.

Clearly, Eisenman aims to operate as an artist even while claiming that the project authors itself, where "artist" is understood in terms of psychoanalytic therapy. As one personally retraces the story of one's past to undo its effect, one's designs also aid in the articulation which overcomes itself. Or, in using the past as an instrument for production of its own displacement/ replacement, Eisenman's work partially reassembles the work of the Russian constructivists earlier in the century. They too aimed at overcoming the established order by four-dimensional collage and produced volumes which were fully articulated yet without actuality. Vladimer Tatlin's Monument to the Third International, 1910–20, modeled though never built, imagined geometrical elements which would have revolved at different speeds, thus combining an openwork structure of wood, glass, and steel with time and change.

In Eisenman's work we see how elaborate theory and the *process* of design make clear the desire to transform the commonly given reality through the power of creative fiction; so too does the *mode* of *presentation* of architect

and architecture: a masterful staging of event, as technically accomplished and easily beautiful. Everything is completely self-consistent: personal appearance and manner, architectural theory, process, and product all under control, in a polished and interesting unfolding of themselves before our very eyes.

Still, even if the judgment of Eisenman's work is suspended, we clearly are in the arena of the power of artistic creation. Straightforwardly and without regret, Eisenman acknowledges that the issue is one of control. He evokes the idea of "auratic" art.[31] The object is the transformation of self and environment from the vantage point of the needs of the architect, not that of patrons or users. Would it be too strong to say that in its way, Eisenman's museum for California State University is not livable?

Evidence for the force of this criticism can be found in Eisenman's recent statements and projects. He now acknowledges that he has decided to attend more to clients' needs.[32] And, as can be seen in Columbus, not only is the Wexner Center built whereas the museum at Long Beach is not, but the Wexner has led to another, though more mundane, project down the street, the Columbus Convention Center. Insofar as this interpretation is appropriate, we come full circle, back to the willful manipulation of building, which precisely while successful in creating a new story of and scene for the things which are supposed to be as they appear, simultaneously suppresses sustained and shared human belonging to what we usually call reality.

Obviously, the task of the fictive destruction and transformation of ordinary reality is not able to be accomplished once and for all. Eisenman's work, as a series of projects, attests to that. Yet, whereas Eisenman does disassemble the natural and cultural constituents for his projects, he practically goes on, at the end of the process, to settle on a new and "random" composite by *choosing* one possibility and letting go of the others. It seems that the decision to specify when "it is done" is a formal, perhaps "aesthetic" one. Is a stronger position necessary in the face of the illusions of reality? Is it possible to keep the choices always open or to move beyond formalism?

Co-op Himmelblau

Wolfgang Prix and Helmut Swiczinsky, a team designing as Co-op Himmelblau, have generated a series of highly original designs, especially for urban infill or renovation projects in Vienna. They are interested in process, rather than object-oriented architecture. Co-op Himmelblau can be understood as advocating a more radical position than Eisenman—choosing building forms which hold in tension what cannot be settled: ambiguous and undefined spatial forms and experiences for today's urban environment.[33] For architects and users alike, the opening and freedom would be maintained, beyond the creative process, in the building itself.

The project, seen through the work of Co-op Himmelblau, could be to generate freeing fictions over and over. As the earlier modern architects stripped away the accretion of false symbols and meaningless architectural vocabulary, with austere honesty as in the case of Loos, today we would need to fight contemporary forms of conservatism. The latter, for example, appears in the forms of postmodernism which attempt to avoid both the past and future by masquerading in the recovery and use of historically valid forms or in the neoconservative movement orbiting around Leon Krier and the Prince of Wales.[34] To face the fear of change would be to confront and reject "an architecture of building"—understood as fixed forms which determine social behavior and are able to withstand change.

The insistent stripping away of the pretense of safe, completed architecture would require a continuous mode of destruction, including the refusal to reassert determined space and correlate proper, programmed use. The requisite architecture would resist reaccommodating itself to convention. The ideology and buildings of architectural partners Wolfgang Prix and Helmut Swiczinsky strive to burst through such illusion and pretense and keep free. The project, then, is to follow a course which is bold and disposed to the non-ending experience of open architecture in today's urban situation.

Even at first encounter, Co-op Himmelblau's buildings appear as destructions, as *explosions*. Building elements pierce facades; in interiors, severe and sharp geometrical elements are flung about. The distorted sheet-metal wings of the angel over the stage of The Red Angel pierce the ceiling; its stainless steel tone line ruptures the facade, bursting outside, then returning. The stainless steel wing and open metal stairway protrude through the front wall and out over the pavement of the studio/workshop Atelier Baumann. These buildings present, not so much the aftermath of an explosion witnessed, as the explosion in process, suspended for the moment.

The freedom of open space involves continuing tension, both in the buildings, and prior to that, in the design process, which would need to accept and sustain the tension resulting from unresolved openness and choice. The account of Co-op Himmelblau's working procedure confirms Derrida's account of the generative power of language. The partners explain the power as proceeding from prolonged discussions that end when, in a communicative act, sketches are produced and a model straightforwardly made. From the word comes design; but, design itself is the complex superimposition of multiple views and cross-sections.

The multiple, tensed dimensions of design/sketch are somewhat resolved as complex, alternative flowpaths for users. That is, any resolution lies not in reduction, but in discerned still-open choice. One acts now, this way, and momentarily chooses a way through the ambiguity. But, the spaces remain open for other users to fill in other ways, so neither space nor behavior is deter-

FIGURE 3.3.
Co-op Himmelblau, The Red Angel, Vienna Sheet-Metal Wings Pierce the Facace

mined by building or architect. The buildings become the stage for human drama, as is recognized in the presentation of Atelier Baumann in *Architecture d'Aujourd' hui* where a script appears as a running account of the events happening there.[35] Given this simultaneous volatile scene for action, the suspended cage-like platforms as much shelter users as provide space for activity in the midst of possibilities.

The buildings, then, remain "taut and tense"—phrases ubiquitous in criticism of Co-op Himmelblau. The inner logic here refuses resolution, holding-off by enduring the tension—a logic manifest in the envelope, facade, and exterior, which gives neither one way nor another. The tension of multiple dimensions, of future choices, are held in and by the features. Because the entire building vigorously holds on to openness and freedom, accepting their tensions, the overall effect is powerful. The feeling of *distortion and twist* is like the experience of massive sheets of winter ice groaning under building pressure, ready to shatter and pile upon themselves as that pressure builds and tension seeks, but does not yet find, release.

Still, in its attempt to locate architecture at the center of an experience of our unresolvable situation, Co-op Himmelblau is tugged, in part, by an ideology it would need to transcend. With Derrida, in the modern voice, the architects insist that "there is no truth"; yet, simultaneously, they affirm the acceptance of the city as it is, and advocate pulling back toward the tattered urban reality.[36] The insistence on urban materials in The Red Angel—corrugated metal doors and interior wall panels, industrial guard rails, concrete and asphalt —discloses at its center, as Derrida held it would, that just when we admit there are no truths or resolutions, we inevitably desire and seek them. Finally, wanting it both ways, we must not pretend resolution. Instead, bound together in undefined space, engaged architects and users would need to accept the tension as a source of honesty and freedom. The common task is to avoid the numbing everydayness by maintaining a "constant, unsettling awareness."

If Co-op Himmelblau, despite its best efforts, cannot sustain itself as the mere destruction of convention without, in the end, reconstituting space according to conventions of its own—as Tschumi and Eisenman also found— then a still more sophisticated and more adequate deconstruction is called for, one which still would emphasize differences with previous conventions and yet also would assume responsibility for reassembly that might serve as a new cultural fiction. *In short, deconstruction requires both displacement of posturing superiority and its replacement with a habitable reconstruction.*

While Coop Himmelblau insists on its buildings as part of our contemporary life world, they nonetheless—in final accord with their core/originary vision and name—appear ready to float away and fly.[37] For all their urban grit, in the refusal to be an architecture of reification, they hover close to disembodiment as noun giving way to verb, object to event.

Ambasz

Is it possible to push, in a similar vein, to an architectural deconstruction that moves not to the sky, but down to earth? Is it possible to move beyond the metaphysics that is directed to dimensions of reality, beyond even Tschumi's, Eisenman's, and Co-op Himmelblau's deconstructions of what, after all, is a world of our own making? That is, can there be an architectural deconstruction not only of cultural meaning and products, including our urban environment, but of the natural world?

While the deconstructions of Eisenman and Co-op Himmelblau are perhaps the purest in their refusal to become fixed environments and while their success as events held as much in tension and process as building allows, even this does not fulfill the fullest sense of deconstruction. To be brought to conclusion, deconstruction not only involves the destruction of the posturing superiority, but its replacement with a reconstruction. The fiction must displace and then replace. Hence, the question remains, not so much what is the purest destruction, but what is the most efficacious reficitonalization. This asks about the architectural deconstruction of not only cultural meaning and products, including our urban environment, but of the natural world in relation to the cultural; and, it asks about a fiction that we could inhabit.

A plausible, habitable discourse is spun and reiterated by Emilio Ambasz's Lucile Halsell Conservatory in San Antonio, Texas.[38] Generally, Armasz has made a reputation by poetically combining sophisticated technology and sensitivity to landscape or site to generate and arrange heterogeneous places. He too displaces a cultural posture—the relation of culture and nature—by a series of inversions. In addition, however, he goes on to reinstate the built complex as a new, autonomous cultural realm with its own conventions.

The official text preceding the project does not disclose the radical nature of Ambasz's project. Of course, the forms displayed in graphics and models are striking; but, the accompanying official narrative stresses continuity with local place: the new complex is said to be integrated with the surrounding hills and climate, to the community's interest in ceremony and processions (a religious allusion). The project announces that it maintains and enhances the diversity already there. This slick program is not very convincing; it sounds as if it is mouthing—dangerously close to parodying—clichés that judges want to hear.[39]

Yet, even a first glance at the building complex makes clear that the conservatory is very different from the rest of the preexisting garden complex. One obvious way in which the new project might be said to fit would be as an element in a heterogeneous garden. The juxtaposition of different forms in a collective "garden" is not unusual. Together, the novel parts serve to attract visitors and provide an interesting experience, one which draws them

FIGURE 3.4.
Emilio Ambasz, Lucile Halsell Conservatory, San Antonio

back again. The unity, parallel to a fair's, comes from the idea of a "variety of garden elements": formal gardens (rose, herb, old-fashioned, sacred, garden for the blind), Texas natural settings (hill country, east Texas pineywoods, south Texas plains), Gazebo Hill Overlook, Outdoor Theater, Xeriscape, and Conservatory Complex. At this mundane level of ensemble, the conservatory does work: it is a *tour de force,* the most "different" and curious component. The building complex and plants surely are a major draw. Equally compelling is the occasion for active and varied participation. Visitors meander and go straight, move from full sunshine to shadow and shade, rotate up and spiral down, pass inside and outside, look, smell, and feel. The conservatory draws our bodies in. We want to move there. In this way, the buildings continue, as well as newly enhance, the overall experience of the gardens.

But, Ambasz's project operates at two deeper levels. The conservatory reverses the dominant concepts and forms of traditional garden culture and, finally, asserts its own reversal. That is, the building and its discourse constitute a new fictive text which deconstructs its predecessors and establishes itself as the replacement.

In a first decentering, the identity of a botanical garden is undone. It seems that Ambasz has proposed a building complex intelligible as a development of the tradition of greenhouses. In the West, we have used technology to cultivate exotic and interesting plants in hostile climates or during hostile times of the year. Glass and glazing have long been techniques to overcome the natural processes that otherwise would prevent our cultivation and enjoyment of the vegetative realm. With greenhouses and, more elaborately, crystal palaces, we assert culture over nature.

Ambasz does more than merely continue this tradition of straightforward domination of culture over nature. He plays with the relationship, establishing the difference between his garden and the traditional forms, rather than their identity and continuity. Specifically, traditional greenhouses impose themselves between natural dimensions: the glazed glass and controlled ventilation are vessels for the delicate plants, holding them in sheltered containment between sun above and earth below. Greenhouses hold the cold earth below at a distance from the plants and bring the sun's light and warmth closer. Thus, the glass building moves the plant away from earth toward sun.

In Ambasz's conservatory, the earth itself becomes a container, protecting the plants from the sun. Here the traditional relationship is unexpectedly inverted: hot sun, not cold earth, is the threat; earth, not glass, is the container. In Derrida's terms, Ambasz replaces the traditional identities of greenhouse and garden and the presence of sun with the difference of his building project and the reduction or "absence" of sun. Of course, nature does not replace culture in Armbasz's conservatory. But nature (earth) temporarily displaces culture (greenhouse), only to be immediately transformed into its own opposite: nature becomes a technological element or instrument used to culturally overcome nature—that is, itself. Unlike nature transformed as happens when sand changed into glass, *this earth is transformed and nonetheless is left to appear as earth: a deft double deconstruction accomplishes the final semblance of matters unchanged.*

A second displacement is carried out in regard to the cultural forms of the botanical garden. Beyond the relation of the binary pair nature-culture just considered, the identity and continuity of cultural forms also comes into question. Again, the official discourse of the project asserts the continuity with the surrounding regional forms. For instance, the text speaks of the "garden patio or courtyard characteristic of Texas."

But, the new addition bears no resemblance to what is already there. No unity is promoted. The vaunted courtyard form strongly contrasts with the already existing gathering place. The open, grassed area articulated by the limestone walls from the old reservoir of the 1890s and a wooden arbor have a convincing simplicity and power of entirely different order. Here, the new complex's contrast and discontinuity with local tradition could not be stronger. Similarly, the evocation of cultural tradition, with religious connotation, is not borne out in the building. The text tells us that the conservatory is as a secular temple with a strong sense of procession. What identifications are evoked? The strong Roman Catholic tradition of the area? The earlier indigenous religious traditions with their pyramids? Or the Egyptian pyramids, as quoted in the Palm House?

Not unexpectedly, on closer inspection, the conservatory has no correlate or finally grounding referent. The building-as-text means nothing by way of reference to and continuation of objective natural or cultural tradition. Rather, the text collapses back into itself. What the building and its discourse accomplish first appears to be an opening to a new mode of building; finally, the signified is deferred and the building remains as a pure sign.

Thus, beyond the destruction of the familiar identity of the botanical garden, of culture-nature relationships, of local natural and cultural identity, Ambasz's non/ultimate greenhouse, through its double inversion and assertion of difference, establishes its own fictive meaning. Hence the eerie effect of the models—the outward look of desert, palm, and temple; the inward realm of oasis and tropical vegetation. These images of the conservatory's new forms in the landscape recall projects for outer space, such as the terraforming of NASA or Ettore Sottsass' High-Tech Star or Amphitheater brought down to Earth. What postures as contextual fit for the Southwest, instead accomplishes a new earthscape, not on another planet, but at the very site which the building's displacements have cleared for itself. In spinning its own tale, the conservatory establishes itself as its own place to be. A stable place we can enter and enjoy.

FROM DECONSTRUCTION TO RECONSTRUCTION

Ambasz's Conservatory, then, goes beyond the cited work of Tschumi, Eisenman, and Co-op Himmelblau as architectural fiction. It not only disassembles the traditional presences and identities upon which it is built, but, forsaking the gambit to remain a liberating destruction only, it completes the needed and inevitable reassertion of new cultural presence and identity.

Architecture proceeds as deconstruction by remaining a strategy in process, not by denying habitable space or interpretable symbolism. The deepest architectural deconstruction disassembles and liberates us from architectural and cultural prototypes and ends with a subtly different, but disturbing or attractive, reconstruction.

Beyond a doubt, in the postmodern era, the task of thinking and building is to remain free from "naive" illusions. Not only our modes of discourse, but the very built environment, whether woven by gestures of the media or architecture, is a fiction, for which we need to take responsibility. The cultural project is to renew the coming of fresh meaning by elevating process over object, so that buildings become interpreted and used as events. Architecture, then, becomes a possibility for freedom and play. The architect's task is to devise strategies whereby we hold off buildings' reification and concretization as conventional meaning systems. Even if we know that, in the end, we will fail to hold them off, the goal is to keep deconstructing and reconstructing, forever weaving our environments afresh.

4

Eliade: Restoring the
Possibilities of Place

It would appear that Foucault and Derrida successfully have followed Nietzsche's trail in working out a way for us to respond to the almost invisible, yet outrageous oppressions of cultural fictions. We need to expose and remove the authoritative accretions of previous discourse and practices, including those of architecture and planning.

For Foucault and Derrida, the belief that we can penetrate to the reality or truth of anything is a delusion, a deception imposed on us for the sake of dominance by one historical regime after another. What is called for is courageously facing up to the situation with a relentless honesty, which means violently stripping away our comforting illusions and forcefully undoing past interpretations by inserting our own. Yet, we need to be critically vigilant that we do not take our own unavoidable substitutions too seriously, that we do not claim or allow any illusory validity to adhere to our arbitrary, though necessary, dislocations and substituted constructions. Here we would become responsible for and open to the only remaining possibility—the free play of language and other sign systems, that is, interpretation as a strategy for liberation from the oppression and bodily bondage of our culturally built world. *At the end of the history of human habitation as dislocation, only violent, liberating displacements would be within our power.*

So it may seem. Still, other powerful thinkers acknowledge the crisis in meaning that our culture is experiencing, but nonetheless contend that the skeptical position of Foucault and Derrida is neither necessary nor the most appropriate response. Specifically, the Rumanian-American scholar Mircea Eliade and the German thinker Martin Heidegger may provide still valid, even more attractive alternatives to solving our dilemmas.

RESPONSIVE CARE VERSUS VIOLENCE

Both Foucault and Derrida locate themselves, as we have seen, as unavoidably at the end of the modern age of the metaphysical West, within history and historicism. Eliade and Heidegger can agree with Foucault's and Derrida's self-locating description and can agree that this is how we now understand our cultural situation, which as Nietzsche says, may only now be beginning its long reign. But, in contrast with Foucault and Derrida, Eliade and Heidegger do *not* believe that the current placement is the only viable theoretical or temporal-historical possibility. They contend that we do not need to despair of understanding things and their meanings. Instead, Eliade and Heidegger attempt the admittedly uncertain and risky route of trying to go counter to the prevailing, contemporary trends. Both of them work to show how our historical situation and relativistic theories occupy a peculiar place in the history of the world and of the West in particular. Perhaps even more importantly for Westerners, both of them seek to explicate (1) how alternatives existed earlier in the not-yet-metaphysical thought that occurred before the classical age of Greek metaphysics beginning with Socrates and Plato and since then with thinkers withdrawn from the dominant metaphysical tradition such as Meister Eckhart, and (2) how alternatives persist today. For example, Eliade contends that we still can be in touch with primal sources of meaning and value that have *not* been eliminated, but only ignored, in Western rationalistic views.

The simplest way to approach the positions of Eliade and Heidegger is through the development of phenomenology and hermeneutics. A radical critique of Western science and philosophy was the basis for phenomenology from the start. Following the story amounts to moving through two tripartite divisions. The first set of three pathways involves Edmund Husserl's forging a middle way between the two extremes that dominated science and philosophy at the beginning of the century. Husserl argued that logical positivism, despite its posture as the heir of objective Western science with its goal of disinterested knowledge, was not scientific enough, not as purely focused on the empirical as it should be. Hence, Husserl formulated phenomenology as a way to see and describe what really showed itself, prior to secondary scientific concepts and abstractions such as 'data,' 'time,' 'space,' 'evidence,' and 'verification,' which themselves were unthought, and unthinkable, in purely scientific terms or categories.

At the same time, Husserl opposed the subjectivistic opposite: psychological reductionism that understood truth as merely a descriptive summary or consensus concerning accidental psychological processes. Under such a view, $2 + 2 = 4$ only because that is the way we happen to think. There would not be any trans-subjective, logical necessity or *a priori* truth to a given mathematical equation, but only contingency based on the features of our mental makeup, which could be otherwise. In short, phenomenology was to avoid the twin chimera of science as impossibly objective—a form of absolutism—or purely subjective—a kind of relativism. It was to be, theoretically and practically, a dramatic departure from the then-current outcome of the modern scientific worldview in order to provide the new foundation for rigorous scientific inquiry.[1]

Husserl himself, in working out his theory of the constitution of consciousness, eventually returned to a transcendental idealism, a grand kind of subjectivism. Following his final position would have reduced the options to the clearly inadequate, and still Cartesian, heritage of modernism: subjectivism or objectivism. Hence the other two major founders of phenomenology, Max Scheler and Martin Heidegger, worked to carry out what started as the middle way—a path that would both radically criticize the tradition and culture and yet open a new and positive way to move theoretically and existentially.

Originally, Scheler and Heidegger came to prominence in the first two decades of the twentieth century as the master-guides in the attempt to throw off the complacency and everydayness that sedate and drive bourgeois life.[2] Their phenomenological program was specifically intended to shatter the illusion and dream of a falsely comfortable world and to face up to the difficult and persisting task of choosing who we are in a revalued world. Heidegger's student Sartre had that right: phenomenology was the methodological foundation for an unavoidable, perennially uncomfortable life of existential thought, decision, and responsibility.

It became apparent to Scheler and Heidegger that authentic understanding and life in our world could neither be based on the ahistorical absolutism that science falsely pretended to offer, nor on some version of relativism. Hence Scheler and Heidegger independently worked to reinterpret the delusions of contemporary modern culture and to reestablish connection with the genuinely objective dimensions of meanings and values that occur concretely and historically. This meant moving beyond phenomenological description and analysis to also interpret the historical and symbolic aspects of phenomena, that is, to elaborate a hermeneutics.

Both Scheler and Heidegger worked out a remarkably sophisticated phenomenological hermeneutics that may remain the best way to avoid the false oppositions of extreme subjectivism and extreme objectivism. Their way may indeed be able to account for essential features that occur historically and culturally, since that is the only way in which potential values and meanings are realized in the world at all, but that also are only partial realizations of the possible set of values and meanings, since only a facet of the potential can ever be fully realized at any one time, for any one group. Further, in the historical unfolding of Being and humans, the essential characteristics of persons, things, and events are transformed from epoch to epoch. For any time and culture, aspects of meanings and values—dimensions of reality—always are partially revealed and partially hidden. While an aspect is partially actualized in specific events the other aspects remain only potential, that is, absent or obscured to people of that place and age. The accomplishment, then, was criticizing and rereading cultural suppositions and developing an alternative approach existentially adequate to our age and to the interplay of the objective and historical dimensions of reality.[3]

Of course, the complex development of intellectual positions does not stay tidy. Thus, as John D. Caputo points out, after Heidegger, and in reaction to him, there develops a hermeneutical right, left, and middle.[4] We have seen the development of the left with Foucault and Derrida. They move out of the phenomenological and hermeneutical nest to criticize it as being itself too close to the metaphysical tradition, as being too fond of essences, truth, and the objective. To the right are those hermeneutical scholars who emphasize the continuity of traditions, the possibility of still recovering constantly lost meanings as has been the desire and project of humanism since the Renaissance. Here, for example, we find Hans-Georg Gadamer (another of Heidegger's students) and Mircea Eliade, the latter with his own tradition of the phenomenology and comparative study of religions as discussed above. In the middle we have the later Heidegger himself, where his thinking, since around 1950, moves against his own early work.[5]

This second three-part quarrel of the last forty years still takes place within the overall context of the initial goal of a way between extreme relativism and absolutism—though the latter apparently is gone for good, since positivism and its patchwork heirs remain discredited. The result is a new figure: Derrida and Foucault taking the helm of the far left, Gadamer and Eliade on the right (now a more moderate and tenable right, where a sophisticated hermeneutics would maintain access to, and would develop, our heritage of understanding).[6] The later Heidegger would be between these two positions, in the middle.[7] The quarrel between this newer left and right is fairly straightforward: do we need to undo the tradition and create whatever temporary meanings and values we can for ourselves, or is it possible to recover and continue to participate in traditional ways of life, appropriately rejuvenated for our time and place?[8]

What is called for, according to Eliade (and Heidegger too), is a turning away from our metaphysical prison and the seductive image of ourselves as technological or literary creators of meaning, in order to open up to realms beyond ourselves, which still come to us existentially, manifesting the dimensions of reality in which we can dwell. *Here we would need to learn to think anew, that is, to attend to and to care for what is given to us,* which also means to understand and respond to the built environment and culture in their proper relationships and historical possibilities. Insofar as our response would be open to the meaning of the world in which we participate, but which we neither create nor are free to ignore, and insofar as we are receptive to the values embodied in historical, authentic ways of building and dwelling, we might yet be admitted into a mode of belonging within the world which would also enable us to more fully live out our potential, that is, play our proper role in remaking our place today.

The question at hand, then, is not whether we need a rigorous, uncompromising criticism of current assumptions and cultural constructions. Foucault, Derrida, Eliade, and Heidegger, all seminal contributors to the debate, agree on this point. The question remaining is whether to embrace (1) the skeptical line of thought as carried out by Foucault's, Derrida's, and others' strategies, or whether better alternatives lie either (2) on the hermeneutical right as represented by Eliade or (3) in the middle way with the later Heidegger.

RECOVERING PARTICIPATION IN THE SACRED

Mircea Eliade is a consumate scholar of the phenomenology and hermeneutics of religions. He uses these methodologies to discern, describe, and interpret the essential features of such phenomena as myths and rituals, religious images and symbols, sacred and profane time and space.[9] Some of his work parallels Jung's, especially in its interest in the mystery connected with the numinous—the eruption of the sacred into human life—and in echoes of the sacred found today in dreams and secular myths and practices. At the same time, whereas Jung as a psychiatrist was oriented to the development of the individual, Eliade focuses on the comparative development of religions. As a phenomenologist, Eliade's approach is rigorously empirical, describing but not judging what appears to become manifest in various religious experiences and traditions. Yet, as a hermeneutical scholar, Eliade does believe it is possible to retrieve the substantive meaning of religious phenomena, even from cultures to which we never did, or no longer, belong.

In other words, Eliade practices phenomenological hermeneutics as a way to understand reality and to find the deep meaning of the cosmos. He contends that a phenomenological hermeneutics of the sacred is an alternative that overcomes the skepticism in which Derrida and Foucault find themselves. They, of course, would include Eliade in the tradition they seek to expose and abolish.

The Situation

Eliade differs from Derrida and Foucault, not only in his analysis of our contemporary problem, but in his assessment of the actual situation and possibilities. Eliade recognizes our anxiety and fear in historicism's wake. As a correlate of believing that there is nothing transcendent to history, modern culture generally believes it is trapped inside linear time, unable to escape.

Hence, our current existence in time is understood via historicism where the flow of time changes and determines everything. Naturally, this leads to anxiety in the face of our impending death and the apocalyptic end of our civilization. We are lonely and estranged from the world.

According to Eliade, historicism and its anxiety has resulted from the displacement of religion as a mode of access to the sacred and the subsequent de-sacralization of the modern world. Further, Eliade holds that we *unnecessarily* "put up with a nihilistic and pessimistic vision of the world"[10] because we have rejected the access to reality which is still possible. We have imprudently discarded the wisdom and comforts available through contact with other and earlier cultures and with a transcendent reality. He contends that we have a viable option to seeing human habitation as only historically delimited and inaccessible: sacred reality or Being still is available to us, either as a means to understand other cultures or in itself.

Built Things

Throughout his work, Eliade explicates the primal difference between the sacred and profane. All things in their ordinary, merely natural or made character, are profane. They are used and understood in an unexceptional way. But, according to Eliade, the sacred manifests itself in this world by showing itself in or though things: natural things, built forms, symbols, and so on. The sacred breaks through the homogenous and establishes the world in its fullness, making it what it is.[11] Eliade calls this act of manifestation of the sacred power or reality, hierophany.[12] Since some things participate in the sacred, they become differentiated from the rest: they become saturated with Being and significance.

Further, our built world participates in the sacred cosmos by homology. It is able to repeat the sacred patterns. That means some built things are able to help establish and hold on to the sacred. They can participate in, and thereby have meaning in, the homology between the human condition and the structure of reality. But, built things and natural things have this meaning only insofar as they are oriented to the cosmic and display the sacred. According to Eliade, this orientation and display crucially depend on myth, because the paradigmatic sacred events themselves are held for us in myth.

Language

Language, too, for Eliade, can be sacred or profane. As distinct from humanly invented and utilitarian or profane language, sacred language is not at all a representation of objects, as modern metaphysics has it. Rather, it is a revelation of world: "the World 'speaks' in symbols, 'reveals' itself through them. A symbol is not a replica of objective reality. It *reveals* something deeper and more fundamental."[13] The sacred language which concerns us here, myth, is a narration of sacred events which occurred in the beginnings, in *illo tempore*. As a result, myth itself is sacred, exemplary, and significant.[14] Myth complexly functions (*a*) to record and hold on to the sacred, (*b*) to enable human beings to understand and interpret the sacred, and (*c*) to participate in the sacred, especially since myth means the repeated story.

As opposed to the modern view, then, which takes myth to be an object of study and curiosity and its supposed source (sacred reality) to be a fiction, Eliade contends that myth is the basis of the lived experience of a culture, since myth makes models manifest, thereby giving meaning and value to life.[15] The repetition of myths, according to Eliade, enables culture to recover or repeat the sacred epiphany. That is, living *mythos* though primarily "sacred story," involves linguistic and graphic symbols, and also actions and deeds (rituals) which display the sacred story. Of course, the built environment is a crucial means of manifesting cosmic order and events.

Eliade claims that, taken broadly to include myth proper (story) and its symbolic kin, *mythos* does give us access to the permanent by holding and carrying on that permanent realm. Through mythic symbols, a culture is able to relate our lives to the structure of the cosmos in its multiple modalities of being and to the world.[16] Thus, objective continuity is asserted insofar as the culture implements the sacred models. This connection to the sacred cosmos is possible since myth discloses a mode of reality that is not available solely in terms of immediate experience. Here language and the symbolic-built things are two dimensions of the same phenomena: the built instantiates the myth and thus the sacred (built form comes from the sacred); the built actively evokes and participates in, that is, recovers, the sacred.

Culture

If the sacred appears to people, revealing structures of reality and paradigms for behavior, the latter clearly are not idiosyncratic or private, but belong to the whole group. Indeed, a group's culture and consciousness is first established by hierophany and is retained only by myths. Human participation in and response to the sacred is what we call culture. Cultural distinctions, actions, and forms homologously repeat the sacred distinctions, actions, and forms. Because culture is the manifestation and effect of the sacred, the continuation of which is the responsibility and power of a people, authentic culture is life in conformity to the sacred paradigms. Insofar as a people hold on to and enact (reenact) the sacred, there is a meaningful, distinctive pattern of life and society. The failure to do so, or loss of participation, amounts to cultural obliteration.

Interpretation

Given his view that the transcendental sacred is manifest, as immanent in history, and repeatable, Eliade holds that there is a mode of interpretation proper to recover it, just as there are modes of interpretation appropriate to purely profane realms such as sociology. For Eliade, finding the origins of religion in the sacred is not a matter of working back to *historical* causes, as has been known since the nineteenth century. Accordingly, Eliade does not do a history or chronology seeking to get back to the first occurrence of the events, but seeks to "grasp the essence of religious phenomena."[17]

Eliade's hermeneutical phenomenology aims to open to the epiphany and transformation of the sacred, to "the emergence of a reality and the disclosure of its fundamental structures."[18] The task is to pass beyond ourselves, to the *other*, in a manner congruent with actual experience of access to the sacred—if not the access of an indigenous participant, at least that appropriate to someone on a genuine quest. Eliade proceeds into religious experience and existence through the "exercise of the phenomenological attitude in opening to this material on its own terms and allowing essences to appear."[19]

Interpretation, for Eliade, is able to gain access to cultural manifestations of the sacred that erupt into the world. In turn, this access enables the interpreter either to understand the culture which participates in the specific epiphany or to interpret the sacred itself. Of course, this approach emphasizes the *care* necessary to accomplish and maintain the recovery of the sacred way of habitation, the meaning of myth, and the sacred itself. It is akin to the care the culture itself takes to recover and live in the sacred.

Eliade himself makes the further claim that it is possible to "remythologize history into mythic text and then to the existential encounter defined by the myth," thereby actually recovering what has been lost in the modern Western world.[20] Sacred time and its transcendent events are infinitely recoverable in the patterns of human life. For Eliade, *time can be overcome and reality reached:* authentic existence for *homo religiosus* begins just where contemporary society leaves off. In the former, time is confronted and surpassed through initiations into maturity which provide fuller participation in the cosmos.[21] Here, Eliade claims, hermeneutic phenomenology could "help us rediscover spiritual positions that one is justified in regarding as universally valid."[22]

Specific Implications for Interpreting
the Built Environment

Eliade's approach specifically applies to the built environment and yet is broad in the scope of what it can describe "from the inside." The majority of all human habitation on earth, from earliest times until just recently in the West, and still in many parts of the world, has been a participation by *homo religiosus* in sacred modes of being and building. In such traditional life, built form and culture belong together, by way of myth, since they both participate in the sacred by being homologous with it. In a sacred cosmos, techniques of orientation are also techniques for the *construction* of sacred space, and built form is an *imago mundi*.[23] Originally the work of the gods, such techniques and forms in human habitation have been reproduced and continued through human work. Accordingly, Eliade's hermeneutical phenomenology is of greatest practical importance to understand how specific peoples dwelt in the cosmos, according to their particular, local version of the meaningful, traditional homology—human body: house: cosmos.[24]

According to this traditional mode of dwelling, the sacred initially established, centered, and ordered the world so that world could be lived in. Because of its origin and foundation, then, a group's sacred dwelling place is opposite "the chaos of the homogeneity and relativity of profane space," and is not intelligible in the latter's terms.[25] For those living immersed within a profane view or otherwise preoccupied with the profane, and hence living outside the sacred cosmos as our contemporary culture is, it would be all but "useless" to look for the sacred. The latter always would be hidden, as unintelligible, since it is wholly other.

Thus, the advantage of Eliade's sympathetic method: allowing the essence of sacred phenomena to appear on their own terms provides access impossible to either merely objectivistic (purely empirical) or subjectivistic approaches, since the deep reality behind the order of the built environment is distinct from both the objective and subjective. Here, Eliade's approach is useful as an attempt to recover the underlying cosmological-ontological meaning and *structure* of primal and many contemporary ways of life. That is, the recovery of meaning via myth is the key to such traditional cultures' entire built forms and to cultural delineation itself.

OMAHA DWELLING AS AN EXAMPLE

An example of the homology of habitation forms with sacred reality is seen in the traditional organization and orientation of the Omaha tribe's dwelling. The mysterious life force, called *Wako"'da* which permeated all things, relating them to one another, gave the pattern for the arrangement and continuity of all life.[26] As narrated in the tribal holy stories, the cosmos proceeded from the union of the two great primary realities: "the Above" and "the Below." In the former *Wako"'da* as revealed as masculine and in the latter as feminine. From this foundation, the sky is seen to be father; the earth, mother. The myths relate how human beings were born from the union of Sky people and Earth people.[27] The way creation came about indicates how life must be continued here on earth. Because the union of these powers is the basis for all life and because its continuation is necessary for human existence, it generates the practices of the Omaha which are especially visible in the tribal organization of the gens or exogamous kinship groups that trace their descent from the father's side only. The vision of union of Sky and Earth is manifest throughout the homology, cosmos: tribe: encampment: individual lodge (as well as in rites and customs). The vision is held and instantiated in a primary image or form which permeates and guides Omaha life: a circle open to the east, with the sky identified with the north half, the earth with the south half.

Sky and earth provide the figural organization for the encampment where each gens has its place, just as does "each member of the family within the [individual] lodge."[28] While on the hunt, the time when the major sacred ceremonies are performed, the Omaha pitched their tents in the tribal circle.

FIGURE 4.1.

Hu'Thuga. Omaha Tribal [Encampment] Form.

A. I^{N}SHTA'ÇU^{N}DA DIVISION. B. HO^{N}GASHENU DIVISION. 1. WE'ZHI^{N}SHTE. Subgens: None. 2. I^{N}KE'ÇABE. Subgentes: (a) Nini'bato^n (b) Wathi'gizhe. 3. HO^N'GA. Subgentes: (a) Waxthe'xeto^n (b) Washa'beto^n 4. THA'TADA. Subdivisions: (a') Xu'ka; (a) Waça'be itazhi; (b) Wazhi^n'ga itazhi; (c) Ke'i^n; (d) Te'pa itazhi. 5. KO^N'CE. Subgentes: (a) Tade'tada; (b) Nini'bato^n. 6. MO^N'THI^{N}KAGAXE. Subdivisions: (a) Xu'be; (b) Mi'kaçi; (c) Mi'xaço^n; (d) Nini'bato^n 7. TEÇI^N'DE, Subdivsions: (a) Teçi^n'de; (b) Nini'bato^n. 8. TAPA'. Subdivisions: (a) Tapa'xte; (b) Thunder rites; (c) Star rites; (d) Nini'bato^n. 9. I^{N}GTHE'ZHIDE. No subdivisions. 10. I^{N}SHTA'ÇU^{N}DA. Subgens: (a) Lost gens; (b) Nini'bato^n; (c) Washe'to^n. 11. Sacred Tent of War. 12. Tent of Sacred Pole. 13. Tent of Sacred White Buffalo Hide.

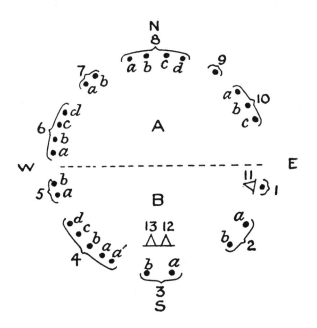

Since this action took place on the wide-open prairie, the form of the encampment not only provided an internal "built" environment, but a cosmic orientation.

The opening of the whole encampment was thought of as the door of the dwelling place of the tribe, an orientation with the opening symbolically to the east, where earth and sky first begin together. The circular encampment consisted of two parts with the south half representing the earth; the north, the sky. In unvarying order, beginning at the east opening, the Earth people (five gentes) were located as follows: first, nearest the opening and keepers of the Sacred Tent of War that stood at the opening, were the *We'zhi"shte*, who were responsible for the thunder which wakens life in the spring and for war which made tribal anger known; next, the *Inke'cabe* were responsible for the buffalo hunt and the maize; next, on the south, the *Ho"'ga* were responsible for tribal governance and the quest for food (and were the keepers of the other two Sacred Tents); then the *Tha'tada,* connected to maize, birds, and rain; finally, the *Ko"'ce,* associated with the rites of wind and clouds. On the north half of the circle were the Sky people (five gentes: continuing around in the same direction, the *Mo"'thi"kagaxe* tended the stones and water connected with creation and its continuation; then, the *Teci"'de,* associated with the crow and the embodiment of human beings; on the north, the *Tapa',* connected to stars and night sky; next, *I"gthe'zhide,* associated with procreation via the Sky powers; finally, again closing the circle on the east, the *I"shta'cu"da,* tenders of lightning and thunder, understood as *Wako"'da*'s power over human life and death.

In sum: the whole encampment replicated the cosmic pattern and the course to be followed by the people. Those on the south side, the Earth people, were responsible for the actions and rites necessary for physical welfare such as protection from the outside, harmony within, and the food and clothing supply. Those on the north side, the Sky people, were the guardians of the rites related to creation, to the stars, and to the cosmic forces governing life.[29]

The model of the generational union of the two primary dimensions and the force enabling life also is repeated in the tradition of two chiefs, two pipes, as well as in myrad details and symbols of the forms of dwelling and the patterns of action. For instance, the organization in which each gens had its place was again replicated in the individual family lodges, where each member had his or her place. Marriage was exogamous, the male and female drawn from the distinct sky and earth groups. Thus, the procreation of children reproduced the cosmic type. Naturally, the pattern was continued in minute details, such as seating arrangements within the family lodge.

The Shell Society, a secret society, typified the replication of the cosmic paradigm in dwelling form and actions. The head of the society sat in the middle of the circle at the back of the dwelling facing east, that is, in the direction of the entrance. On his immediate right, toward the south, sat the "eldest son" and his lodge; on his immediate left, toward the north, sat the "second son" and his lodge. To the leader's far left, on the north, sat "the daughter" and her lodge; to the far right, on the south, the "youngest son" and his lodge. These positions were drawn from the mythical story whose preservation was the Society's purpose. Similarly, the meaning of the mode of body painting. The eldest son was painted blue to represent the sky, "with no clouds to obstruct the passage of the sun's rays"; the youngest son, the color of the earth; the second son to represent the night sky. The daughter had the moon painted on her. Again, the earth on the south, the sky on the north.[30]

The same pattern also was manifest in the ceremony connected with the Sacred Pole, the means whereby the people were kept together. The Sacred Pole was the manifestation of the power of thunder, the power necessary for the hunt, defense, and for food. To begin the ceremony, each lodge would be visited and a pole selected, from which the ceremonial lodge, representing all the people, would be constructed. The resulting semicircular lodge, opened to the heart of the tribal center, was the scene of the ceremony in which a sacred figure would be carved before the pole. The figure, called *ushi"'eti*, was aligned to the east as the source of life, and, as enacted in the surrounding songs and rituals, also repeated the cosmic model.[31] "The design was said to signify the wistful attitude of the people, looking for the good that *Wako"'da* was to send to them in the house, the dwelling of the family, and is in a larger sense, the *hu'thuga*, the dwelling of the tribe; it also brought to mind the fathers who established these ceremonies that opened the way for the reception of good gifts from *Wako"'da*."[32]

In this ceremony, and at the base of the other examples just considered, we find a key word, *hu'thuga*, which speaks and preserves the Omaha vision. The central homology of cosmic, tribal, and individual environment and action is held in this central Omaha word *hu'thuga* because it evokes and calls into memory the two great cosmic divisions and the sacred orientation of that which it names: "the [figural] form or order in which the tribal organization ceremonially camped, in which each one of the villages or gens had its definite place" and, at the same time, as a very old word, "carries the idea of a dwelling."[33] In short: the entire life of the Omaha, sustained by its participation in the cosmic life force, was a dwelling built up by way of replicating the revealed sacred patterns.

The North American case cited here is only one example of a "cosmic" settlement and way of life. Worldwide, a large number of such traditional cultures and forms have been documented in which buildings, settlement's spatial organization, and ritual uses incarnate a sacred mode of dwelling.

Many of the scholarly interpretations acknowledge or utilize Eliade's approach. These are found in the ethnographic literature, which generally remains too unused by specialists in architectural and environmental research. More promisingly, numerous participants in the "Built Form and Culture Conferences" and some members of recently developed International Association for the Study of Traditional Environments are well aware of this body of research.[34]

Eliade, of course, also argues that mythically constituted sacred worlds *continue today* in many places, both for continuous "primal" groups and for major religions from Islam to Roman and Greek Orthodox Catholicism. His approach also would seem to fruitfully apply to new-age communities and parts of the radical ecology movement. Finally, his ideas and values continue to resonate in the emerging field loosely identified as "sense of place" or "place and identity" studies.[35]

In addition, Eliade demonstrates how significant aspects of profane modern societies remain informed by myth and argues that the meanings of these dimensions can be interpreted adequately only with some version of hermeneutical retrieval. Hence, his emphasis on the "mythology of the modern world" and on "survival and camouflages of myths" is intended to encourage us to look for deep meanings not only in tonight's dreams, stories, and art, but in planning, architecture, and environments as well.[36]

5

Heidegger: Retrieving the
Still-Coming Source

Obviously, Eliade's assumptions and approach contrast markedly with Derrida's and Foucault's, thus clearly focusing the *question* of how we may interpret the built environment and culture. To push the tension among the alternatives further, perhaps to a point where it might be resolved, it is crucial to consider the position of Martin Heidegger—since his complex work not only prepared the way for both Foucault and Derrida, but also frequented the same neighborhood as Eliade. The prospect of a middle path between the hermeneutic left (Foucault and Derrida) and right (Eliade and Gadamer) is most fully laid out with the later Heidegger since he continued to move radically against metaphysical thought in order to help us again become open to what has been obliterated during metaphysics' twenty-five hundred year reign. In the process, he had to revise his own earlier approach to try to respond to the possibility of a new mode of dwelling.[1]

In the end, Heidegger's pathway and Eliade's have the same orientation: Eliade's attempt to recover the meaning and possibility of dwelling by interpreting dwelling's origin in a sacred cosmos is parallel to Heidegger's quest to retrieve and restore the source which continues to exfoliate a multidimensional world. Yet, in attempting to interpret the world non-metaphysically, Heidegger is not as traditional as Eliade.[2] To understand his difference from a traditional hermeneutics it is helpful to read and interpret Heidegger in light of what Foucault and Derrida found in him and in light of what they missed. As recent scholars are beginning to argue, the most profound and radical Heidegger moves beyond the position followed by Derrida and Foucault.[3] This Heidegger has not yet been understood, much less assimilated.

Foucault and Derrida follow and depend on Heidegger's interpretation and critique of metaphysics and history, developing their positions from a point Heidegger reached midway in his own thinking—and what is most important—a point beyond which they do not pass, but that was place of *departure* for the venture Heidegger attempted with varied success for the last twenty-five or so years of his life. Foucault's theory and analysis depends substantially on Heidegger's interpretation of the epochal unfolding of Being as the force behind the history of Western culture. Foucault tells the social, economic, political equivalent of Heidegger's ontological tale. Derrida depends on Heidegger's description of the metaphysics of representation, of identity and difference. Derrida plays out, even plays against Heidegger who started the game with Nietzsche, the hand that Heidegger mulled over from the 1920s to the early 1950s—the task of *overcoming metaphysics.*

Heidegger, from the beginning of his career, believed that the traditional philosophical and cultural apparatus since Plato had obscured fundamental truths about Being and human beings, though not in any avoidable way, given the mode of what undeniably was worked out by philosophy, science, technology, and political practices. Heidegger is the source of the idea and terminology of deconstruction. But, deconstruction as he originally formulated it in the 1920s was an integral phase of the recovery of meaning. It was a preparatory step, a clearing away to rebuild. The dismantling was necessary because the cultural edifices erected over the course of history hid what was sought: the still potent original meanings that needed to be retrieved. Heidegger argued in 1927,

> Even the ontological investigation which we are now conducting is determined by its historical situation and, therewith, by certain possibilities of approaching beings and by preceding philosophical tradition. The store of basic philosophical concepts derived from the philosophical tradition can hardly be overestimated. It is for this reason that all philosophical discussion, even the most radical attempt to begin all over again, is pervaded by traditional concepts and thus by traditional horizons and traditional angles of approach, which we cannot assume with unquestionable certainty to have arisen originally and genuinely from the domain of being and the constitution of being they claim to comprehend. It is for this reason that there necessarily belongs to the conceptual interpretation of being and its structures, that is, to the reductive construction of being, a *destruction*—a critical process in which the traditional concepts, which at first must necessarily be employed, are de-constructed down to the sources from which they were drawn. Only by means of this destruction can ontology fully assure itself in a phenomenological way of the genuine character of its concepts.
>
> Construction in philosophy is necessarily destruction, that is to say, a de-constructing of traditional concepts carried out in a historical recursion to the tradition. And this is not a negation of the tradition or a condemnation of it as worthless; quite the reverse, it signifies precisely a positive appropriation of tradition. Because destruction belongs to construction, philosophical cognition is essentially at the same time, in a certain sense, historical cognition.[4]

Thus, while Derrida and Foucault take up Heidegger's idea of disassembly, they hold that his project of retrieval is untenable. Heidegger himself saw the destruction as necessary, but also as only making sense insofar as it was a preparation for the positive recovery that is the real goal. For Heidegger, the phase of deconstruction is intended to remove historical additions and to repair defacements in order to restore the original for use today.

Heidegger argued that we must overturn what is simply given and what appears as the everyday in order to responsibly come to our own understanding and to become open to discovering what we are oblivious to insofar as we are full of the habitual, the everyday, and our willful selves. Hence, Heidegger is not on the right with Eliade and Gadamer, more directly staying within and continuing the tradition; he is more radical than that. Here Heidegger agrees with Foucault and Derrida, and we can see why they use him.

But, on his own, *Heidegger also went on to think through the need to give up merely trying to overcome metaphysics,* since in this activity, as with Nietzsche's revenge against the past, we remain stuck to it as to a grudge or hatred that never allows us to be free to move on. We need to let go— Heidegger's term is *Gelassenheit,* meaning a releasement from the metaphysical and an opening to the mystery that is non-metaphysical. While all of this is obscure and dangerous, Heidegger believed that at least a fleeting leap into the non-metaphysical could occur.

That is, a non-metaphysical way of thinking, saying, building, and living may yet happen. We have enough hints about it to at least strike out on the pathway, though there are no guarantees. Heidegger spent a lifetime taking apart the western metaphysical tradition and apparently—may have— emerged for at least brief moments into a no-longer-metaphysical realm. Whether or not such a discovery of meaning and value is possible is the real point of contention with Foucault and Derrida.

FROM TECHNOLOGY TO DWELLING

The Situation

Heidegger describes our age as homeless even though we are entering the era of our greatest power and technological mastery over everything, including ourselves, and seem to be able to be at home everywhere on our planet. This is a great paradox: though we more and more are able to do what we will, to most fully control whatever comes within our reach, and to live anywhere as we wish, we also find ourselves alienated from the world and from our own human nature. Reality is far from us, in large measure, according to Heidegger, because it is separated by the particular developments of the historical unfolding of metaphysics since the rise of classical Greek thought with Socrates and Plato.[5]

Yet, reality also is nearby. Even while it withdraws and conceals some of its aspects, primal reality still does disclose itself to us, emerging as what he calls World.[6] Heidegger contends that while we obviously cannot return to the original not-yet-metaphysical past, we can move beyond metaphysical homelessness, toward a condition of becoming no-longer-metaphysical. Here we would again come to be at home in the world.

Heidegger's task is to work toward such a homecoming, through the imaginative and intellectual recovery of the originary source which continues to come to us for the future.[7] He names this way of retrieving meaning and value, "originary thinking." The first step in recovering from the homeless condition of our age would be comparatively seeing and thinking the reigning technological framework and its originary alternative.[8]

Built Things

In the reigning epochs of metaphysics over the last twenty-five hundred years, things have been understood as beings and the built environment as the culturally made patterns of beings. Since the time of Plato, the built, that is, what is made, has successively been understood as (1) "that brought forth into presence" (by the Greeks), as (2) "that created by the Creator" (by Judeo-Christian onto-theology), as (3) "the set of objects perceived by subjects" (by the modern era), and now as (4) "a standing reserve or stock" (in our technological era).[9]

In the possibly emerging no-longer-metaphysical epoch, according to Heidegger's interpretation, originary things are understood as (5) the *sites or occasions where the four fundamental dimensions of reality—earth, heavens, mortals, and the divine—concretely gather together into a world.*[10] In built things and forms, in bridges and houses and gardens, there can happen the belonging of humans in a disclosed reality, in their own nature as mortals with their proper relation to the earth and its waters, hills, and nourishing soil, to the heavens in their weather and seasons, rain and light, and perhaps to the increasingly hidden divine. Here the built is thought of as a *place* which makes space for an ontological event: the gathering together of the four dimensions of world—which also means *the opening of a place for human beings to originarily dwell,* as mortals.[11]

This happens when, together, people take up their problems and ideals and talk with one another as may occur in community marketplaces, at a kitchen table, or with an interviewer who genuinely listens, as happens with Studs Terkel in Chicago.[12] Clearly, things are not seen globally in these cases, but in terms of specific places, which we usually call "locality" and "region." Thus, planning and building take place in the midst of what is local—within local traditions, materials, skills, needs, animal and plant life, climate, dress, customs, foods, dialects, and so on. Things that would be able to delineate specific places and articulate local ways of life would be *distinctively individual*—rather than homogeneous as are the objects of modern mass production and the standing reserve of technology. The word ''craft'' gives a helpful hint as to what such individuality means. What is crafted, whether fully by hand or by hand and tool is composed so as to respond to materials, to proper use, to its place with that to which it belongs. It is the manifestation and fitting-together of what takes on form only in the fitting.

Consider two cases of handmade doors used in restaurants. The first case involves the unexpected misfit of doors made by hand in Mexico for the Casa Gallardo restaurant chain. The restaurant owner, intending authenticity, ordered handmade fixtures, including hand-carved doors, for all the restaurants being built in the southeast United States. But, whereas all the restaurants were built according to precise and standard technological instructions, the well-crafted doors would not fit. They could not. Each handmade door was different, according to the specific piece of wood and the different craftsmen and the way the carving developed. Such a hand-made door only fits together with a building—which it secures and to which it helps bid guests welcome— when it and the building are built together, each mutually ''informing'' the other, as in the case of Fonda San Miguel Restaurant, pictured here, which took the door into account with a responsive design.

In short, originary things are not interchangeable. Things still wear out, but refurbishing and repairing can take into account the character and use, even idiosyncracies of a thing. ''Mend'' names the essential restoration to working order which is akin to healing. ''To mend'' echoes ''amend'': to put right again, to take out the fault. When we *mend* a thing, we tend to the way it and the world wear on one another and attempt to preserve or continue the style of the encounter in its concrete character and appearance. In mending a shirt or table, we do not attempt to make it appear as brand new, which would counterfeit its reality, but, instead, try to make it authentically whole.[13] We do not mend or even repair digital watches or plastic shoes; we dispose of and replace them.

We still remember and are able to participate in non-interchangeability at times. One wedding ring is not ''just as good as,'' or identical with, another. Here, things are not disposed of, but *kept*. To be kept means to be thought of as what lasts and endures. For a thing to be kept requires that it be designed and executed so as to hold up and hold on to its essential features, power, and even charm. This is what we have in mind when we talk of the upkeep of a house, or keeping up a yard and garden, or keeping bees. To keep also means to store so as to retain special potentials. We see this in seeds. We see it in

FIGURE 5.1.
Fonda San Miguel Restaurant, Austin, Texas. Handcrafted Door.

things intimately important to our personal lives, such as clothing and jewelry used when we participate in and commemorate significant events or when we carry out our vocation. A craftsman's tools and garments, a judge's robes, heirlooms, holiday decorations and dishes, and even recipes need to be kept. Indeed, often such things as a locket or watch, a well-made table or chair, a tended garden or house, or even a city seem to assume a deeper value and meaning as they endure through our lives, or generations of lives.[14] Most of our technological clothing and houses, obviously, would have to undergo a radical, essential change in order to so deepen their character and qualities.

Language

Language, in Heidegger's view, is closely related to things. Genuine saying, as happens in poetic words, is a kind of thing, as are artworks and also buildings, originary thinking, and political actions. In such saying we discover an essential character of things since here earth and heavens, mortals and the divine are gathered and disclosed in their proper belonging. Not surprisingly, then, Heidegger argues that language and building *do not* primally *refer*. That is, their meaning finally is not intelligible in terms of functioning as representational signs, as semiotics contends.[15] Rather, language has its power as the site where the primal dimensions of reality occur, thus making a way for our life on earth.[16] Because it shows this belonging to us, Heidegger says the world is granted to us, not by, but through language.

That would not make sense if language were understood in its usual sense as the written or spoken representation of thoughts, feelings, and objects (the definition Derrida and Foucault pursue toward its radical end). Instead, Heidegger thinks of language as saying, that is, as the showing which enables something to emerge or come forth.[17] Language enables features or dimensions of reality to emerge and also allows us to understand facets of those things and hold on to them in thought and deed.

Culture

Our culture, according to metaphysical understanding, is what we have made. It is the objectification of will in order to organize and efficiently use the natural and human resources at our disposal. Hence, culture generates a variety of built forms: forms of individual buildings, of cities, of whole regions. For instance, the entire web of the technologically formed energy, communication, and transportation resources is understood as a system of relations. These logistical systems making up a culture unfold and impose our will upon the land and behavior, upon the West and the rest of the world.

In contrast, understood originally, according to Heidegger, culture is not the merely human, though, of course, he does not deny all that we make and do. Rather, Heidegger situates what we call culture—the humanly made systems—in the broader context of historically unfolding epochs in which there is a variation in the relationship between human beings and the primal concealment and disclosure that gives a world. Here the governing relationship between "that which gives a world" and human being is beyond our power: humans, for all our power and technology, cannot provide any ground by which we occur. For Heidegger, there finally is no such stable foundation. Rather, the event of the unfolding of an intelligible world, which Heidegger sometimes calls *Ereignis*, is *given* to us, for human experience to deal with and to work out as part of our way of living. Culture is the human working out of the possible, that is, of what is given in and by the occurrence of ultimate reality.

Heidegger sees the possibility of an entirely new form of culture, where instead of the metaphysical, systematic domination and control of beings, we would respond to the world we are given, which includes ourselves, as responsible caretakers or guardians. This is the possibility of a culture of originary, meditative dwelling and becoming at home.

ORIGINARY DWELLING

"Originary" is distinct from "original." Whereas "original" refers to the first instance or beginning point at the beginning of a history and as lying in the past, "originary," names a continually coming source understood as both (*a*) belonging to and retrieving what has been genuine in our own tradition, and (*b*) disclosing or manifesting the sources which still come to us and afford new possibilities in the future.[18]

Heidegger does not use the word "dwelling" or "originary dwelling" to mean a human behavior, or a feeling of being "at home" just anywhere, or a comfortable manner of living with good food and housing—that would be a sort of everydayness, perhaps in the bourgeois mode, out of which we continually must break. Rather, for Heidegger, *"dwelling" names the manner in which mortals belong on earth, under the heavens, before the divine.*[19] The appropriate manner occurs when we spare and preserve the earth, heavens, the divine, and our own nature *as they are disclosed to us.* Dwelling, then, is not merely a human process, but ontologically occurs as the difficult securing and keeping of these four dimensions of reality which are given to us. Heidegger speaks of the character of their relationship dynamically. He says that the fourfold gathers together, into 'World.'[20]

Because dwelling would be a way of living where we would have our proper placement in relationship to the earth and heavens, and to the divine and ourselves as mortals, it names the recovery of place which many people seek. In short: dwelling bespeaks genuine becoming at home with ourselves and the world. And how to accomplish this dwelling? As noted, Heidegger is clear that dwelling, as the recovery and preservation of the fourfold, is not anything we can make or create by ourselves since this primal reality is far more than the merely human realm. We must become open to the other dimensions of reality in order to hope to be given the possibility of such a belonging. At the same time, thought and action are called for, since we have a necessary part to play. While we do not create reality or meaning, neither does the fourfold somehow gather together abstractly. The fourfold occurs, World happens, by way of things such as buildings.[21] Accordingly, we have a responsibility to help the fourfold occur and be preserved in natural and made things.

It is somewhat easier to speak of this fourfold relationship, even though with some loss of meaning and danger of misunderstanding, if we use the more ordinary, but at least proximate terms: human society, nature, and the sacred. As a paraphrase of Heidegger's words, we can say that we would come to fulfill our human nature and to recover our place precisely when we do our proper part to let come and to preserve, in their own way of being, human society, nature, and the sacred, through such things as the built and natural environments—in buildings and bridges, in cities and landscapes, in poems and novels, in plants and animals. Persisting in thinking by way of Heidegger's terms involves attending to the basic characteristics of originary dwelling and the fourfold both existentially and ontologically, that is, respectively, as concretely disclosed to us and as dimensions of historically unfolding reality.

Heidegger reminds us that we deeply, potentially, are human beings only insofar as we remain genuinely *mortals*. We are embodied and finite beings, who can only be understood—who can only live properly—if we remain related to earth and place. Humans are *humus:* we die and return to the soil.[22] Our bodies are the finite *place* which we are. We are the site or *place* where Being appears intelligibly: this is the meaning of Heidegger's word '*Dasein.*'[23] Mortals are those called upon to care for and nurture what lies before them. This essential trait would mean people have the vocation of safeguarding and keeping open their hearts and a place for the fundamental dimensions of reality, and also a place where we can come into our own nature. That is, we would become truly ourselves insofar as our character and potential would occur only at one and the same time as would our proper relationship to the earth, heavens, and divine. But, before this could happen, we need to learn what the rest of the fourfold and things are. We first become open by passing over to an originary thinking and listening to more than ourselves.

Technologically understood, when we consider it a source of energy, the earth itself is a reserve. We sketch and carve our systematic designs on it and in it, as aerial photographs show. Highways, canals, buildings, lights, pipelines, fences, communication towers and stations all mark and allow the distribution of materials and services. The earth is where this takes place. Seemingly diverse groups who identify and differentiate themselves as conservationists, preservationists, environmentalists, laissez-faire developers, and centralized resource allocators actually all assume and share the taken-for-granted viewpoint that the earth is a reservoir to be used and replaced. There is no genuine debate of real alternatives here. The question merely is how, where, and at what rate to use the earth as a material resource under our control. Water is a good example of a stock in reserve when it is dammed, redirected, polluted and purified, or run through machinery to generate power or be desalinated.

But, originally thought as the abiding source, the earth is our ever-coming home, which keeps on unfolding as a place for life, that is, in part, a place for human lives within its larger complexity. On the earth we participate in and learn about growth, preservation, transformation, harmony, and strife. The earth is nothing homogeneous because it is a plenitude of emerging and mutually enabling aspects. In its diversity, earth appears as the paradigmatically local—as locality. Earth is what supports and sustains.

It seems odd to note that above the earth, are the heavens. The point needs to be made explicit because we are so used to a double (dis)appearance of the heavens. As we build and control enclosed shelters, cars, and even whole areas of cities, and as we work, play, and travel day and night, the hours and seasons are separated from our lives. Our interior, humanly shaped lives, especially in an urban environment, have almost nothing to do with the night sky, clouds, moon and planets, or stars—save that we fear the dark. On the other hand, the heavens now appear as space, interpreted largely as a purely empty container into which we are able to project our communications, travel, research, and production systems. The heavens become limitless and homogeneous space.

Importantly, in these two contemporary attitudes, the earth and the heavens no longer belong together. From below, we no longer look up or are drawn up. Following from the concept of absolute homogeneous space, the earth becomes a mere launching pad or coordinate point which we leave behind in order to begin to inhabit and utilize the universe.

In contrast, originarily, the heavens belong intimately with earth. The heavens above provide the place for the course of sun and moon. The latters' presence and movements yield light and darkness, proximity and distance, which in turn give us day and night, seasons and weather. Overall, the sun and moon provide a measure and give rhythms. The moon and winds and clouds are here disclosed as neighbors to the earth. They belong to the interplay of heavens and earth. The heavens embrace and bear on the life of mortals on the earth. Humans and earth respond to the heavens' influence, for instance, when we ship bottles of wine across the seas. The wine is the fruit of our work and the gifts of vine, soil, and rain coming forth in grapes; bottles are the result of our head and hands melding fire and sand, the latter of which itself results from the water and wind wearing down rocks for years and years. The seas move in waves and tides. Clearly, water is thought of quite differently here than in calculative or representational thinking.

Scientifically, past associations of the heavens and the divine are put to rest by means of the univocal concepts of absolute or relative space, of vacuum, gas, matter, and force-fields. Or, the heavenly and divine is reduced and banished to the more earthly realm as divinity is psychologically assumed to be a figment of our imaginations or desires. Insofar as we continue to attend to absent or silent divinities, we now do so in religious practices which also are generally understood sociologically as aspects of alternative cultural systems. As the historian Oscar Handlin observes, our forebears lived in quite another world where the divine was manifest or given, locally and immediately. In no way could they have thought of religion as something to select when "attending the church of our choice," as American immigrants learned to do.[24]

The final dimension, the divine, is not the same as gods or deity, that is, divine being(s). In all ages, according to Heidegger, some dimensions of deity are concealed. In the modern age, the age of the "death of god," either god is so remote as to be concealed from us almost entirely, or nonexistent. Lest originary thinking attempt to say more than it is able, Heidegger is clear that we cannot say whether or how god(s) might come again. The divine, as Heidegger understands it, is the abiding manifestation of deity, even where the latter is absent and concealed. The divine is what remains in relation to the other three dimensions of reality and in epiphany in specific phenomena, such as places and events. In this way it is similar to the sacred as understood by Eliade. The divine, then, is not the Judeo-Christian or any other god. It is a fundamental dimension of reality which belongs with mortals, the heavens, and the earth come together.

Obviously, the fourfold, and especially the divine, is an unusually difficult subject matter. As he himself was careful to say, Heidegger's thinking concerning the fourfold World always remained underway. But, at least, it *does* point and hint. What is clearer because of Heidegger is that the homelessness of the modern and technological epochs actually is a concrete, existential manifestation of the fracture of the four primal dimensions from their originary belonging together. Before any gathering back together, that is, before any originary disclosure could occur, much would have to change. Mortals would have to do their part to safeguard the essential character of the fourfold by first interpreting and then building things.

To recapitulate: according to Heidegger, dwelling occurs when we participate in the occurrence of the fourfold. We play our proper part when we let the fourfold come in its own way, which we do by such deeds as originary thinking, saying, and building things. Heidegger teaches us to try to restore the originary meaning of things by two-track thinking, simultaneously explaining the originary mode of habitation and things by contrasting them with the metaphysical mode, which currently appears as the technological.

Interpretation

For Heidegger, the task of interpretation is to think and help reveal reality, which means understanding *both* its metaphysically and non-metaphysically disclosed dimensions. Though referring to Heidegger's approach as either hermeneutics or phenomenology is correct for his earlier work, he generally gave up these terms in his last twenty-five years. Following his own preference, his deepest thought is called "originary or meditative thinking."

Originary thinking aims to take care with its subject matter, sparing what is given and preserving it, in order to heed that subject matter according to its own mode of disclosure and thus, help it come forth in its own way.[25] To let the subject matter come and lie before us as it is, in its own nature, we must learn to give ourselves over to what calls for thinking. We do that by learning to hear and attend carefully. Heidegger often speaks of evocative "listening," in part to avoid the dominant metaphysical metaphors of light and sight. To "listen," the interpreter first must clear away obstacles which confuse or conceal—principally these are obscuring metaphysical assumptions and attitudes which have occurred over time, both through everyday forgetfulness and through the active force of metaphysical willfulness. In addition, we must give up our own assumptions, agenda, and calculative rationality. Such metaphysical thinking is not able to force or produce any genuine result with method or technique, since the latter conceal what is given. Letting go of the metaphysical tradition and method, and the dictates of our own will, prepares us to give ourselves up to what must be questioned and thought. Such releasement enables us to become open to hidden meanings.

Once we have begun to open ourselves to the saying and showing which occur in the phenomena of language and things, we need to *pass beyond our ordinary mode of thinking,* that is, beyond metaphysical or representational thinking as exemplified in science, *to originary thinking.* Such a move from the common to the strange will require a leap, not a gradual progression, and will demand that we learn to think in a dual mode. We need simultaneously to attend to (1) the metaphysical thinking we are leaving behind and within which we still live, and to (2) the originary thinking we are trying to learn. The procedure requires that we pass beyond the univocal meanings which characterize scientific thought to recognize multiple meanings. The latter realm is uncommon because it involves what has been obscured by metaphysical concepts and also that which at first does not seem to go together.[26]

The next step is to clarify the various meanings without reducing them: each different meaning needs to be understood and then the way the many meanings go together needs to be brought forth. Here we seek to discover the unity or principle of organization behind the polysemous. If we manage to find that simple unity, we then enter into it to work out the manner in which the previous phenomena and meaning (partially disclosed, partially hidden) now display their fuller and deeper senses. Here, the phenomena are properly understood as specific, but not arbitrary, dimensions of an enclosing and more complex reality, or occurrence, as Heidegger prefers to call the unfolding of world.

The goal of originary, interpretive thinking is to find that previously concealed, and thus unthought, historical unfolding within which we belonged. Though it may seem that we have become separated completely from the hidden during the time it has fallen into oblivion, in fact, all along we have remained influenced by it and still are embraced by its call and gift. Because Heidegger is concerned with a way to recover the dimensions of reality which have been disclosed, but are so easily lost, he also names his approach ''memorializing'' or ''recollective thinking.''

Interpretation for Heidegger, then, is a way of heeding a historical world's possibilities. To heed the nature of things in their epochal ontological disclosures is (1) to listen beyond ourselves in order to near what comes to us, (2) to care for what comes, by safeguarding its own nature and mode of occurrence, and (3) to take to heart and hold on to what is given by way of our originary thinking and guardian-like action. Because originary thinking retrieves the original unfolding of meaningful phenomena within which we have our place and purpose, even if the place has become obscured, *interpretation can help disclose—and thus restore—the source of dwelling which still comes to us and also our proper future responses, that is, our possible modes of genuine habitation tomorrow.*

Specific Implications for Interpreting
the Build Environment

The implications of Heidegger's thinking in regard to the built environment are substantial. He provides a thorough, self-critical way to recover an understanding of the environment.[27] By means of his interpretation of the West in terms of historically unfolding epochs, Heidegger both grounds and provides a concrete way to interpret the changing, but not arbitrary, relationships of human beings, natural and made things, and what had appeared as Being itself.

His approach is not at all nostalgic, for Heidegger explicitly and repeatedly refuses any interest in the past which aims to escape from today's situation and any wish to go back to live in what is past. This characteristic apparently is passed on to Foucault's attitude toward history and his analysis of how past social constitutions bear on us today. That is, Heidegger wants to look at the past and present nature of things in their historically *existential* and concrete aspects precisely because this is an aspect of recollecting their *ontological* dimensions. Only such a retrieval, he contends, is adequate to avoid nostalgic or historicist preoccupation with the past because the retrieval allows us to see how historically given things actually are aspects of the still-occurring, epochal unfolding of what once was called Being but now is thought of as the event of the fourfold world.

While this approach is especially useful for recovering the meaning of Western built environment and culture since the Golden Age of the Greeks and is suggestive for describing modernity and technological building, it also is important for understanding earlier and current cases of originary dwelling, which is a crucial step in accomplishing our own belonging.

VERNACULAR SWISS DWELLING AS AN EXAMPLE

As a case study, consider a Heideggerian interpretation of the indigenous dwellings and landscape of Switzerland, proceeding beyond the well documented study of Richard Weiss' *Häuser Und Landschaften Der Schweiz.*[28] Both Swiss vernacular houses and the landscape are built: the result of the mutual collaboration of the natural place which is given, with highly localized and vivid characteristics, and the human ways of interpreting and acting in response. In their attunement to what is given, the Swiss have built their environment of fields and hillsides and the houses and outbuildings intensely and for a very long time.

The astonishing variety of distinctive house forms and different landscapes, for a land as small as Switzerland, recalls the old pattern where locality, the local spirit of place, prevailed everywhere.[29] For a given people, the life-world covered a relatively small area, with its subtle but recognized nuances of natural features, climate, and character, with correspondingly specific human customs, dialects, settlement patterns, house forms, and ornament.[30] Local place is the site for the emergence of particular ways of being human; simultaneously, those ways of human existence enable the earth to emerge as a landscape.[31] The specific point is how the dwellings for each canton, in their own place within the landscape and its congruent ways of life and language, are sites for the uniquely Swiss gathering together of the four dimensions of world.[32]

Even thinking of a house as nothing more than four walls and a roof begins to show how house belongs to world. In Switzerland, vernacular houses have walls made of wood, or stone, or *fachwerk*. Whether a given house has wood, stone, or *fachwerk* walls is a matter, not really of local custom, but of the potentials of wood and stone as those are disclosed to the builders, who also are dwellers in the place. That is, a response to the given earth and heavens is what develops into custom in the first place, which then is safeguarded and remade with appropriate variations.[33]

In one place, softwood is given; in another, hardwood. Each allows and limits what can be done if their nature is acknowledged and respected. Softwoods, commonly in the form of long tree trunks made into logs, seem to call for being laid lengthwise on the ground, so that a wall of stacked horizontal elements rises up.[34] Their uniformity enables them to fit closely together, not only when joined at their ends, but along their entire span. Such wood easily forms the pattern of the "log house." At the same time, the log house displays the character of the logs, and thus the trees, letting them show their linear strength and ability to be close by other trees of the same kind with which they grew in forests.

Or, in another location, large hardwood trees are found. Their wood, which is very different from softwood, requires more work to be usable for a house. More distinct and different pieces must be discerned and cut, each from a specific part of the tree, to respect its character and strengths. Trunk, limb, and crotch all yield different pieces, with remarkably different properties. This dense, stronger wood stands upright and bears hugh loads, even at angles. The tree itself shows this, the massive girth, height, and load of its limbs going off diagonally, even horizontally, from the trunk. The house made of such wood, not surprisingly, in response to its material, displays upright forms and diagonal dynamics.

Stone, too, is given. Fieldstone and fallen stone, the curse of the farmers who would plant, much less plow, presents itself abundantly in some locations, even before anything else, to be taken up and used to make a house and fence. This same clearing of the fields enables farming to occur. Stone calls for human response. To one who knows the character of stones, they show how they can be shaped, how they can be gathered in rising walls which stand solidly for a very long time, tight and solid.

The roof, as Weiss notes, is not just a fifth side to a house. Rather, it completes the four walls, making them into a house. The roof—as roof, over the walls, covering them and enclosing their inner area—allows the walls their difference, shows them as walls which stand and enclose, not as vertically rising fences or pens. While the roof depends, then, on the standing of the walls which hold it up and allow it to span and cover, the roof simultaneously allows the walls to stand, as walls.

The roof also is a response to what is given by earth and sky. Trees grow from earth into sky and because of the rain and sun which the sky gives. Hence, the tree mediates between earth and sky. There is a further mediation of earth and sky in the house, which gathers them together, first in its walls

FIGURE 5.2.
Vernacular Dwelling, Switzerland. Building as Response to Potential of Wood.

FIGURE 5.3.
Sawmill outside Grindlewald. Dense Hardwood Stands Upright, Bearing Hugh Vertical and Horizontal Loads.

Vernacular Dwelling, Switzerland. Roof Responds to Earth and Sky.

rising between earth and sky, then in the roof, not only placed between earth and sky, but even between house, as rising earth, and sky. Wood carefully split into shingles, according to its grain, and placed in patterns as roofing, keeps wind and snow and rain from blowing into the house. In further mediation of earth and sky, the wood roofing rising up to the heavens may be capped, and held down to earth, by one of the most earthly elements, stone. Or, flat stones overlapping one another, or straw in dense, strongly linear bundles, or overlapping tiles (themselves the product of earth and water—clay—and fire) form other kinds of roofs, which each join earth and sky in a different manner.

But, a house is more than walls and roof. A house can have its essential features and form as a house only because, first of all, it is a site for a home. As many others have noted, a crucial feature of most homes is the presence of fire and the patterns of human actions associated with it. While barns and sheds are also buildings with walls and roof, it is the tended fire which enables walls and roof to become a dwelling by giving warmth to a family and allowing the cooking of nourishing meals, by drawing them into a circle as a family and as tenders of fire and dwelling itself.

How does all this happen? Chimney, fireplace, and stove are the things which provide a place for fire and its effects, safely within the house which it could destroy. Chimney, fireplace, and stove contain an intense blaze or, more usually, coals burning for long periods. By holding fire, protecting it from draft and water and allowing more fuel to be added and assimilated, chimney and fireplace and stove keep fire going and, thus, *free fire to burn and heat*. At the same time, because it is kept within their containing, fire is *kept in bounds*. Its danger is rendered safe.

In the hearth, fire—the overwhelmingly powerful force of the heavens that comes from sun and lightning—is brought "down" and kept within the house. And, consumed earthly fuel and fire are let go again, released back to the heavens, by the chimney, in the forms of smoke and heat. Human life thrives at this juncture and interchange of earthly and heavenly elements.

Because chimney and fireplace and stove enable us to heat and cook, they lead to table and chair, to knife and spoon and plate, to cupboard, to beds and mattresses. Much has been said about the hearth in the dwelling place. Perhaps the following is sufficient here to hint at its role in the Swiss house. The *sitzbank,* made of tiles which retain the heat of the oven whose outer "wall" they form and whose fire within is a beloved place in the kitchen, a room that itself already is one of the most intimate of all places in the family dwelling.

There are, of course, other things: cistern and wood pile, doors and windows, stairs and loft, the rooms themselves. Cistern and wood pile are gatherings. Wood, given by nature, is collected and chopped by human work, and sheltered so as to cure and remain dry. Thus, the wood pile is formed and tended as partly natural, partly humanly "made." Stone or wood cisterns gather water, which sun and sky have collected earlier from earth and its lakes and seas, to let freshly fall as rain or snow, or to be purified and retained as it flows through the earth to cold underground streams. Cisterns hold this water for inhabitants who use it for cooking, for drinking, and for washing their bodies and clothes so they can come together decently.

Door and window open out and let in; they close off and keep out. As often has been discussed, much about the essential nature of the door can be discovered in its characteristic appearance as threshold.[35] The door is a site through which the family enters to partake of their inner life together. It is the site whereby a stranger may be invited in. The door also secures the house. It shuts against the outsider not privy to the action within; it shuts against thieves and other threats to the family's well-being. The family, however, passes freely through the door, which joins and witnesses their inner and outer spheres of dwelling and life.

Windows especially allow the outside and inside to gather together because, almost magically, windows also keep them distinct.[36] For example, glass windows separate outside and inside, while letting light in and our glance out. Windows can be opened to play on this balance between inside and outside. Fresh air can come in along with light. Through ventilation holes in the base of windows, the phenomena occurs in a small way, as a pie on the window sill cools and spreads its aroma before being served for supper.

The special, focal gathering of inhabitants and their surroundings by windows is marked with window boxes of flowers. The window boxes hold out soil and seed to rain and light. The red geraniums which come forth release their color and scent back to heavens and earth, back to those who live amidst these cosmic dimensions.

Stairs, as notched logs or cantilevered stones or rising planks on the outside of the building, may go to an upper floor or loft. Here things are stored; here people sleep; here older or younger generations live under the same roof. Stairs allow coming and going. Or, stairs may go to the cellar, where food is kept, preserved. Like the door, they enable passage, now between higher and lower levels of the house.

Stairs allow for the routing of family members as they go about their chores and responsibilities, each contributing to family life and the maintenance and use of the dwelling and animals. Stairs allow them to come together and share too, at table, over storytelling and worrying and grief, in the marriage bed.

Obviously, the house does not stand alone. With it, and part of the dwelling place, are outbuildings. The barn, with its stalls, shelters draft horses and cattle, some at night, some during the long winter. In sheds, the animals' hay is kept, readily available; ladders, forks and shovels, harness and rope, milk buckets and the one-legged milking stool are housed here. Also in barn and shed, through the milk they give, cattle contribute to the life and well-being of the family which keeps them. The close belonging together of family and animals is witnessed in the oldest form of habitation, where both dwelt under one roof.

Patterns of farming—the daily and seasonal work of planting, harvesting, and storing, of letting cattle go to pasture, calve, and be milked—and also building and settlement forms make clear that Swiss dwelling belongs to the surrounding and containing sphere of earth and sky.

Standing back from, or coming upon, the house, barn, and sheds, we can see their relation to the surrounding landscape. They are situated not only in regard to the hillside which immediately bears them, but to the entire valley and the weather which comes there. Settlements are sited so as to recognize and receive the wind which is channeled by and into the valley, the attendant moisture and temperatures, the patterns of season and growth. Accordingly, these settlements manifest a local understanding of the way cold and frost come, how snow drifts and melts, the way spring rain and breeze and summer heat appear.

For example, the prevailing wind currents, humid out of the west and cooled as they move across the hills and mountain glaciers, drop moisture as they come. Hence, house and barn nestle back into the hillside, their roofs echoing the hillside's slope and their wide overhang sheltering the house's walls and inhabitants from snow and rain. Sloping down the valley side, the neighboring buildings and roofs repeat the pattern, as houses are spaced between streams which bear torrents of rain and melting snow, and away from avalanche areas.

Other winds come too, regional and local. The *Bise*, which descends from the northeast, clearing sky of clouds with its cold, dry air, bites into house and inhabitants. Farmhouses, for example in western Switzerland, turn a windowless wall to it. Walls and roofs, chimneys and windows also are oriented in regard to *der Föhn*, the hot wind from the south, which sets yet another tone, scorching springtime buds, blowing sparks from fireplaces which cause fires, and bringing headaches with its high pressure.

Indeed, in the context of the landscape's dynamic, what we have too simply called "house" itself appears as only part of a larger rhythm of life. Typically, dwelling—home—is not narrowly fixed, fitted to just one plot of land. Rather, it moves across three kinds of settlement: alps, "May-village," and permanent "church-village." "Alp," in the sense used by Swiss mountain farmers, names the high meadows which serve as summer pasture. These meadows, which reach up to rock and snow, are temporarily inhabited during the summer by a man and a boy or two of the family, who move with the

FIGURE 5.5.
Swiss Dwelling. Seasonal Dwelling in a Vertical Landscape.

cattle. The seasonal life is stark and isolated with punishing nineteen-hour workdays. Milking is done; cheese is made in rude huts, where a copper kettle holding simmering milk and a cheese press, stove, and plank table are the only furnishings. A pig to eat the whey and a few hens are the only companions. The sound of cow bells is not romantic here, though it is useful and even comforting. The clear, pure tone, after all, tells the herder where the cattle are, if not penned. This amidst the sound and play of winds, thunderstorms, and waterfalls.

Lower, connected by well-worn paths, and, likely, fences, are the hayplots. There is a sort of rough village, with stalls for cattle and hay, occupied by the menfolk in May (amid spring wildflowers and the calls of songbirds, the smell of soil and vegetation) and in the fall. Often, the entire family may be here for a part of the summer. This is where the great task of haymaking takes place, a crucial event because it gathers and stores the harvest of food for cattle, and hence the livelihood of family and community. The harvest is the fruit of earth and the heavens and human labor. With an eye to the sky for indications of sun and rain, the family scythes the ripened grass from the meadows, pitches and hangs it on racks to dry, threshes it on the barn floor or more likely on sheets laid out in the open, stores it, and later carries it further down by sled.

Lower still, below even forests and commonly held wild hay-plots, lies the valley floor, with the permanent village and church, the houses and gardens, the barns and stalls with which we began our description. Here the chores continue: milking, feeding, removing manure. Here the strong smells of ammonia from the stalls, the odor of milk culture and hay.

The specific modes of belonging of family and animals and buildings to the rhythms of earth and the heavens carries over in the relation of neighbors in the hamlet or village. In the regular interchange of place and work, inhabitants are separated during summer in the high alps, gathered together in spring and fall to help with haying and with barn raising and hut building, then joined in town for holiday festival and holy day, and in winter's deep. Family members, moving through these landscapes, settlements, and life patterns, move through experiences of isolation and private and communal intimacy.

As the family finds the most enduring social life in the town, so too it comes to church there. The church, in turn, sends its steeple from earth to the heavens and mediates humans and divinity. The church bell sends its call and order not only throughout village, but far beyond into the surrounding countryside, into the sky and against mountainside. The bell's sound tells not so much the hour, as more the time for the phases of day and life: midday break, evening prayer and meal, Sunday service and holiday, funeral and wedding.

FIGURE 5.6.
Swiss Hay-Plot

Clearly, a village house is more than a temporary location for a family. It endures. That means it not only has a lasting relationship to the surrounding landscape, and to the family's life over decades, but to the community which has long gone on nearby. That means it also is related to the course of past and future generations. This connection is seen in the house that provides for several generations to live together, with a place for all that also allows them to grow and thrive. It also is seen in the way the house and family are related to the dead, to those who have lived there before. Hence, the house does not omit the encounter of humans to their own mortality. Rather, the house helps humans encounter their own mortality—and the divine, long associated with the hope for and promise of a life after death.

Houses are made so that a corner of a room is set aside for the holy and the memory of the dead. Often a crucifix and fronds from Palm Sunday or pictures of the Sacred Hearts of Jesus and Mary are placed here. This corner is a special place in the home for prayer and recalling family, which yet remains open to and part of the household's daily life. By way of this corner, the household and divinity stay open to each other. They continue belonging together.

Here we find an example of how language is crucial in interpreting the home. The language of anthropology reduces this corner of the building and aspect of being to an "objective category" by considering it through the concept "*die Kultecke*" ("cult corner").[37] But, of course, it is no such thing to the family living there. To them it is a place which allows and manifests their mode of living devoutly, in daily connection with deceased loved ones and divinity. They call the place "*der Herrgottswinkel*" (the Lord God's corner or niche). This corner, a key to orientation of mortals to the heavenly realm, sets the form for seating around the table, which itself is the scene of the gathering of the bounty of earth and the heavens before the family.[38]

The rural Swiss, in all these ways, dwell between the heavens and earth. The mountains are the place where earth rises up, with power and exquisite delicacy, to meet the sky. The valleys are the place where sky dips down to touch the earth. Mortals spend the course of their lives in between. In the simultaneous mutuality of natural and cultural realms there is no contest to see which is first or which can dominate, no struggle whether human desire can be imposed on a material realm or whether elemental features determine the built. What occurs is the round play of the natural and cultural, which dances forth as style or manner of living in a place, and in house and settlement as dwelling places, where earth, the heavens, the divine and human are mutually attuned, where they mutually attune themselves to one another.[39]

Heidegger's approach, of course, is not limited to evoking the meanings of past or disappearing settlement forms. Rather, it is useful to retrieve the deep meaning of any life-world, a meaning usually lost in the reductive conceptual analyses of representational science or functional operations. The power of his mode of interpretation is that it concretely brings into language the unfolding of the fourfold world that occurs in our shared, local ways of dwelling, thus rescuing dwelling's possibilities from both the oblivion of unthinking everydayness and of conceptualizing metaphysics.

Since Heidegger contends that, along with unavoidable contemporary concealments, such genuinely potent meanings of dwelling still are given to us today, his approach, as well as Eliade's, is suspect for Derrida and Foucault. The next question, then, is whether Heidegger is still roped to his forebears from Plato to Nietzsche and thus falls prey to the avalanche in which metaphysics is being swept away. Or, did he manage to free himself with originary thinking and leap over to even a small clearing in a new, nonmetaphysical realm?

Part II
Practical Directions

6

Using Heidegger: A Critique
and Shift toward Praxis

It seems that in the postmodern era the task of thinking and building is to remain free from "naive" illusions. The freedom from the illusion of the metaphysics of presence, both in theory and in practical endeavors such as architecture and planning, should be a permanent gain. The question of *how* to go on continually needs to be asked, however, since it is not clear how the act of deconstruction can persist. Here the difference between Derrida's and Heidegger's understanding of deconstruction is crucial. Derrida sees deconstruction as the only option, one that inevitably will generate new discourse and conventions, including his own work, which in turn will need to be torn down. In contrast, Heidegger sees the destruction as a clearing away preparatory to a new building. In Derrida's strategy, we stay within the eternal recurrence of disassembly; in Heidegger's, the next move is through and beyond deconstruction to positive gathering together.

The strongest indication of how to accomplish the latter goal comes from Heidegger himself. His later work shows how Derrida and company are not radical enough. Because their tactic is to invert and displace metaphysical ideas, they remain still tied to the metaphysical system, necessarily moving within its way of thinking, structural categories, and history, even as they approach its end. Heidegger admits that he himself remained entrapped, long after he thought he had "overcome metaphysics."[1] Yet, Heidegger apparently also did manage to break through to the no-longer-metaphysical.[2] According to Heidegger's most radical lead, the next task would be to pass beyond a deconstruction of Deconstruction in order to recover an appropriate belonging with a meaningful world. Indeed, it can be argued that Derrida himself, an exceptionally talented reader of Heidegger, does not finally or unequivocally deny Heidegger this task.[3]

OND DECONSTRUCTION

Heidegger agrees with Nietzsche, Foucault, and Derrida that the illusions of the past need to be displaced and stripped away. Yet, against Derrida and the others, Heidegger contends that the revelation of the power of our fictive grasp of the world simultaneously conceals within itself—and from itself— the historical unfolding of the natural and cultural worlds which need to be brought into "unconcealment." In such a move beyond deconstruction, "reality" and "truth" are not understood as some reassembly after our disassembly of the false, posturing relations of sign and signified. Rather, Heidegger advances the interpretation of truth as the disclosure (*aletheia*) of the dynamic granting (*Ereignis*) of the natural, human, and sacred dimensions of the cosmos. Further, according to Heidegger, it is possible to establish a genuine belonging with what is given to us, rather than an ironic or disassembled relationship with it.[4]

Thus, Heidegger does insist on soberly facing the withdrawal of the traditional sphere of comforting meaning, a withdrawal that is only beginning to assert itself in the powerful illusions of our symbolic languages, actions, and built environments. At the same time, he holds that we have a post-deconstructive prospect, a possibility that is itself concealed precisely insofar as we still remain enthralled by metaphysics, which includes deconstruction. We can thoughtfully and responsibility remain open to the possibility given for a no-longer-metaphysical dwelling by saying "yes" to a self-releasement from the prison of willful power and purely fictive discourse. For Heidegger, the preparatory destruction of tradition readies us for releasement *from* subjectivity, nihilism, and representation and opens up the way *to* a no-longer-metaphysical world which may emerge. This post-deconstructive alternative would not amount to a false and easy switch to a secure realm, but, full of risk and uncertainty, would attempt a first turning toward the required new mode of thinking, interpretation, and building.

The wonderful gift handed on by Heidegger should not be derided from a supposedly chic, skeptical, and nominalistic post-structural posture, especially insofar as the most radical and penetrating thought actually is that of the later Heidegger. The deepest thinking shows how such a destructive pose represents an incomplete phase of development that needs to be replaced by a releasement involving giving up our clever, willful attitude and the glamour of facile cynicism in favor of a more humble reverence and dedicated attention to the simple.[5]

Today we still need a middle way between absolutism and relativism if we are to adequately understand, plan, and build a socially pluralistic and ecologically appropriate environment. The amazingly powerful absolutist apparatus of academic and institutional positivism remains on the right. Though intellectually discredited for over fifty years, it still is politically and economically the dominant force. The radically relativistic approaches now acted out by Foucault, Derrida, and others are on the left. A radically self-critical hermeneutics appears to be in the middle.[6] Hence, from the right, the heirs of positive science claim that hermeneutics is too qualitative or subjective. Even a sophisticated, moderate humanistic geographer, David Sopher, speaks for many when he says, "the social scientist learns to be wary of poets; and I myself read them, if at all, with the utmost care."[7] From the left, the disassembling strategists argue that hermeneutics is conservatively holding on to a passé belief in the real, objective, and essential.

If we do want to inquire hermeneutically into the problems and possibilities of dislocation, belonging, and dwelling in the technological era, it makes good sense to proceed with Heidegger as a guide since he has thought the matter through perhaps better than anyone else in the century. As Heidegger argues, for all our scholarship and intellectual cleverness, we continually fail to think because we insist on moving too quickly to the next new and interesting idea, without pausing to meditate on what we are doing, where we actually are right now, and what our options are at the end of the twentieth century for thinking, living, and building, for planning, architecture, and environmental research.[8]

ROMANTIC NOSTALGIA OR APPROPRIATE RESPONSE?

There are, however, two potential problems with following the way that Heidegger opens up for rethinking our world. It would make no sense to use him as a guide for environmental practices if he goes in the wrong direction or if his thinking leads to tyrannical results. These two concerns are raised respectively, by those who argue that Heidegger is retrogressively conservative and that his connection with Nazism renders him permanently taboo.

To pick up the dynamic from the earlier chapters, those who seek to follow Eliade or Heidegger hold that there is some positive opening through the use of philosophical, historical interpretation to go deeper into things around us in our ordinary lives, to see them as we had not before, to emerge with fresh insights that will help guide us in what we do next. But those who cast their lot with Foucault and Derrida shake their heads in disagreement and mutter that with Eliade and Heidegger we hear a tale of failed nerve, a story showing that hermeneutics does not have the courage to finish without a happy, "uplifting" ending.

The skeptics contend that even if hermeneutics could do a decent enough job of exposing the obviously untenable cultural underpinning of pious nature cults or exploitive doctrines of "manifest destiny," it doggedly tries to rescue a lost and even undesirable cause by piling on tales of a lost meaning to be found beneath the surface of environmental phenomena. The semblance of attuned caring for a great mystery would appear to be nothing but a lapsed romanticism, a hopelessly nostalgic exhortation to return to past environments that never were valid. This sort of argument is made from several opposing camps. In addition to those we are focally considering, the Marxist critique could be added, as when Henri Lefebvre, while acknowledging his admiration, also criticizes Bachelard and Heidegger for nostalgically focusing on the house in what he takes to be an obsession with an almost absolute space.[9]

To what extent is this so? Do Eliade and Heidegger eventually advocate a quaint world of villages, rural retreat, and philosophical folk? Doesn't the hermeneutic bias show in the very examples it uses—in the focus on exotic, primal, and traditional environments and in the exclusion of "disapproved" environments such as modern and postmodern cities or technological landscapes?[10] Doesn't the language assume a mythopoetic, even pseudo-religious, tone that pretends to an authority hypocritical in light of the uncompromisingly critical rigor required of us today?

Insofar as these charges are true, they would point out a major shortcoming in hermeneutical research and perhaps a fatal flaw in the approach itself. The description of "what might once have been" or "merely is wished" would be deceptive if it postures as "what is" and "should be." Moreover, any self-serving selection of topics and atmospheres would be ideologically prejudiced.[11] Hermeneutics, then, might appear as a neoconservative movement, suspicious of the energy of today's mass media, sprawling cities, and technological innovations.[12] It would appear to advocate a return to an environment *given* by traditional cultures and forms, not actively and freely *created* by liberated individuals. If so, hermeneutics would be dangerous and misleading because what is given today is precisely the postmodern rejection and overturn of imposed traditional conventions of environment and behavior.[13]

If valid, these criticisms would show the self-vitiating inconsistency of hermeneutics' own program and advocates and would indicate that it is illegitimate in environmental research and practice.[14] To focus on two of the most famous (or notorious, depending on the outcome of judgment) founders, Eliade continually seeks spiritual symbolism and inspiration in the mystical world of archaic societies and in India, where he spent a youthful phase and to which he apparently longed to return. The parallel case considered above involving the vanished world of Native Americans seems a projection of white peoples' nostalgia for a lost paradise which was constructed only insofar as the already tattered way of life and environment were being destroyed.[15]

Similarly, Heidegger pleas for authenticity, being-in-the-world, guarding Being, dwelling, and belonging, while analyzing Greek temples, harvest jugs of wine, and farmhouses in the Black Forest (and, in the example I provided, leading us to focus on places such as rural Switzerland). Do these value-charged environments and interpretations really show that the world we might desire is to be found only in the hazy past, or in peasant life, which people have been trying to escape for a long time and whose harshness and limitations on individual possibilities have fed the growth of cities for centuries? It would be no coincidence that Eliade and Heidegger would advocate rootedness in the past and be hostile to the dawning technological age or to cynical reason.[16] The rhetoric which exalts the mundane and presses the virtues and values of these places upon the reader implies that the past environment should still be lived in.[17]

Obviously, we are in danger if there are no boundary walls and no entrance gates to help us stay clear on the difference between fantasy-lands and escapist entertainment on the one hand and, on the other, the actual, dangerous world with its oppressive academic and political structures. Without such a discernment, action and moral responses to the environment would not be possible.

In fact, Heidegger does diagnose the problem of contemporary culture as homelessness. He analyzes how we no longer are rooted in patterns which previously related cycles of human life and death to specific locations and modes of appearance of earth and the heavens. He discerns how we are disconnected from the divine with the current absence or silence of the gods. He also recognizes the disclosure of new dimensions such as subjects' freedom gained through political processes and power acquired through technology, which controls environments and resources and produces amazing wealth. These new dimensions obviously need to be seen and described. With each historical epoch, Heidegger contends, the specific aspects of reality which are disclosed and concealed vary: we discover new freedom of choice and mobility and forget our old sense of place and cease to die in the midst of family.[18]

Heidegger is not opposed to the modern era in any simplistic way.[19] That would be pointless. Quite the opposite, he contends that the dawning technological age has been incubating for centuries—since the Greeks and Romans began work on logic, engineering, and military logistics; since medieval categorization and machinery; since the modern differentiation of subject and object. The technological is unavoidable and is not subject to the control of individual human agents. Its "ontological"-"structural" changes underlie the very possibility of our experience. While Heidegger recognizes that technology is just beginning to show its power and global reign, he also argues that what is at risk is too precious to forget. Essential dimensions of our human nature will be lost if we let fall into oblivion phenomena such as the focal experience of death as part of human existence, the modes of belonging to and reverence for the cosmos and the life given to us which is beyond our creative powers, the attendant proper fear of *hubris,* the power of language to name and hold in memory, and the built environment's power to shape a world full of meaningful possibilities for us.

How to avoid being purely negative about the contemporary era, how not to be a Luddite? What concrete examples of positive value could Heidegger point to? How could he describe, practically, what we might do in the future to complement technology's power? Heidegger is explicit on the duality of the challenge: we can not, and should not wish to, go back to live nostalgically in the past; we need to find a way to incorporate technology into future life.[20]

As a strategy, to be able to specifically describe and interpret alternatives to the present situation, Heidegger looks to key events where some major environment and corresponding values have been disclosed. Here, the constitution of a new environment would amount to the emergence of a new viable mode of life-world. Just as the young Heidegger found illuminating keys to personal experience in encounters with death and anxiety in *Being and Time,* twenty-five years later the maturer Heidegger explores how meaningful—and paradigmatic—environments are disclosed not only for the Greeks by their temples, but for his own Black Forest neighbors by their homes, country paths, church towers and bells, as well as for dwellers and the stranger passing in the snow outside the house's threshold.[21] These examples are *not* meant to describe the entire set of possible or desirable environments. Drawn from what Heidegger had deeply experienced and thought, they intend to show that in these environments meanings and values actually have occurred that made dwelling possible. In addition, the analyses contend that environments are not fundamentally understood in scientific terms, while also acknowledging that scientific knowledge has its strengths in other areas. By looking meditatively at how valid modes of living have opened up for others in specific places and circumstances, we too can catch a glimpse of what matters and perhaps a hint about what to do.

But, if Heidegger's (and Eliade's) hermeneutics are so wholesome, why the suspicion and misunderstanding? In the practical interpretations above, I have taken care to develop examples that are the same kind used by Eliade and Heidegger themselves. The Native American example for Eliade and the Swiss landscape for Heidegger are chosen deliberately, as entirely typical of the two thinkers in order to show both the fundamental strengths and weaknesses of their approaches. These examples do force us to ask why the seemingly conservative drive for the exotic and rustic. There are two major reasons. First, Heidegger erred in his understanding of "belonging and rootedness." Second, followers practicing hermeneutics as well as critics often have erred in not attending to the other aspects and examples used by Eliade and Heidegger and also by too narrowly focusing on or exaggerating the role of past environments.

In describing the homelessness of our technological era, Heidegger often identifies authentic dwelling with being rooted in a place, especially in the works most read by environmental researchers such as *Being and Time* and the essays collected as *Poetry, Language, Thought.* That identification is too simple; it is wrong. Nomads, for example, display profound patterns of belonging to the cosmos, living in forms subtly attuned to seasonal change, biological rhythms, and environmental variations. To fish and hunt by moving as part of the environment is a different, but valid mode of being at home. The proper distinction, then, is between (1) rooted and nomadic modes of being at home and (2) homelessness as obliviousness to necessary world or environmental relations. As a consequence, Heidegger exaggerates the contrast between traditional stability and contemporary mobility, and the latter is not seen in relation to its proper historical precedents and future potentials.[22]

The error is all the stranger because it belies Heidegger's own conviction that human life remains always underway.[23] This latter position is a constant motif throughout Heidegger's work that somehow is overshadowed when he deals with rootedness. Partly this is explained by seeing that Heidegger always speaks about the meaning of ultimate reality and human life in a manner that avoids any physicalist reduction. That is, the search for an authentic life and proper belonging in the world primarily is a spiritual and symbolic, not literal or physical, journey. As a case in point, Heidegger's wonderful explication of Hölderlin's poem "Homecoming" makes the case that one has to move away from what is so familiar and taken for granted that it is invisible in order to be able to understand it for the first time and then choose responsibly and freely to engage with it. But, one may stay in one physical place and undertake this journey that searches for a change in meaning, as happens with a terminally sick person from their bed or a scholar in his room.[24] Thus, being underway as human does not necessarily correlate with a special physical placement or movement.

Still, when Heidegger does use the image of people as rooted, as growing from native soil and a local dialect, he is pointing to one way of life, one way of belonging to the world. But he finally does exclude others by never choosing an example that concretely points to mobile possibilities. He does have a lacuna in regard to rhythmic or life-cycle movement, a blind spot which partially explains the persistent misunderstanding and mutual hostility between Heidegger and mobile Americans.

In this lapse by Heidegger, we can see more clearly the danger of over-emphasis on the local. The inherent dangers of provincialism and of the exclusion of differences are ignored as are the corresponding traditions and benefits of cosmopolitan and urban worlds. Of course, Heidegger deliberately and consistently is undertaking a critique of the cosmopolitan movement that resulted from the Enlightenment's view of reason, human nature, and the earth. From the Greek and Roman building of theaters and marketplaces, from Latin as a universal language and the original meaning of "catholic" as "universal" which emerged in the Middle Ages, the West has worked to develop a way in which people can be at home in many parts of the world. Neither St. Paul nor St. Augustine, nor even Caesar, are regarded by conservatives as "rootless" and "inauthentic." At the same time, being at home in several places and languages need not be reduced to sterile homogeneity as the worse examples of the built environment might indicate. This issue opens to the current debates about the possibility and desirability of regional architecture and design.

As to the error of exaggerating the role of past cases and exotic environments, phenomenological and hermeneutical analyses have done a disservice insofar as they have focused too narrowly on historical accomplishments and traditional examples, at times to the point of ignoring urban and common landscapes or by proposing a future that ignores the dynamic, unavoidable, and healthy tension between the achievements and dangers of technology and the achievements and dangers of complementary meditative-poetic dwelling.

In part, the problem has resulted from working in a new area. In beginning the phenomenology and hermeneutics of the environment, it was natural to start with obvious and clear subject matter as Bachelard did when describing attics and cellars. Closer attention shows that neither Eliade nor Heidegger ignored the contemporary situation. As noted above, Eliade wrote at length about "Survivals and Camouflages of Myths," "The Myths of the Modern World," "Religious Symbolism and Modern Man's Anxiety," and the continuation of mythic elements in mass media and popular heros, in the art of Chagall and Brancusi, in the initiations of elite intellectuals via *Finnegan's Wake, tachisme,* and atonal music, and in Marxist Communism.[25] Heidegger attended to the contemporary environment in his less read work on technology: atomic energy, jet aircraft, radar stations, airports, highways, and power generating systems are deftly described as we will see below.[26]

As to the body of current environmental research, there has been a corresponding change and broadening of subject matter. Naturally, as researchers became able to move beyond repeating or varying the examples of the great thinkers and beyond the simple, clearer cases, the focus enlarged. Thus, to some extent, the lingering image of romantic nostalgia stems from a stereotype where hermeneutical and phenomenological research are not recognized as covering diverse environments or as having more recent states of growth.[27]

Further, it is the case that both Eliade and Heidegger want to find the meaning of what lies hidden within the actual world around us because it is the nearest of all—the splendor of the simple as Heidegger calls it.[28] For his part, Eliade says,

> The most commonplace existence swarms with images and symbols. Let us repeat . . . that symbols never disappear from the *reality* of the psyche. The aspect of them may change, but their function remains the same; one has only to look behind the latest masks. . . . The life of modern man is swarming with half-forgotten myths, decaying hierophanies and secularized symbols. . . . They are of no less interest for all that. These degraded images present us the only possible point of departure for the spiritual renewal of modern man. It is of the greatest importance, we believe, to rediscover a whole mythology, if not a theology, still concealed in the most ordinary, everyday life of contemporary man; it will depend upon himself whether he can work his way back to the source and rediscover the profound meanings of all these faded images and damaged myths. But let no one object that these relics are of no interest to modern man, that they belong to a "superstitious past" happily liquidated by the nineteenth century . . . or that it is all right for poets, children and the people in the Tube to satiate themselves with nostalgias and images, but for goodness sake let serious people go on thinking and "making history." Such a separation between the "serious things of life" and "dreams" does not correspond with reality. Modern man is free to despise mythologies and theologies, but that will not prevent his continuing to feed upon decayed myths and degraded images. . . . All that essential and indescribable part of man that is called *imagination* dwells in realms of symbolism and still lives upon archaic myths and theologies. . . . Hence the failure of man "without imagination"; he is cut off from the deeper reality of life and from his own soul.[29]

But, even if the methods, intentions, and achievements of Eliade and Heidegger finally focus on the common world and avoid both the elitism of pointing only to examples of valued environments associated with high culture and the suffocating nostalgia of lapsing into the way things never were, there remains the deeper problem of whether there is some sort of meaning and "reality" there to be found—the major point of contention between the two sides. Hermeneutics *does claim* that meaningful environments have existed, still exist, and can be described and interpreted. The implication is that one can discern the nurturing from the harmful, can evaluate the better and the worse, and can apply the insights gained to future action and design.

Thus, to an extent, hermeneutics stands by the work criticized above. Whatever the shortcomings in emphasis and partial treatment, the traditional environments of Native Americans and Alpine peoples and many of America's past environments do manifest meaningful patterns for human life and still can be instructive if appropriately retrieved. This assumption is straightforwardly part of the hermeneutical tradition, even while we now try to reject any reductive relativism or historicism and to pass beyond any anthropocentric humanism (as Heidegger argues in "Letter on Humanism").

INVOLVEMENT WITH NATIONAL SOCIALISM

A second and far nastier problem with using Heidegger's thinking has to do with the credibility, even propriety, of using it at all. The issue, of course, is raised by the current controversy concerning Heidegger's involvement with National Socialism. The issue and problem are not new, having arisen three times before. The first occasion was in 1945. During the de-nazification hearings held by the occupational powers Heidegger presented his account of his term as Rector of the University of Freiburg during 1933–34 and requested permission to teach again. Permission was not granted until more than five years after the request. In the early 1950s a second wave of controversy came with the publication of a lecture course, *Introduction to Metaphysics,* that had been delivered in 1935. The issue at the time revolved around a phrase concerning "the inner truth and greatness" of National Socialism that Heidegger let stand from the lectures, without revision, comment, or retraction.[30] Some argued that he refused to recant his interest in the movement; others contended that he was manfully opening himself to criticism without trying to hide or explain away what had been said. The third outbreak occurred in 1976 after Heidegger's death and the posthumous publication of the famous *Der Spiegel* interview, actually given ten years before, in which Heidegger declined the final opportunity to "explain himself."

The general response "on behalf of Heidegger" has been that his involvement was born of philosophical and political naiveté, was brief and regretted, but not explained because it was Heidegger's way not to be pressured, because any additional comments would only appear as evasions of responsibility and would muddy the waters even further, because embroilment in issues of ideology and "personality" would prevent genuine questioning about what is the most question worthy of all: Being, *Ereignis* (Event of Appropriation), *Es Gibt* ("It gives"). This position acknowledged what was known and allowed most, including me, to proceed with good conscience.

The immediate occasion for the latest and current controversy, Victor Farias' notorious book, is in itself only of minor importance, markedly flawed, and even wrong in places.[31] The book and several subsequent inflammatory reviews and letters to the editor in such usually balanced publications as the *New York Times* in fact present little new information that is not careless and misleading.[32]

What actually makes the latest phase different from the previous ones is that with new archival material the historian Hugo Ott has conclusively shown that Heidegger's break with National Socialism after his resignation from the rectorate in 1934 was not as complete and his involvement neither as short-lived nor casual as he pretended and as many of the faithful believed.[33]

While the entire sensational affair goes on, the best, most open and thoughtful, general analyses are those of Karsten Harries, Thomas Sheehan, and Michael Zimmerman, as well as the more specific reflections of Derrida, Lacoue-Labarthe, Lyotard, and Dallmayr.[34] As to the boom created in the media market and the resulting rush of books to press with alluring titles (and promotions making the most of the related issue of Paul de Man's earlier writings), readers will need to judge for themselves.

The fundamental issue, of course, goes beyond any curiosity about the famous philosopher's involvement with a despicable political movement and its horrible deeds. The substantive issue is that a philosopher supposedly is a professional thinker who is responsible for *truth* and for an *ethics* consistent with the highest standard set by Socrates. The difficulties in making a judgement on such a matter, and of our justifying our own ground for doing so are great enough. Greater still is the vibrating question: was Heidegger's involvement with National Socialism no accident or error from which he withdrew, but integrally bound up with his thinking and somehow inevitable? That is, is Heidegger's thinking essentially flawed and erroneous, so that it contaminates what it touches, so that it needs to be purged and avoided? If so, he would be quite the opposite of an insightful and trustworthy guide.

This is the issue taken up by responsible scholars such as Ott, Derrida, Lacoue-Labarthe, Lyotard, Sheehan, Harries, Dallmayr, and Zimmerman (the latter of whom also has undertaken a thorough reevaluation of the issue of the historical relation of technology and National Socialism to Heidegger's thought, especially in its earlier phases).[35] In written presentations and in special sessions at conferences such as the Annual Meeting of the Society for Phenomenology and Existential Philosophy held at Duquesne University in 1989, the same point is reached time and time again: we need to reread Heidegger in light of the new evidence, new suspicion, and new problematic.[36] Yes, yet again. The issue will not yield to snap judgment or simplistic responses, but only to what Heidegger called for all along, a deeper questioning and interpretation. As radically critical, we always must take up the task ourselves; we cannot transfer opinions from someone else.

HEIDEGGER AS A GUIDE FOR ENVIRONMENTAL RESEARCH AND PRACTICE

In the context of this controversy, I have two reasons for proceeding with the chapters below, which, begun long before the most recent questioning of Heidegger's thinking and revised several times since, use Heidegger to investigate the technological era. These reasons need to be given in order for readers to decide whether following the exploration in the spirit of Heidegger is a worthy venture or not.

First, having thought through the issue three times (when I first took up Heidegger seriously after several years of teaching, as I prepared for a sabbatical in Freiburg just before his death, and now with the most recent controversy), I believe that while Heidegger was not an admirable person in many ways, he was in others. His faults, while considerable, do not vitiate his thinking. From personal testimonies it always has been clear that Heidegger was a powerful personality and often impossibly difficult. At times he was petty, prejudiced, certainly hostile to most things and people American and to democracy, not forthcoming, manipulative, and even vengeful and self-serving.

But, he also often was open, charismatically generous with ideas, willing to risk himself to help others during the Nazi oppression, admired by numbers of his Jewish students, and rigorously responsible for stripping down what he had said in the 1930s and 1940s, down to its foundations in his understanding of and implication in the Western development of "willfulness," "destiny," "power," and "nihilism." As a person, then, he was very complex, a mixture of the admirable and reprehensible. How to judge this? How to judge in light of my own life? How to judge by comparison with valid moral measures? My *tentative* position, after rereading Heidegger critically in light of the new information and others' reflections, is that what Heidegger says largely is true, though it often is challenged and misunderstood by scholars and others who should know better.[37]

Second, Heidegger did, in fact, change his thinking after his encounter with National Socialism and his subsequent withdrawl and meditation via Nietzsche and Hölderlin.[38] He emerged not as a nihilist, but with the new mode of thinking that characterizes the later work such as appeared in the 1950s and after. And that is the work on which the following interpretations of technology depend. While Heidegger naturally does develop ideas that he had earlier, he worked as hard as he could and with more success than almost anyone else to think and say things in a new manner—to pass out of his earlier position and beyond the thinking on which he had built his reputation because it still was tangled in the metaphysical tradition and stance which he had struggled to overcome.

The struggle to overcome, he came to see, was itself yet one more willful act in the drama of metaphysics, and needed to be given up. In 1962, he presented *On Time and Being,* signaling the distance he had been establishing from the assumptions and approaches of the period of *Being and Time* by reversing the title of that classic published thirty-five years before (1927). He also tied to that early work his subsequent efforts at and references to "overcoming metaphysics'' which occurred regularly in the interim. From the other side of the reversal, he concludes *On Time and Being* by saying,

> The task of our thinking has been to trace Being to its own from Appropriation [*Ereignis*]—by way of looking through true time without regard to the relation of Being to beings.
>
> To think Being without beings means: to think Being without regard to metaphysics. Yet a regard for metaphysics still prevails even in the intention to overcome metaphysics. Therefore, our task is to cease all overcoming, to leave metaphysics to itself.[39]

This continuing effort and openness to releasement from any tinge of metaphysics and willfulness, this ability to give up the not inconsiderable overcoming that he had accomplished is the achievement that warrants using him as a guide.

Of course, even if these insights and arguments explain why the hermeneutic path laid down by Heidegger deserves to be followed—or is chosen by the author—*Foucault and Derrida finally are not refuted. Nor are they intended to be.* That is neither the goal of these chapters, nor the proper task. Our first goal has been to explicate what both sides say—and what the implications and potential for environmental interpretation would be—as clearly as possible in *their own terms* so that readers can make up their own minds. What would be the point of covert coercion or pretending to settle a major and lively debate that is occurring in our society?

The fundamental responsibility and contribution of these chapters, then, is to help keep the questions of environmental meaning open, to not let them settle comfortably into a ''now we have it.'' I have tried to keep this project underway in the writing and rewriting—which hopefully comes across to the readers.

At the same time, I have chosen one path to follow in the chapters yet to come, while staying in self-critical conversation with the other alternatives (as substantial revisions from the first to final versions of the chapters witness). My choice partly is the result of the thinking presented in this book and partly the result of sustained inquiry undertaken before and while these essays were in progress, the approaches and results of which need not be repeated here.[40] I also am encouraged by the fact that similar conclusions have been independently reached in the work of scholars such as Caputo and Bruins.[41]

Pondering the topic for over sixteen years has led me to believe that the radical critique and deconstruction of historical and cultural edifices does need to be done, as all the thinkers explicated here agree, and that the positive difference and prospect pointed to—*shown,* I am convinced—by Eliade and Heidegger leave the skeptical position of Foucault and Derrida as an un-

necessary self-impoverishment, intelligible to be sure at the end of metaphysics, but not to be embraced when a non-metaphysical alternative is available.
Heidegger claims no final authority, no exclusion from mistakes and dangerous errors, no exemption from the need to start over and over. Usually this
attitude is dismissed as "merely" rhetorical, as false modesty, or as a empty
ritualistic formula. Actually, as I have shown elsewhere, in such remarks and
in the form of his writing Heidegger genuinely acknowledges the difficulty
and failures of his adventurous thinking.[42] At the same time, out of the fire
of thinking itself, out of the reexamination of metaphysics and his own errors,
he also has flashes of success. He does receive the gifts of insight and, at
times, of being able to say a great deal about the historical unfolding of the
inner character of technology, unavoidable displacements, dwelling, and the
world we need in order to become fully human. It is to these pressing issues
that we now turn.

It is not possible to forecast what will or should happen in the future.
But, we do understand enough to begin to do what is required of us. As
Heidegger shows, we can try to open ourselves to what is needed for human
dwelling, and perhaps, for the vitality of all life forms if they are to come into
their proper natures in the midst of the technological epoch. We at least understand from Heidegger that we should not seek some new style of design,
but instead the necessary meanings and values in a new interpretation of what
is given to and asked of us.[43]

The issue nearest and most pressing is whether we can release ourselves
from the fascinating play of current intellectual games and let ourselves into
the interpretations and practical problems facing us as social and moral
agents, as inhabitants, researchers, and practitioners. Thus, instead of alternating among contending theories and their interpretations of historical and
avant-garde buildings and landscapes, the next task is to join in the dance that
happens in the opening made by, or given to, Heidegger. *This dance has its
own dynamic that moves powerfully back and forth between meditative thinking and the emerging technological epoch and environment.* By participating
in this dance we may come to rethink technology and its displacements in
order to understand, plan, and design today. The following chapters, then,
take up questions concerning the character of the technological environment
in which we find ourselves and the nature of our current dislocations in order
to approximate the kind of belonging we now want. They examine how we
might somehow free ourselves from constraining ties and obligations to previous places and ways of life and yet realize satisfying relationships to the
world which will enable us to reach our potential and fulfill our hopes.

7

Taking Responsibility for the Technological Landscape

We live in an increasingly technological world. Our daily actions and patterns, our built and natural environments, the very possibilities and limitations of our existence appear to result from the influence of technology. We suppose that our very mastery and control over the earth and its resources are improving our ability to solve the problems facing human habitation.

Naturally, then, we are busy in the process of making a world in which to live, in the tradition of the scientific and technological West, through such disciplines and activities as building, architecture, and urban and regional planning. As the Greek root word *techne* indicates, technology is not only a making, but fundamentally a way in which humans participate in bringing things into the world and, accordingly, a mode of knowing.[1] We are just beginning to understand that *the technological sphere has its own inner logic and principles of organization* which unfold in the world, regulating the very forms and materials which manifest technology and enable it to work.[2] Here we can see the importance of basing our practical interpretations and proposed design strategies on sound theory, since only changes which proceed from insight into the essential character and dynamic will be efficacious and appropriate. Before we can even consider whether we want to try to change or overcome technology's formation of the world and our lives, much less whether we could even do such a thing, we need to try to become open to technology by reflecting on how technology *makes* a place for us in today's and tomorrow's world.

HEIDEGGER, THINKING, AND THE TECHNOLOGICAL ENVIRONMENT

Only reluctantly do we face up to a difficulty. The technological, while successful in its application, simultaneously seems to produce forms of displacement and a reduction in the meaning and value of life. Perhaps more profoundly than anyone else in our time, Martin Heidegger has decisively articulated our dilemma and the dual threat and promise of technology. In works such as *The Question Concerning Technology,* he provides a series of insights which, if we follow them, help us encounter our contemporary situation.[3]

Suppose we begin to ask about the possibility of a dwelling place in a concrete way: what is a building, a road, a bridge, a river, or a field? According to Heidegger, in our technological epoch, *things have come to appear as stock.* That is, when we ask what a house or street is, we find that they are stock, understood as something accumulated and *standing in reserve,* waiting to be used. Think of an elevator. We go into a building and walk to the bank of elevators. There may be six or eight of them. We push a button indicating that we wish to go up. The one button operates all the elevators, bringing the closest one to our floor. We wait a bit. We push the button again. We are annoyed if a door does not open quickly so we can be on our way.

In this ordinary scene we can see that the individual elevator holds little interest for us. Any one will do. That is why there are several in a row; we have a reserve of identical items so that if one is not close to our floor, going in the direction we wish, another is likely to be. The reserve minimizes our wait because what is on reserve is standing by waiting to be called up and pressed into service.

What is important, though almost invisible in our ordinary experience, is that things about us have their character precisely as "being in reserve." Heidegger cites examples of hydroelectric power and airplanes.[4] To be an airplane is to be a complex thing which is standing by, in reserve, ready to taxi down the runway and take off. We await our flight, our plane. It does not matter whether the particular plane is just now arriving from Italy or Miami, whether it was at the terminal overnight, whether it is newly produced in California or conscientiously overhauled in New York. What matters is that it is ready at the proper time—emerging out of the general reserve for our current use. In so emerging, it also comes forward as defined or constituted as a thing disposed to be ever ready.

Here, things appear as part of a system, or systems of production, storage, ordering, payment, distribution, and so on. Think of electricity, water, and natural gas. For things such as electricity to be ever ready, we require elaborate generation systems of tunnels, pipelines, and dams, hydraulic turbines, and generators. Once produced, the current moves through transformation systems of lines, switch gears, transformers, and control-room equipment; through networks of transmission conductors and lines, poles and wire, insulators and circuit breakers; to distribution network systems of final transformers, so that it always is standing in reserve. The same is true of our dishes and cups, our tables and refrigerators, our cars and houses, and the land itself. In short: things are produced and moved about according to the

FIGURE 7.1.
Richard Rogers Partnership, Lloyd's of London Redevelopment. Elevators as Stock, Standing in Reserve.

rules and ways of *logistics.* We live in the midst of logistical systems of what stands in reserve. Things have their value, their meaning and use for us, precisely insofar as they successfully come forward into the world and remain standing as available, as stock.

Accordingly, things are related to human will because it is the will that moves things to come forth and remain available for our needs.[5] Human needs, whether regular and constant, or periodic, or unpredictable, demand the presence of things which satisfy or fulfill those needs, or which at least serve as instruments to aid in the quest for satisfaction. Because of human need, we will that a reserve of food, shelter, transportation, entertainment, and companionship be available. Need demands that there be satisfying things in reserve. Since the need can occur at any time, it requires the reserve to be always standing ready. That is, will exerts itself against needs spread over time, thus expending its energy in ordering the realm of things.

In the realm of will a challenge is issued. In technology's challenge, nature is challenged to provide what is needed, when it is needed; humans are challenged to direct and control the things and processes which are brought forth. Indeed, will itself is challenged to move ever forward and also to retain mastery over things. We will easy-to-care-for clothing, inexpensive food, comfortable and affordable houses. Consequently, fruits and vegetables from California, Texas, and Mexico are called forth all year long. Trees are called up from the American Northwest, Brazil, and the tropical Pacific to be processed into pulp and then paper and cellulose, or from cellulose into plastics and textiles; alternatively, trees are converted into charcoal, rubber products, rosin and turpentine, gum, resins, and oils to be logistically disposed to food, soap, printing, and pharmaceutical industries. Such a list barely evokes the scale and scope of the challenge and response. Clearly, though, the challenging of nature and humans to maintain things as stock is dispersed across the whole world, to places where things were not, or still are not, locally understood in the way they now appear technologically. In this pervasive challenging-forth, the nature of our contemporary era is disclosed.

The technological challenging, which is now making tomorrow's world, thinks, plans, and builds according to the dominance of standing reserve. The latter's character involves several major facets. First, technological things are and increasingly become *modular.* That is, each thing is delimited or given in a fixed and determined way, which is carefully worked out beforehand and executed according to a set plan—designed or engineered we would say.

Each of the elements of a system for the collection and transfer, storage, distribution, use, and recapture of potable water—the collection and storage devices, filtration plants, pollution monitors, pipelines, pressure gauges, taps, sewerage systems, and so on—appear as *the modular.* That is, each whole is composed of parts which are engineered in a fixed way, as determined by the rest of the system: each element is identical and interchangeable with others of the same type and suitable to its function in the network of elements. The filtration elements and pollution monitors are suited to each other. The output pipes, distribution network, production capacity, and demand correspond to one another. Thus, the water system for an entire region may be a collection of modules. At any level, from individual valves, to hugh resevoirs, to entire Municipal Utility Districts, the modular elements stand in reserve, to be used, replaced, or expanded according to the consistent rules of the system.[6]

Importantly, and in contrast to the way objects once were understood, no individual technological element is taken to have an inherent character or purpose. Rather, in a system, the meaning of each element is a function of its relationships to all the other elements, which also have their meanings according to the complete set of systemic relationships—a striking correlation with the theories of infra-referentiality laid out by Derrida and Foucault, though only Foucault picks up the connection from Heidegger and develops the relationships among technology's linguistic and symbol systems and its practices and built forms.[7] Clearly, technological things are subordinated to their systems and operate according the systems' consistent rules, which we call logistics. Today, autos, roads, bridges, rivers, fields, and forests all are transformed and used according to networks of *technological systemics.*

Obviously, technological systems are highly designed. In fact, technological design is amazingly vigorous, since the system itself exposes any flaw, any blockage, weakness, or inconsistency in the system. The elements not properly configured fail: transformers and light bulbs alike burn out; expired credit cards are rejected by automatic bank-teller machines, water hoses and nuclear plants rupture from surges beyond the levels of normally tolerated and constant capacity. It is not surprising to think of computers designing other computers since here we find the same movement. The system itself, the entire set of constituent elements and their relationships, indicates how it is to be designed and implemented. Hence, an energy system with a given nuclear generating plant calls for a specific size and number of transmission conductors and lines, spaced just so far apart, finally inserted into an urban fabric as dictated by the requirements of maximum systemic efficiency.

We assume that things are this way. A nut and bolt, a brass knob and plate, a three-by-eight-foot piece of polished wood, and a set of hinges are fixed in character by design. Collected together, these parts add up to a front door; at the same time, they appear as they do precisely because of the way the door and entire house are designed. Things are modular partly because they are expected to measure up dependably, that is, to remain usefully as stock and to enable more complex systems of things to stand by.

We see this modular character in building and all its technologies: in the divisions of working, living, sleeping, and recreational spaces and in the furnishings of these defined use-spaces in rooms and clusters of rooms, as these form the constellations we know as house, hotel, or office. Think of how we "add up" different, but fixed, types of rooms into aggregates to make, alternatively, public housing, affordable development housing, a budget hotel, a restaurant for a fast food chain, a hospital, a Tudor-style mansion. Think of how the defined shapes and areas are filled and bound with systems of color schemes, furnishings, utilities, landscaping, and roadways. All these things are produced and arranged according to our understanding of the modular, where each is an element.

The modular prevails across a wide range of scales and contexts. We find it in children's building blocks and other toys, in the use of precast pieces to assemble highway bridges, hotels, and towers of all sorts. In light of overall design and engineering specifications, the pieces are cast prior to construction somewhere else, each piece made of many smaller pieces and ready to fit together with others on the construction site to become the final thing. Like the firm's preceding designs, such as the Dallas-Fort Worth Airport, the Airport at Managua, Nicaragua by Adler, Goodman, Kalish, is a refined assemblage of terminal modules linked by a network of roads, communication and transportation systems, and runways. Each pod is set precisely so as to allow direct passenger and baggage access to and from the planes. The assemblage allows the larger systems of airlines and ground transportation to operate. In short: things appear in and as the modular.

For the modular to be as it is, modules must be combinable. Naturally, given changes over time and the nature of materials, we find a *turnover* in combinable things and parts. A large unit, or thing, may be renewed by replacing a smaller one. A house is repaired with a new roof, window, or furnace; a furnace with a new valve or thermostat. On a large scale, machines and even buildings are replaced entirely. Here, things are disclosed as the *disposable:* they need to be disposed of because they wear out or are otherwise used up. Interestingly, once things are understood as disposable, they may be disposed of because they are out of fashion or no longer pleasing. A chair may be replaced because it does not go with a new couch we have introduced, because it is not currently stylish (fashion itself is an elaborate codified system), or because it does not present us to others as we wish. Commonly, we demolish materially sound houses in order to construct something more congruent with our current tastes, needs, social position, and capital.

In order for something to be disposable, it also must be *replaceable.* What replaces is the "not yet disposed of." The replacement is the new "equivalent" of the old, either as an "*identical*" item in the cases of window panes and fuses or as the "new and improved" version in the cases of a redone kitchen or air-conditioning and heating systems. This understanding is found in the concept of manufacture by assembly line or wherever the

FIGURE 7.2.

Adler, Goodman, Kalish, Airport at Managua, Nicaragua. A Refined Assemblage of Modules.

LEYENDA
LEGEND

1 Area de la Terminal y Estacionamiento
  Terminal and Parking Area
2 Area de Carga
  Cargo Area
3 Area de Mantenimiento de Aeronaves
  Aircraft Maintenance Area
4 Area Comercial
  Commercial Area
5 Area Industrial-Puerto Libre
  Free Port Area
6 Aviación General
  General Aviation

7 Aviación Militar
  Military Aviation
8 Sistema de Combustibles
  Fuel Farm
9 Extinción de Incendio, Rescate,
  Mantenimiento y Seguridad
  Fire, Rescue, Maintenance and Security
10 Torre de Control y Administración
   del Aeropuerto
   Control Tower and Airport Administration

11 Ayudas a la Navegación
   Navigational Aids
12 Suministro de Energía Eléctrica
   Power Supply
13 Sistemas de Comunicaciones
   Communications System
14 Colector de Energía Solar
   Solar Energy Collector
15 Suministro de Agua
   Water Supply

16 Sistema Sanitario
   Sanitary System
17 Dirección de Aeronáutica Civil
   Civil Aeronautics Administration

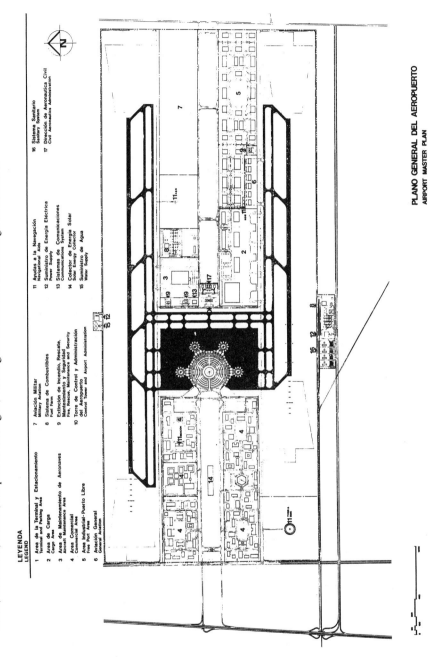

PLANO GENERAL DEL AEROPUERTO
AIRPORT MASTER PLAN

interchangeability of standardized parts occurs, that is, over all the technological world.[8]

The concepts of the disposable and replaceable in the sphere of turnover
govern more than things as we usually think of them. The city too is understood this way. Urban renewal is defined by the concept of turnover through
replacement of the disposable on many levels: one population is displaced and
replaced by another, one network of social relationships and movements by
different ones, one sort of local economic system by another with complex
substitutions and transfers of funds and rights of control. Buildings are turned
over either by demolition and replacement or, more rarely, by renovation and
restoration. Whatever the submechanisms and specific parts (rooms and
buildings, streets and freeways, subways and sidewalks, fountains and pla-
zas), cities are changed by having entire sections turned over into something
different through disposal and replacement.[9]

The same concept governs our understanding of human beings. Each laborer is disposable and replaceable by others in the labor pool. Workers, ev-
idently, like tires, become worn out or, like old floral wallpaper, become
things of which we tire. How do airlines and passengers perceive aging stew-
ardesses? Certainly, our very bodies are seen this way as we embark on replacing—transplanting—our original parts with parts from eye banks and
kidney donors, not to mention with mechanical hearts and plastic surgery.

These specific dimensions of things clarify what it means for them to
appear as *reserve*. In order to be available whenever needed and wanted, as
the modular, and in order to replace the disposable in the course of turnover,
things are interpreted and dealt with through the concept of "holding in reserve to be used." What is held in this manner is a part of, or belongs to, a
reservoir. That is, things now have their nature or are disclosed to us as part
of such resevoirs. Again, think of all the components of our energy systems.
Or, consider credit: money itself, not to mention the cruder gold or silver, is
no longer needed. Rather, credit is a standing reserve which can be built up,
depleted, transferred, held, drawn on, and so forth. The same is becoming
true of our food, clothing, and building systems. Further, nature itself appears
as a giant reservoir of raw material from which we can produce what we want
by way of physics and chemistry. Oil yields plastic and medicine and fertilizer and gasoline; grains become food or methane. Genetic research already
is opening the reservoir of genes so that we can engineer with them, creating
new forms of life.

To take another step, for things to be understood in terms of a reservoir,
they must be thought *via distribution*. Here, things show themselves as the
yet-to-be-distributed. That is why they stand by. New houses, apartments,
condominiums, and offices are constructed to be distributed. Why else? The
process requires a network of capital, land, materials, and designs; of finan-

ciers, developers, designers, builders, realtors, apartment and business location services, and newspaper advertising.

Accordingly, we have all sorts of systems, systems for what we produce, transform, and use. This also means information, communications, and banking-economic systems. It seems obvious, or even inevitable, that computers and computer languages would be created in order to facilitate the systems' flow and to generate new systems. But, computers also are themselves possible just because we conceive of things as standing in reserve in need of distribution.

Clearly, the technological is not merely a local matter. Under the sway of technology, resevoirs of the modular, networks of the disposable, become global in operation. Our communications, credit, and products encircle the globe, our companies are multinational. We have geopolitics and a world economy. English and computer languages vie to be the world language.

Insofar as the technological epoch discloses things to us in the manner seen so far, it changes what things are, or what they have been. Plants, for example, no longer are seen as objects with given features and uses determined by local surroundings and environment, but as pliable biomasses which can be manipulated to grow, even thrive anywhere in the world. The intention may be good: to produce strains of grains which will grow in places where food is needed desperately. And to support the project of world cultivation, we mobilize our networks of research and technical expertise and our resevoirs of fertilizer and machinery. We replace inefficient local plants or "nonuseful" growth with different crops. Or, if the soil is depleted or weather so difficult or intemperate that nothing seems to grow, we make every technological effort to replace those conditions too.

In a related example, our system of food production, distribution, and consumption, has developed "oranges," "tomatoes," and "lettuce," which have displaced and replaced the texture, color, and taste of earlier or indigenous local products. Native products are rejected because they look odd or imperfect: ordinarily "real" oranges are not acceptably orange or uniformly round. Clearly, things become something different than they were. A different world is being made.

In the process, things not only are understood in a global perspective, but the entire globe comes to understand things as stock. That is what the Americanization or Westernization of the rest of the world means: things everywhere are understood and used according to the same prevailing technological manner.

We can see that it is not an exaggeration to say that *the technological is making tomorrow's world:* it defines and disposes not only constructed furniture and houses, but the inner character of all things as well as our own appearance as we maneuver for progress and well-being. The whole of nature, the humanly made, and we too are dealt with as standing reserve in a way which challenges. The challenge unfolds as we plan, design, and build today for tomorrow, according to the essence of technology. *Technologically, we make or create our own world.*

Even in so brief a sketch, we can see that the nature and power of the technological is only gradually becoming clear to us. We could say that the technological era and the changes in our environment and lives are only beginning.

If the technological is so pervasive and powerful, if it promises to spread its changes and progress everywhere, it may seem an obvious course of action to enter into its spread and development. As a specific case, by exploring building, design, and planning as the means for implementing and elaborating systems of urban and regional living, we could intensify and maximally utilize the transformational character and force of the technological.

Still, without denying that the technological will become even more dominant, deeper questions remain. The changes in things have been seen by many as losses rather than advances. The technique governing tomorrow's world, including human life, may be more powerful than that of the modern world in which we have lived. But, will what is coming be good or desirable?

It is obvious that there are problems with the technological world. One way of seeing the limitations is by contrasting the technological with the richer, more complex relatedness the dimensions of the world have had to each other in the past. To cite an example at the root of global urbanization, the bewilderingly swift and apparently irreversible displacement of indigenous people by our technology, consummating what began with the age of modern commerce, is deftly delineated in Gabriel García-Márquez' description of a South American village, transformed by the food system, in this case, a banana company:

> [A] group of engineers, agronomists, hydrologists, topographers, and surveyors arrived who for several weeks explored the places where Mr. Herbert had hunted his butterflies. . . . The suspicious inhabitants of Macondo barely began to wonder what the devil was going on when the town had already become transformed into an encampment of wooden houses with zinc roofs inhabited by foreigners who arrived on the train from halfway around the world, riding not only on the seats and platforms but even on the roof of the coaches. The gringos, who later on brought their languid wives in muslin dresses and large veiled hats, built a separate town across the railroad tracks with streets lined with palm trees, houses with screened windows, small white tables on the terraces, and fans mounted on the ceilings, with extensive blue lawns with peacocks and quails. The section was surrounded by a metal fence topped with a band of electrified chicken wire which during the cool summer mornings would be black with roasted swal-

lows. No one yet knew what they were after, or whether they were actually nothing but philanthropists, and they had already had caused a colossal disturbance. . . . Endowed with means that had been reserved for Divine Providence in former times they changed the pattern of the rains, accelerated the cycle of harvests, and moved the river from where it had always been and put it with its white stones and icy currents on the other side of the town, behind the cemetery.[10]

The process of systemic technological appropriation, which fractures individuals from their natural and built environments and stable social forms is constant and widespread. The breaking up of traditionally profound ways of life occurs everywhere: in the cities and in the countryside, in the global human homelessness of political refugees and workers migrating to foreign lands, and in the pollution of the earth, seas, and atmosphere.

Thus, we encounter something very strange. Just when we feel we are more and more making the world the way we want it to be, just when we are attaining increasing power over the environment and ourselves through our techniques of engineering transformations in things, we also grapple with homelessness. We become separated from ourselves and what we belong to during the very course of what appears to be technological mastery.

Seemingly, our methods of travel, communication, and living allow us to be ''at home'' anywhere. Is this not the point of our homogeneous stores, motels, and restaurants which allow the comfort and dependability of having everything just the same no matter where in the world we are? A striking, and quite ordinary, example of the modular appearing as ''at home anywhere'' occurs with mobile homes. As Rudolf Arnheim notes, ''instead of adapting its size, shape, and color to the lay of the land, to the avenues of access and vistas, to light and weather conditions, the mobile building, like the automobile, must be designed to serve adequately in all situations and with distinctive appropriateness in none.[11]

This non-accommodation is a mode of oblivion which conceals local place in order to make possible an opening to any and all spaces. To be built anywhere and used anywhere also is the dream for the factory-made house. In short: the design of our things, services, and businesses is just beginning to see how radical autonomy from local place will work, not only in the United States and Western Europe and in places where tourists and business people go, but everywhere.[12]

The process began over 2,000 years ago, even if it has exploded lately. We need to think through the early impulse and mode of belonging in Greek and Roman colonies, the spread of a ''world'' civilization and Roman rule by way of Latin, law, and engineering. To be a Roman citizen was to be a universal person. Then, later, 'Catholic' in 'Roman Catholic' meant ''universal.'' Cosmopolitan life was a major goal of modern political rationalism.[13]

How this tendency finally resulted in such phenomena as the international school or style of design and building is part of the same story.

In any case, somehow, many who supposedly are at home everywhere—as an abundance of our ordinary experience and the witness of contemporary art, literature, philosophy, and cultural criticism attest—*are not genuinely at home anywhere.* We "necessarily" or "inevitably" design cities and build housing which will be for anyone, anywhere. Since people move so much, anyone could live there over the course of several years. This sort of building seems to be what people want and need.

But, just when it appears that we are successful at this task, it also seems that the international style inserts us into, and fits, a "nowhere."[14] We plan according to complex regional and national networks of energy, water, transportation, housing, economics, and employment. At the same time that we have more comprehensive and powerful theories of these systems and, in fact, also more actual systems in operation, at our disposal on an unprecedented scale, we are in danger of creating a homogeneous no-place for anyone and no one. "Placelessness" and "displacement" are now catchwords for this phenomena, once called "alienation." *Who* we are and *where* we are, are lost as *person* and *place* are technologically masked. Thus, globally, masses of refugees and masses of seemingly comfortable inhabitants undergo technology's uncanny homelessness. Many manifestly yearn to belong in a local place with its specific characteristics and qualities—in short, for a place where they can be satisfied.

Yet it can be argued that past worlds are gone, and new possibilities and measures have taken their place. It may be only an apparent paradox that the hyper-designed technological landscape results in monotonous order or spatial disorder. The problems with our perception and behavior in the technological landscape actually stem from *the essentially non-spatial and non-visual character of technology.*[15] Of course, the technological displays itself in a striking way because of its rigorously systemic and modular character. Highway cloverleafs are manifestations of systemic interchange. As seen above, in air-transportation systems, the modular physical basis of the system appears in the linked networks of airplanes, airports, and supporting transportation systems, where each plane, runway, terminal, hanger, highway connection, parking lot, toll booth, baggage area, and vending station is identical with others in the same constellation. The form operates at every scale: we find modules connected in the same manner on the micro-scape of the silicon chip and on the macro-scape of subway systems.

These systemic physical elements, however, often are experienced or perceived as disorderly or oppressive because the principle of organization behind the physical manifestations is not inherently spatial or visually well-formed. That is, the abstract and internally consistent systemic relationships

FIGURE 7.3.
Highways Manifest the Systemic and Modular

are not essentially connected to any specific external spatial location or pattern—not even the abstract spatial co-ordinates of the modern world. Further, the *systemic*, because it is spatially undetermined, is *not inherently connected to places*, understood as sites for human modes of belonging in the world.

Hence, the technological landscape, because its order is a function of abstract relational systems and their logistics, frequently is experienced as dislocating and placeless, as happens with the design and use of transportation, credit, and information-communication systems. Indeed, the systemic principle so fully dominates that in the case of subway systems, we need to overlay the logistical flow chart with a traditional map to make any connection between the system and the local landscape. Because modular physical elements are merely the instruments of the system's operation, even where the resulting technological shape of the earth and human life are objectionable as in the case of the telecommunications tower inserted into the Clarksville neighborhood pictured here, we confront only a symptom of the underlying technological transformation and ordering of the world.

DESIGN AND PLANNING ALTERNATIVES

Even if we more adequately understand the technological as the systemic and modular which stands in reserve, how can we achieve a more satisfactory relation to the technological and approach a landscape better suited to the human and the natural? Consider three *possible* modes of design and building.

The most *timely* and effective response might be one which operates as part of the circulation systems of technology itself, drawing power from and also shaping technology's logic, practices, and progress. Or, in contrast, we might transform technology so that it realizes archetypal dimensions of the person-world relation, providing us with a contemporary manifestation of "*timeless*" patterns of human life and environment. These two alternatives will be treated in this chapter. A third approach—fitting placement—would be more distinctly *originary* in Heidegger's sense of the future occurrence of a proper mode of belonging to a fourfold world, and thus is considered separately in the next chapter.

A Technological Aesthetic

First, we could insert ourselves into the technological systems more wholeheartedly, submitting our desires and intentions to the powerful shaping of the technological itself, so that we could act *from within technology*. This strategy would be an attempt to push the technological hard enough so that its features would appear more and more overtly. The result would be a rigorously consistent aesthetic and a more coherent landscape.

FIGURE 7.4.
Clarksville Neighborhood, Austin, Texas. Technology Unconnected to Local Place.

Part of our unhappiness with the technological arises from the contrast and clash between the technological and our older "natural" and "cultural" landscapes. *Thought technologically,* from the inside, such tensions and confrontations would appear to be merely the signs of failures. Like the weak or inappropriate element that fails because it is not in proper relation to the rest of its system, perhaps because it is too old or the wrong size or capacity, native stands of oak trees and romantic gardens would not be suitably incorporated into any contemporarily valid and vital system, except for such phenomena as tourist or conservation networks. Such remnants of past landscapes would need to be transformed and integrated as standing reserves for a technological world.

In fact, design has proceeded this way before. At the beginning of the century, Futurists such as the Italians Balla and Severini, the American Stella, and the Russian Goncharoua or Picabia with his machinist paintings attempted to let the machine's geometric forms and repetitious rhythms, the motion, speed, and power display themselves. The problem was that the idea surpassed its content. That is, the machine turned out to be not the form introducing a new age, but the grand climax to an old era of industrial production.

The machine as object producing other objects was a final manifestation of the modern age. The machine and its commodity culture now are being eclipsed by the technological systems which are replacing them. "Things" are no longer objects, as we have seen, but increasingly appear as reserves of stock in relational networks of services and interactional processes. Suppose, then, that the idea of the systemic-technological came forward in art and the landscape in a way parallel to that attempted earlier for the machine by the designs of industrial "streamlined" forms (popularly thought of as "form following function"), by Tatlin's tower and machines, and by Lasio Mohoiy-Nagy's objects and constructions.

The resulting landscape already is appearing, for example, in the "high-tech" architecture which allows the support systems ("infrastructures") to manifest themselves ("putting the plumbing on the outside"), as happens with the Georges-Pompidou National Center of Art and Culture in Paris by Renzo Piano and Richard Rogers, in the Patscenter Technology Laboratory at Princeton, New Jersey by Richard Rogers Partnership, and in Lloyd's of London Redevelopment by Richard Rogers Partnership.

In a somewhat different manner, high-tech is fused with biomorphic forms, continuing the dream of a hybrid between the organic and the mechanical that has run from Icarus to the Architectural Association's work in the 1960s and following. For instance, Christopher MacDonald and Peter Salter's ICI trade pavilion for the Royal Agricultural Showground, 1983, appears to meld the organic dimensions of skeleton, nerves, and skin with mechanical metallic and functional elements. One advantage of this approach is that it is honest and, perhaps, "courageous" in that it faces up to the technological. The style may even appeal to the American idea of a "macho" culture and our longstanding attraction to technological devices, moving out

FIGURE 7.5.
Richard Rogers Partnership, Lloyd's of London Redevelopment. Support Systems Manifest Themselves.

of comfortable natural and cultural landscapes and on into difficult, sometimes dangerous new environments.

Still, a technological aesthetic is an *aesthetic,* that is, a relationship of spectator to *object* which depends on a certain distance so that the latter's form and content can be appreciated. The aesthetic of the technological appears according to this distanced relationship of extreme scale and observational distance: in the highway and crop systems which are etched into the earth and seen from the air, in the vapor trail of a jet overhead at 40,000 feet, in a laser display in the night sky, or, at the other end of the scale, in the circuitry of the microchip. It is precisely at the very large and small scales that the beauty of the technological is most obvious, precisely because here there is maximum distance from ordinary experience and action. That is one reason post-structuralism has revived interest in the sublime.[16]

Learning to see and design a new technological aesthetic for the macro and micro scales is not easy as is seen in proposals for settlements in space. Some of the most imaginative and purest renderings have come from Sotass, who clearly and playfully understands technology—though, sadly, his work is the exception. Perhaps not surprisingly, the projection of landscapes in hypothetical terraforming projects, with their autonomous scale and distance, is disappointingly bland.[17] Typically these visions are of comfortable small towns, with orderly rows of growing vegetables. No doubt these images are the result of a rhetoric intended to make us comfortable with the idea of living in space and funding projects by ''de-alienating'' them, as well as by a failure of imagination. Stronger examples of technological imagination are found in the visionary landscapes and cityscapes for tomorrow's millions by C. A. Doxiadis, whose Ecumenopolis would spread across the earth, and by Paulo Soleri, whose Archology has cubic megastructures ribbing the planet.[18]

Yet, just here, we confront our problem again. We do not live on a macro or micro scale, but in the middle. No matter how interesting or spellbinding systemic form is at extreme scales, we inhabit a middle landscape. And it is as inhabitants that many do not want to live in the technological environment because technology is one thing as a tool for our use or as purely aesthetic form and quite another as the realm in which measure is imposed by the systemic. As seen above, technological systems would be an inadequate principle of spatial and behavioral organization for a landscape precisely because systemic logistics inevitably transforms people and earth into something they have not been and are not inherently. Thus, the deep issue: that in the technological landscape, human and natural characteristics would be dominated and distorted rather than nurtured. Of course, systemic technology and its landscape will continue to evolve, most likely in dramatic and captivating forms, despite resistance. But, an alternative might be pursued actively and positively.

Past and Archetypal Landscapes

We could argue that the technological is beyond our power and turn our attention and energy to what we clearly have the ability to control. We know that we can have a landscape better suited to humans and the earth than the one now evolving from technological systems because we have had such landscapes in the past, for thousands of years. Moreover, we want them again. We could say that we yearn to compensate for the technological with familiar forms which have worked well and have comforted us in the past. Pastoral forms, for example. In short, we could turn back and get away, as the double meaning of "retreat" implies. We have done things in the past which apparently have worked well, so it is natural to return to them, to do them again. Turning to the past by continuing to carry on its forms and patterns would seem to provide a way to cope with technology. This attitude is articulated by the ending of *Candide,* where we hear that, given the world's ways, we should cultivate our own gardens.

Yet, while this may be a comforting dream, it properly remains in the sphere of dream and desire. To unthoughtfully—literally—transpose the desires expressed in the dream into waking life is to live a delusion, and a dangerous one at that. The freedom and healing of dream and sleep only remain healthy and helpful when desire is transformed into consciousness and responsible action, as Jung, Frankl, and others have shown.[19]

If we responsibly are to face the challenge of technology, we can not utilize past designs and behavior as a refuge. Continually constructing the past in the present as a means of holding off the technological future is an attempted escape which dissolves into mere nostalgia and fantasy. A public, national or regional landscape, capable of fostering our vital belonging within social and natural environments, cannot be nostalgic.[20] Hence, the mere reproduction of past landscapes, however beloved, substantially would appear to avoid what is necessary for responsible design.

Not that we need to move forward under the spell of historicism or abandon our heritage of landscape forms and elements. Quite the opposite. What would be needed would be the *retrieval* of the inner logic and essential force of older landscapes in order to appropriately let them continue to manifest the world's potential to us. Past landscapes will continue to be treasured, with old ones maintained and new ones built according to *archetypal* needs and patterns. The primeval landscape and the power of nature in gardens, which appeal to the collective unconscious, inspire the "collective landscapes" of Sir Geoffrey Jellicoe, as in Modena and Brescia, Italy, and the Moody Gardens in Galveston, Texas.

In proposals for the Moody Gardens, to be built on 25 of the 142 acres of the site's marshlands on Offatts Bayou, visitors are imagined as moving by foot and water-bus through the history of 3,000 years of gardens. These his-

FIGURE 7.6.
Sir Geoffrey Jellicoe. Proposed Plan for Historical Gardens, Moody Gardens, Galveston. Collective Landscapes.

torical gardens are surrounded by a twelve-foot dike and consciously juxtaposed with the adjacent wetlands in their ordinary state. In the current versions, through less obviously than in the first proposal, Jellicoe demonstrates a powerful restraint. By establishing the botanical gardens as the site of historical recollection and education and by providing for imaginative, even—in his words—"surrealistic" experience, Jellicoe designs a place that mediates the human and natural realms. Still, he insists, the basis of the design and intended experience is in the idea of the primacy of nature and, thus, of the garden as a "haven for plant life," not people.[21]

In a parallel way, Charles Moore explores the perennial human attraction to archetypal natural and built elements that are part of our shared store of American experience. The unity of Moore's buildings and archetypal landscape practices is striking and points out the enduring draw of lookouts, of hiding places, of camping out, of flowing water and crackling fires in fireplaces, of the desire to draw together to talk, eat, and laugh. These dimensions are all the more joyful in the midst of our everyday humdrum lives. Utilizing the tradition of fairs and circuses, of open summer cabins and lodges, of campfires and swimming pools, of memories of toys and games, he provides for a need for adventure, fun, and surprise that is based on and takes off from the comfortable and familiar.

He successfully develops interior spaces and their relation to the outdoors by drawing on vernacular forms and materials in his imaginative variations on porches and lofts, benches and bunkbeds, windows and stairs, fireplaces and fountains, the colors and patterns of children's playthings, and unpretentious building and town forms. His work taps the resonant power that springs from our common ground, where people already recognize and understand their surroundings and have a shared store of meaningful experiences. The buildings both awaken memories and resonances of what is familiar and beloved and also masterfully rearrange these so that we have an environment deliberately different from any taken-for-granted everydayness. His humorous and humane design rejuvenates tradition in the *playful mode*.[22] Or, interested in the same goal and using similar strategies, architect Fay Jones is interested in "reinvesting the old with new meaning."[23]

The crucial point: rather than fleeing from the technological by returning to past landscapes in order to live in them again, we always will need intimate landscapes as places which allow the timelessly human to unfold, both privately and within the public spheres of work and action. Following this course, we would remove our egotistical willfulness in order to discover the enduring energy of the archetypal dimensions of the landscape. Such an approach seeks the original character of gardens (the antithesis of wilderness and desert) and of houses as forms of enclosure and containment, as scenes of accomplishment and control, and as nurturing sites of sensuality or repose

FIGURE 7.7.
Moore, Lyndon, Turnbull, Whitaker, Sea Ranch, California. Architecture of Collective Memory.

and meditation. These microcosms help make the broader cosmos habitable. Thus, the garden and house do not avoid the outside world—not even by clever play with images—but become a means for authentic design and living.[24]

In a highly original manner, Swiss architectural anthropologist Nold Egenter proposes a strategy akin to, though more historical and empirical than, those I have been considering here.[25] He too insists that we need to reread the past with adequate macro- and micro-theory and recover the meanings of potent dimensions that have been installed in building from prehuman times. Egenter's striking argument is that we completely misunderstand the action of building and the character of architecture when we reductively see it in pragmatic terms of "shelter" or production processes and consumption.

Following an ingenious inductive method, he distinguishes four phases and types of construction and architecture: (1) subhuman architecture, in which the three species of higher apes daily build nests, (2) semantic architecture, or nondomestic built elements, used for ritual purposes and serving as cognitive models, thus producing symbolic meanings and establishing architectonic forms, (3) domestic architecture, the end result of the first two phases of constructive behavior, in which internal space is produced, (4) settlement architecture, also deriving from local semantic architecture and the rituals of cyclical renewal, by which a group's narrative origins and social hierarchy are preserved.[26]

If Egenter is correct about the manner in which the primal origins in natural (prehuman) and nondomestic sacred (semantic) rituals lie at the heart of building,

> buildings essentially structure human environmental space. This would mean that man—as always—not only perceives, but integrates the spatial structure defined by buildings and reproduces this structure in other contexts, thinks with it, works with it. . . . [T]his type of spatial structure generated by buildings, influences man along an anthropological continuum and lives in our language, in our thoughts, keeps the arts living and even supports originally metaphysical ideas.[27]

What a revolutionary reinterpretation. Egenter's bold argument, then, is that our ancient construction practices and our earliest ritual and symbolic production of forms first enabled us to think of the world and act as we do, and only subsequently led to building enclosures in which we could live.

The implications of this view for research and practice would be enormous. Through the "perception of [these] new classes of construction" such as the subhuman and the semantic just noted, we would be able to move from the confines of *a priori* metaphysical thinking and aesthetic deduction, to dramatically widen our understanding of architecture and to open the possi-

FIGURE 7.8.
Nold Egenter, Phaseological Schema of 4 Types of Architecture

PHASEOLOGICAL SCHEME OF 4 TYPES OF ARCHITECTURE (up to the present)

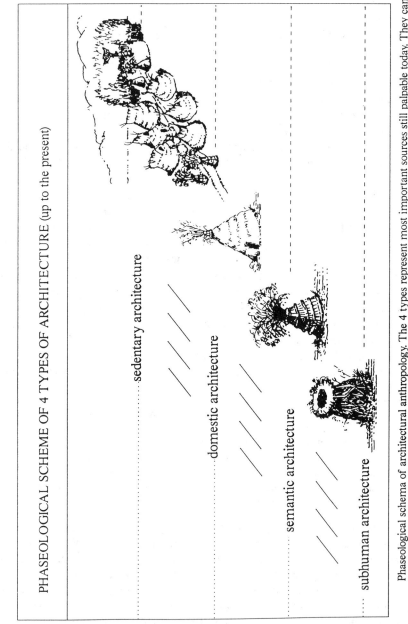

..........sedentary architecture

..........domestic architecture

..........semantic architecture

..........subhuman architecture

Phaseological schema of architectural anthropology. The 4 types represent most important sources still palpable today. They can be used to reconstruct a constructive continuum which parallels human evolution.

bility of an interpretive, yet objective inductive approach. By tracing out our "ancient constructive and dwelling behavior," we would be able to "describe empirically [and] document by criteria *imminent to architecture*, such as the materials and types of construction, resulting form, spatial and temporal conditions, social relations, etc."[28]

And, not only would we gain a new understanding of architecture through the study of past forms and constructions, but we would revise our interpretation of ourselves and become able to "reconstruct essentially new outlooks." Explicitly positive factors could emerge for today through architecture anthropology if we can retrieve "the actuality of the primitive: a really humane and generally valuable architecture could be based on well founded principles."[29]

Both with the radical theoretical reassessment of primal human constructions and architectural meanings and with the practical, creative transformations of archetypal designs, then, we find pointers for dealing with the technological landscape. We need to let the powerful forms of the enduring past come forth in a way that is fully appropriate to our time and place.

8
Fitting Placement

Though a directly technological aesthetic or an architectural transformation of basic architectural and landscape elements are promising, if technology is irrevocably shaping the world, including human and other life forms, its dominance may not be as beneficent or open to archetypal transformations as the first two design and planning alternatives assume. If so, it would be necessary to ask whether technology can be encountered in a deeper, more originary manner. This chapter examines what an originary approach would be like by developing two modes of fitting placement: camouflage and display. These two modes aim at attunement between human and natural patterns.

Obviously, the originary does not reject technology in a nostalgic longing for the primitive; rather, as Heidegger, E. F. Schumacher, and others argue, questions of scale and use are decisive. Heidegger contends,

> We can use technical devices, and yet with proper use also keep ourselves free of them, that we may let go at any time. We can use technical devices as they ought to be used, and also let them alone as something which does not affect our inner and real core. . . . But will not saying yes and no this way to technical devices make our relation to technology ambivalent and insecure? On the contrary! Our relation to technology will become wonderfully simple and relaxed. We let technical devices enter our daily life, and at the same time leave them outside, that is, let them alone, as things which are nothing absolute but remain dependent upon something higher.[1]

Even the popular phrases "appropriate technology" and "voluntary simplicity" catch something of the idea. The use of solar devices, windmills, and computers need not overwhelm us by absorbing us into the technological, but may aid the development of community in a more sensitive response to the environment. Here technology keeps its place as a tool, rather than displacing us. For example, black plastic sheeting serves as an aid in the reconversion of water-intensive lawns in the Southwest back to habitats for native species, where the latter help the inhabitants to become more attuned again to local climate and native life forms.

Since technological systems neither inherently determine spatial organization nor result in specific spatial designs, we have a marvelous opportunity. The situation is open because there is no "given" conglomerate of built elements and forms. Perhaps in fear or paralyzed before the technological, like an animal frozen in the glare of oncoming headlights, we too often become fixed and, following old but now unhelpful reflexes, forget to look around— or within—at the possibilities we have. Today, we do not begin with the massive forms of the modern era's landscape of objectivity: factories and mills producing objects for consumption, canals and roadways and railroads transporting goods, banks and trading houses dealing with objectified money and commodities, mass housing for workers made into objects. Freed from what was given in the past, we are liberated for the possibility of using technology without technological dominance of landscape and life. This, in part, is what Heidegger means when he says that it is possible and necessary to be free of technology, letting it be and using it without being controlled by it.[2]

How then to let technology and the essentially human come into healthy relation? The question is one of *placement*—placement in the landscape and its embracing natural and cultural contexts. Specifically, the question of the technological landscape may be the question of the fitting placement of technology into a world of human scale and vital affairs, into nature's fecundity and simplicity. Though there surely are many approaches, here we will consider two major modes of fitting placement derived from natural and cultural forms, which we can call *camouflage and display*.

Camouflage

Usually we think of camouflage as indicating a hiding or disguising. Hence, we camouflage tanks, aircraft, and soldiers. Insects and snakes often are camouflaged. This sense of "camouflage" connotes the counterfeit and fake, even the lie. The snake is a counterfeit branch so that it may deceive and kill its prey. The toad is a counterfeit leaf so that it may escape being eaten by the snake or may eat the moth. Yet, a more fundamental sense of camouflage is important for us. Something can hide or counterfeit only because it first of all *fits* in. This fitting in is the deeper meaning of camouflage, more basic than the specific derivative meanings which quickly become rhetorically weighted depending on one's goals and situation.

To "fit in" is to assume a certain position in relation to the rest of the world or one's surroundings. For the humanly made it would involve an attitude of not pushing forward ourselves or the things we make. By not calling undue or inappropriate attention to ourselves and our built environment, we may avoid counterfeiting and, instead, be modestly self-effacing, holding back and even letting our technological world recede into its proper social and natural context.

Thus, the tone would be one of deferment without denial. Yes, the technological is technological, but it need not impose itself and dominate. It would be let go into its own necessary forms and nature, yet also would recede and blend in with the landscape of human well-being. In short, with regard to technology, "camouflage" means not deception to the end of survival by deadly strike or innocuous escape, but the quiet fitting in which allows technology to be technology and yet puts and keeps everything in its place. After all, camouflage does not prevent, but enables, the frog and moth to be what they are and to belong in their ecosystems. "Camouflage" would name a fitting attitude or relation of technology to the landscape.

It is crucial to notice that "camouflage" itself gives us a hint about the place of technology, its range and scale in the landscape. To speak of something camouflaged so that it blends in and becomes unobtrusive immediately evokes the realm of our lived world of behavior and perception. It is in the movement of daily life that things would be camouflaged, whether we notice them or not. Put another way, subatomic particles and black holes are not camouflaged. They need no blending in with the rest of our ordinary environment because they are too small or too large to appear in themselves.[3] Thus, "camouflage" bespeaks the phenomenal realm of our lived existence, between the spheres accessible by microscope and telescope. We will return to this point shortly.

As Gestalt psychology shows us, human sensory experience is so organized that we take in and deal with complete patterns. We experience simple and unified arrangements of diverse elements, rather than the diffuse or unrelated constituents themselves. At the phenomenal level of the landscape, we perceive, understand, and act on things as wholes.

It is because experience operates within gestalt that camouflage can be a principle of landscape design.[4] To return to camouflage in a biological context, it is possible for an organism to blend into a background only because organisms perceive wholes. That is, by shading, marking, and coloring, the shape of an organism is "broken down" into complex parts which are harder to see as a unified whole than is their apparently more congruent arrangement with background elements. A green ear appears within the gestalt of leaf, a gray leg in the gestalt of twig. The other's eye sees tree, leaf, and twig in mottled sunlight and shade as wholes, rather than an autonomous creature whose markings and contour are not "of a piece." Camouflage works biologically, then, because of gestalt as a principle of perception and behavior. Once again, the primacy of "fitting in and together."

Consequently, camouflaging the technological can be seen as the blending of technology into its environment so as to produce a holistic landscape. Since we are not speaking merely of the biological realms, we can say camouflage becomes an issue of fitting technology into natural and culturally built environments, including, finally, cultural behavior and values. Of course, camouflage works for this or that thing in specific situations. What is camouflaged in its proper leafy environment may be exposed in a desert or on a sidewalk. That means that the natural and cultural contexts are themselves local.

This insight corresponds to the position and conclusion of an independent body of research, which argues that human well-being and responsible relationships to nature require place, where place, as biocultural region, is opposed to abstract space.[5] Though the issue is beyond our scope here, it would mean that camouflaging the technological would have to be done in ways responsive to different localities. The design of the technological according to patterns of bioregions would allow the dominance of the heterogeneous over the technologically homogenous (modular) and the emergence of place instead of the systemically nonspatial (the systemic goes anywhere and everywhere, but genuinely fits nowhere).

Further, the fitting into the bioregional indicates that technological forms and materials must blend in with and be subordinate to the local. But, if the technological is to remain the technological and not counterfeit something else, how will it do so? The principle here would not advocate steel counterfeiting wood, plastic imitating leather, or shutters that do not close.[6] Rather, it asks about strategies of design and setting, building materials, and techniques which simultaneously respect the character of technology and encourage the emergence of modes of local landscape.

Consider how we can draw on tradition in applying lessons from the past. One way to live in a tradition is to recover and maintain the essential forms and forces, transforming them in a new setting. Landscape architects can draw from the experience with the industrial landscape to find ways to blend in the technological. Some elements of technological systems, for all the fundamental logical and dynamic differences, are phenomenally similar enough to modern, objective-industrial elements to respond to evolved traditional landscape practices. Because technological nuclear generating plants and highway systems *appear* much as do their counterparts of the industrial era, landscape architecture can contribute proven solutions for blending large elements in by siting and contouring, by burying the clutter of supporting structures, pipes, and lines, and by planting and using local materials as well as water, as Dame Crowe points out.[7] Such blending-in emphasizes goals of smooth transition and the unification of new elements with their surroundings, not total concealment.

Or, we can learn from what Olmsted did with roads in his day—lowering the grade of roads in Central Park so that riders and carriages would not intrude or take over. His landscape design neither denied nor falsified the roadway, but helped them come into their own by keeping them in their own subordinate place—and thus allowed the park its full and complex character. The lesson was absorbed by Stein and Wright in their *New Towns For America* and thus passed into the design tradition, though too often it still is forgotten or used without understanding.[8]

Camouflaging parking garages, as is done in Zurich today, not only keeps the automobile and garage in their proper and useful place, but allows them to more completely become facets of their systemic context. No longer are they so much objects with inherent characteristics confronting our perception, but dimensions of the flow of transportation systems. Here we find successful camouflage in our sense: arrangement of the same elements into a more acceptable gestalt and the production of a genuinely different landscape than would have existed otherwise.

In this regard, landscape design and construction can learn from the camouflage "practices" of the natural world. Briefly, design and siting can further develop ways to make the shapes and materials of the technological continuous with the surrounding patterns and contours, blending by means of marking and colors, shapes and postures, by orientation and flaps which modify shadows, and perhaps by surface masking. Correlates to the natural means are found in uses of local materials (such as adobe in Soleri's earthcasting and Fathy's projects in the American Southwest), in planting and contouring around large elements, and in landscaping over or on top of buildings (including earth sheltered and buried structures). Switzerland, Austria, and Germany provide successful cases of settlements fully integrated into the landscape which are both humane and ecological.[9] The point is that while we can cite some pioneering examples, the hard work of design is yet to be done.

In addition to innovative adaptation of traditional and natural means of camouflage, a still deeper resource lies in the natural unfolding of the phenomenal world itself. As noticed earlier, to speak of camouflage is to indicate neither the subvisible realm nor the supra-cosmos beyond direct perception, but the phenomenal world in which we live. Hence, there is a strict parallel between nature and the technological and, more important for our problem here, between nature's forms and ours.

Nature is highly determined, regular, and "mathematical" at the micro and macro scales. The understanding of mathematical physics most clearly and powerfully applies to the subatomic realm and to galaxies and the whole cosmos. Yet, the regular and obvious mathematical forms of molecular structure or geometrical features become scarcer, almost disappearing, as we proceed beyond the level of cell, crystal, and snowflake to organisms and snow-covered fields, much less to whole inhabited landscapes. Even when phenomena such as shells and horns display strikingly visible mathematical forms, their regularity is elegant and subtle within nature's profligate variety. Hence the natural attitude, in which the geometric or mechanically repeti-

FIGURE 8.1.
Parking Garage, Zurich

tious is contrasted with the organic, since the phenomenal natural world is curved, complex, and variable in ways mathematical and technologically formed objects often are not at the phenomenological level.

The parallel extends, then, so that technological forms, highly regular and often emphatically geometric, may be like natural forms at the extreme scales. If the issue is how to let the technological be technological without dominating or imposing its form on animal and human life at the level of phenomenal landscapes, we may find an answer by asking how nature, so regular and "mathematically precise" at the smallest and largest scales, brings forth such a varied, interesting, and valued world in the middle scale. Of course, it is just this middle scale that is the realm of our usual range of human experience. Here, in the middle, there is landscape.

From one direction, we need to examine how nature moves from smaller regular or geometric forms to larger ones, for example, in the honeycomb, the dragonfly wing, and cells in simple organizations. For all the regularity of their constituent dimensions and even granted their similarity to others of the same kind, tide pools, trees, and cats display interesting individuality. Theoretically, similar treatment of the systemic, technological elements could generate a positive and powerful landscape, from the bottom up.[10]

In the other direction, we need to learn how nature achieves its wonderful effects in larger massings. For instance, forests, deserts, mountain ranges, and coral reefs are massings, on hugh scales, of similar elements (and often of a relatively small number of different kinds of elements). This is not to suggest that such features are simple, since they really are complex as ecology increasingly shows. Rather, the point—simplistically—is that "individual" grains of sand, or pine trees, or corals are very similar if seen in one way; yet, occurring in large numbers with complex relationships to other elements, they constitute patterns which appear to be paradigms of what we might seek and strive for. Again, if technological elements are to become present in unprecedented numbers, and interconnected to the components of their systems, the issue may be how to mass such elements in ways that phenomenally are neither homogeneously trivial nor overwhelming.[11]

Ecology says that nature is systemic; but the natural does not appear that way—which is the exact point: nature appears as mysteriously rich, not visually problematic and spatially impoverished or oppressive.[12] The recent "discovery" of fractiles and their potential to provide insight into the relationships and means for generation of new forms and designs "naturally" is exciting in exactly this regard.[13] Fitting the technological into the landscape by letting it recede to levels below and above the normal range of sensory experience or by providing fractile patterns would allow the ordinarily experienced middle scale to be *phenomenally non-systemic*. Here, the technological would appear in new, culturally discovered "natural" forms. How the technological should "appear" also evokes the issue of display, though display is the alternative to camouflage's fitting-in.

Display

"Display" names a second mode in which things show themselves. Rather than receding, what is displayed comes forward into prominence. Again, to speak of organisms, a creature may display, rising up to show bright bands of color, to scare off an enemy, or to woo in courtship. Just as camouflage both aids capture and escape, display involves the capacity to both attract and repel, thus emphasizing that our concern is the life-world of specific situations and places, of particular and complex perceptions and behavior.

The idea is that to complement the strategy of camouflage, the technological also can *show itself* at the phenomenal level but without dominating, so that it may be kept in its place in human and natural contexts. Three specific approaches to design suggest themselves as a means of display: *contextual display, "wrapping," and figural unity.*

1. Contextual display Again drawing from our experience with the industrial landscape, we see that some elements have strong and clean designs in themselves which can contribute to an interesting and ordered landscape. Great dams and their reservoirs often are congruent with their settings. As Dame Crowe and Nan Fairbrother point out, it is crucial that the humanly-made elements be in a scale proportionate to the natural context.[14] Thus the simple power of a dam and reservoir may fit with the mountains and sky in the American West, but would be grotesque in smaller valleys elsewhere. Even here, where the landscape may succeed with the direct display of the major built element, the result is rendered problematic by the surrounding clutter which needs to be buried, that is, camouflaged. Our experiences with bridges and highways are similar.

The requisite principle of display for siting and design would be the same for the elements of technological systems: let the clarity and strength of the elements manifest themselves in a direct manner which complements but does not overwhelm or subvert the surrounding natural and cultural worlds. Direct display is especially important since, given the increase in scale and dimensions of the humanly built environment, it is not always possible to preserve the traditional landscape or absorb the technological into it.[15] The task becomes one of finding the "beauty" of new forms and working out transitions and unity between the old and new landscapes. Clearly, design and site planning, sensitive to contextual scale and forms, can make major contributions to gathering these dimensions together.

The major components of energy, communication, transportation, and recreational systems often can be sited so that their large size is appropriate to the natural spaces and built forms surrounding them and can be planned so that their interface with supporting infrastructures is simple enough not to confuse or distract from the general gestalt. They can be designed so that their general forms are clean while their materials and details are cogent and interesting, perhaps even evoking locality when entered or used.

The Dallas–Fort Worth airport can be cited as a successfully displayed technological environment. The strongly modular form derives straightforwardly from the flow of passengers through the systems of runways, terminal pods, on-site light-rail transport, parking and highway networks. The minimal spatial obstacles between means of arrival and departure make the airport successful at its primary function; thus, a case where systemic form and function are meaningfully interdependent. At the same time, the airport is contextually successful. Its scale is appropriate to the natural surroundings. The low buildings and runways do not loom over the prairie's open spaces and scattered vegetation. At the same time, the strongly modular and systemic character of the large complex provides an order and clarity in the rather homogeneous open space, analogous to the poetic "Jar in Tennessee." In short, appropriate to the edge of the plains, the Dallas–Fort Worth Airport creates a new landscape of its own without destroying what is around it.[16]

The internal configuration and relation to the surrounding site follow one clear and "friendly" pattern at Governor's State University at Park Forest, Illinois. Designed and built in the early 1970s according to rigorous systems thinking, the social and physical programs were thoroughly integrated with the intention of providing a sense of openness and individuality for students, while also providing a sense of welcome and community. The flow of commuting students and faculty to the site was focused primarily on small collegiate units, each of which was thought of in terms of a "house plan." The opportunity for interpersonal interaction is displayed in the personalized "home bases" for community members, which are the result of arranging the general academic and office modules, as well as those with specific uses such as laboratories, around each college's core.

To balance the strong sense of belonging promoted by the concentric cores, openness and social interaction at the larger community level are enhanced by dispersing study, eating, socializing, and service areas throughout the campus and by carefully linking the major and subcores together. The "core concept" keeps the modules on a relatively small and cost-effective scale and leads to an informal relation of colleges, easily accessible to each other and the parking and railway commuter stop. This system is further integrated with the surrounding area by picking up on the Hantock Farmstead as the focus of campus, since as "the high point of the land unit" and "located centrally, from this point one can overlook the entire environment." As one of the project architects, Lance Tatum, explains it, some of the buildings are patterned on farmhouses previously located in the area and by deriving

FIGURE 8.2.
Brodsky, Hopf, & Adler, Dallas–Fort Worth Airport Technological Display.

FIGURE 8.3.
Governor's State University, Park Forest South, Illinois. Schematic Plan for the Subcore Concept.

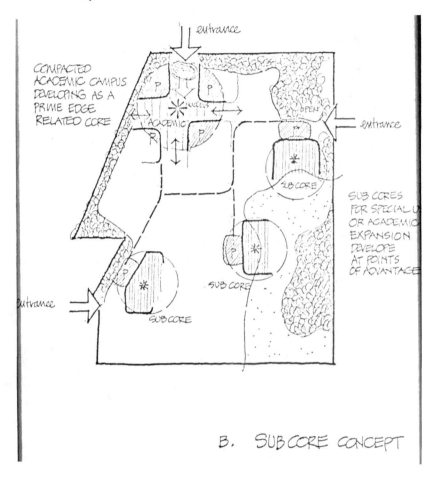

the color and painting schemes from the railroad cars that regularly pass by on the IC Railroad.[17]

2. Wrapping The task of appropriate design and siting is made somewhat easier by another dimension of technology's essentially nonspatial and non-local character: the miniaturization of components. Not only are the very large elements limited in number for most systems (compared to the total set of components), but there tends to be a rapid reduction in the elements' size. Attendant with their power to organize behavior and society itself, technological devices allow a spatial handling which seemingly becomes easier and easier.

The correlate strategy again focuses on the middle-scale landscape, setting aside elements on one end so small as to be almost self-camouflaging, and at the other, the large elements requiring contextual display, as just treated above. We are left with the bulk of mid-sized modular components which physically manifest systems, providing for systemic transformation and use (powerlines, cables, and wires; water and gas pipelines and pipes; parking spaces, roadways, cloverleafs, and bridge elements, bank-teller machines, housing units, and so on).

A strategy for handling these elements is suggested by vernacular modes of design. Think of the famous image of the Japanese wrapping of five eggs. Thought of from a Zen tradition, "wrapping" provides another mode of letting technology be itself, fully present yet freely let go. Here the simplicity and purity of the eggs, or tofu cubes, and so on which are wrapped is similar to modular elements.

The idea of wrapping involves the interesting presentation of the homogeneously modular, that is, the multiple modules of the same sort or of those systematically related in clusters at the scale, for example, of a building or building complex. On the same scale, and on smaller ones too, we can think of the pattern of a "series" of modular elements. Note that the wrapped small and mid-sized modular components likely will result in a large systemic element which as a whole will require contextual display, or camouflage.

Given "wrapping" as a mode of presenting, the question becomes how to "wrap" our automatic bank-teller machines, computer terminals, subway cars, housing and building units, household appliances and furnishings, exterior and interior lighting, and so on. Of course, powerlines and pipelines can be buried or camouflaged, but usually it is too costly or even environmentally harmful to do so. As an alternative, there should be interesting ways to present power and communication lines by wrapping. Here too, natural and vernacular forms might be inspirational, suggesting ways to wrap powerlines according to the example of nature's curved self-containments, thus replacing the awkward mechanical aggregation of the merely technologically engineered. Surely, designers can do better both on individual modular forms and in their external correspondence to surroundings.

In technological terms, the modules of interchange and access for credit or transportation systems have the serial order of logistical transformation and flow. But, while the inner systematic organization would continue to govern the operation of the technological elements in question, the spatial organization could have an entirely different principle of organization and, hence, display quite another phenomenal pattern. That is, we would have a different landscape.

FIGURE 8.4
Wrapping Five Eggs

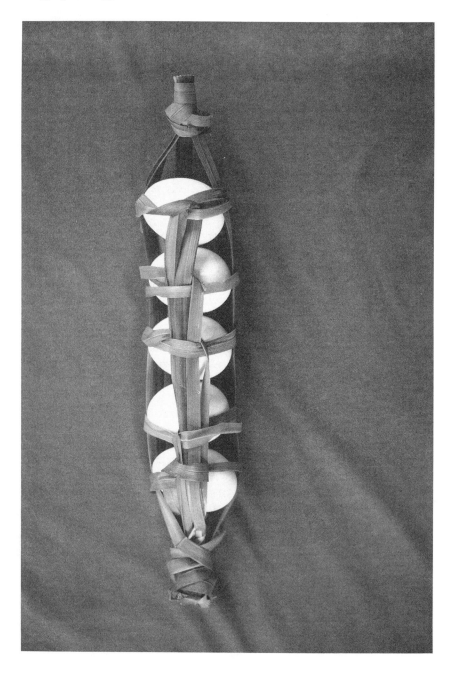

FIGURE 8.5.
Louis I. Kahn, Kimbell Art Museum, Fort Worth. Wrapping on the Scale of a Building.

On the scale of a building, Kahn's solution for the design and arrangement of the galleries of the Kimbell Art Museum in Fort Worth is a fine example of "wrapping." Indeed, the result is so simple and strong a display that it is easy to overlook the highly technological character of the elements: sixteen narrow rectangular vaulted elements (modules) composed of poured concrete and travertine infill walls, roofed with concrete cycloid shells which support concrete channels housing the electrical and air circulation systems. Because the elements are so masterfully wrapped, joined and finished with stone, wood, and metal, with openings for light, and with surrounding pools, trees, and vegetation—all executed with exemplary craftsmanship—the overall appearance is quiet and secure. Out of the modular, Kahn has made a landscape welcoming our entry and contemplation.[18]

3. Figural unity Drawing from tradition a last time: in the West we have recognized that science has a different principle of organization than literature and the arts. Scientific thought and discourse proceed according to sequential logic, while novels and poetry have what often is called a figural unity.[19] In the latter case, the organizing principle is a figure, such as a natural form, a persona, or an image; the configuration and meaning of specific elements of a work embodies the exemplary figure. In fact, primal peoples often arranged their settlement forms and patterns of living in the environment according to mythological models of the cosmos or gods. A village might be laid out in the form of a totem, for instance.

Whereas technological systems parallel science and sequential logic, the non-technological can be aligned with the figural mode of display, as mythology, the visual arts, and architecture often have demonstrated. Applying the style of the latter to the elements of the former, we can find patterns for the non-technological spatial arrangement of systems and modules both in our own figural imagination and by drawing on natural processes and forms. A case in point: the forms of flowing water—which have fascinated thinkers and designers from da Vinci to Theodore Schwenk and John Wilkes—can be applied to the "linear" systems of technological distribution.[20] The goal would be an intelligible order and interesting coherence.

Consider how technological credit systems require new spatialization. Since we now contribute to or draw on our standing credit reserves by computer, the older spatial forms and organization of banks on Main Streets, or across from courthouses, or with attached linear drive-though facilities, have given way to modular automatic teller units. The problem is that these modular units, by being able to appear anywhere, add confusion to our spatial forms and behavior. They appear with no special connection to their immediate surroundings, inserted into randomly placed kiosks or building facades. There is no way to predict where to find them or to be confident of adequate security, such as provided not only by light and privacy, but by social clues and norms governing the behavior of others nearby. People using them form lines blocking pedestrian flow on the sidewalks and winding dangerously though vehicular traffic in parking lots.

Far better to provide some figural unity or pattern. Modular location need not be so mechanical as placement on the same external corner of every shopping mall or so as to form the symmetrical center of nine-block areas downtown. Obviously, the design or patterning remains to be done.

Or, when subway entrances follow the systemic logic of abstract flow-charts and are laid out monotonously, the landscape is debilitated and our behavior confused by the lack of inherent or integral connection to the rest of the physical or cultural environment. Instead, the stations of a whole city and region could be arranged and decorated so as to form images appropriate to the place. While the resulting figure would not elaborate sacred events or natural forms as was the case with primal villages and medieval cathedrals, the challenge for design is to imaginatively articulate the events and forms appropriate to our age and locality.

The transportation system might delineate cultural forms associated with the city's image or nickname or the mascot of the local sporting team; or natural forms such as the major constellations overhead or the contours of the city's dominant landscape features, such as seven hills; or, more aesthetically, mathematical forms, such as purified spirals derived from atomic physics. The goal of the figural tactic would be a system which would present a pattern that experientially and imaginatively is coherent to the users. The resultant simple mental image or map guides movement and thus facilitates individual use. This procedure would add a layer of social meaning to the landscape's organization by evoking and elaborating the deeper structural forms behind the city's natural and cultural appearance.

A simple case of this sort is the unbuilt design for a new airport terminal in Austin, Texas. To emphasize a sense of place and the identity of the city as the capital of the "Lone Star State," the modular terminal ports were delineated in the figure of a star as it appears on the state flag.

What such figural design might look like at the urban scale is hinted at in the Design for the city of Nuran—The City of Illumination—at Isfahan, Iran by The Mandala Collaborative and Nader Ardalan and in Hans Asplund's ekistic design for an urban settlement, *Twotown Grand Grid.*[21] At one end of a spectrum, the city plan by Ardalan and the Mandala Collaborative for the Atomic Energy Organization of Iran continues the heritage of premodern "sacred geometry." Nuran's figural site plan, arranged along both material-geographical and spiritual axes is derived from Iranian culture and theological tradition. At the other end of the range of epochal principles, we find the highly systemic, yet not narrowly functionalistic or scientistic, approach advocated by *Ekistics.* Hans Asplund's town planning experiments with an Eki-

FIGURE 8.6
Nuran, City of Illumination, Iran. Masterplan by the Mandala collaborative, Nader
Ardalan, Principal-in-charge of Design. Figural City Design.

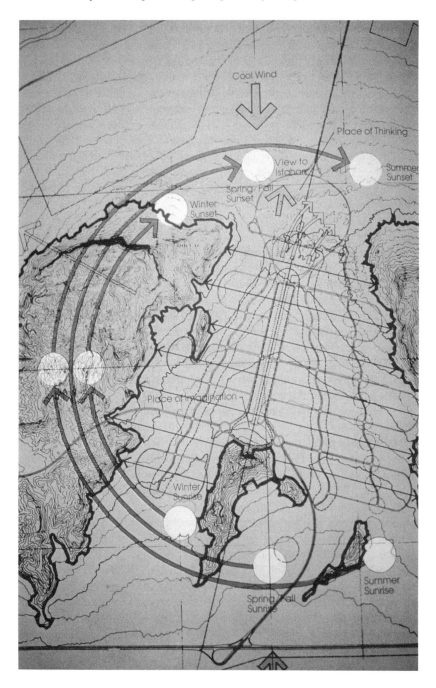

stic, linear "Twotown" form discovered that the best arrangement resulted from the intersection of two groups of parallel linear settlements. The overall pattern: a distinctly floral configuration. Clearly, and essentially, technology is flexible enough to be shaped according to profound figural principles. Systems and cities could be laid out in more powerful, primal and imaginative forms, corresponding to natural and cultural needs and responses.

In sum, through the three proposed modes of display, and surely others, technology itself would be displayed: technology would come forward (a) according to its own logic, (b) as useful[22] not tyrannical, and (c) as fitting for and fitting into natural and cultural life. Here, in response, a technological landscape would emerge.

Attunement

We need to let technology come into its essential forms and yet do so in ways allowing a satisfying life that spares and preserves the natural world supporting us—the world we and technology threaten to fully dominate and destroy. Given the major alternatives, it appears that we either could let the technological develop according to the maximal unfolding of its own forms, processes, and materials, or subordinate it to those of traditional cultures and nature. On the one hand, Soleri argues that we can follow the first alternative, and even need to, in order to let the technological emerge in a restrained manner insofar as we incorporate into our daily life-patterns the technological forms, density, and richness of megastructures, so that we leave external nature alone as much as possible.[23]

Or, we may more modestly let the natural alone by the responsible development of archetypal forms that are both timeless and timely or by appropriate placement accomplished through camouflage and display. While it is crucial to work out the differences among the alternatives and the issue of how to proceed, it also is important not to overlook the areas of agreement. We need a transforming combination of innovation and retrieval of tradition. We need *restraint* enough to preserve nature and archetypal and innovative cultural dimensions.

The approach advocated here would bring us back to the ancient roots of landscaping and our human role, which have been obscured only in the last several hundred years by our Faustian energy and power over the earth. Traditionally, we have cultivated nature by learning her inherent features and then modifying them so that the result is both natural and humanly enhanced. The ancient word "husbandry" names this relation and a principle of landscaping that we still need to apply to the technological environment.[24] The Old Norse *hus* and *bondi* speak of the house and householder and need for stewardship. To husband is to use sparingly and prudently so as to conserve and therefore let something be itself, freely.[25]

The restraint necessary to listen to nature and our archetypes in order to respect them already is part of our tradition, as Dame Crowe reminds us. She notes that, akin to the Japanese manner, she tries to ask of the tree, "Where do you want to be planted?"[26] So restraining our willful plans would allow us better to listen. We could become open to hearing nature's and our own patterns and needs; we could become better attuned to them. Becoming attuned means that we come to follow the same processes and patterns in a newly appropriate manner, since now we not only must cultivate nature but also the technological environment. Attunement between the human and natural could provide the basis for designs responsive to technology's challenge and, hence, the opportunity and the strategies to delineate a dwelling place for humans on the earth in tomorrow's technological world.[27]

9

Homelessness and the Human Condition

In the chapters above we have seen the ontological dimensions and some concrete examples of our personal and cultural displacements. We have explored the theoretical alternatives and the possible appropriate responses to the technological era. This chapter continues the shift from theory to praxis and to the historical, existential dislocations that face planners, urban designers, and architects as well as social and environmental professionals.

It is easy to mistake *one* problem for *the one and only* problem. I do not want to do that. To repeat: I want to examine the existential dimensions of homelessness in light of the theories and practices of environmental interpretation developed above and to consider possible strategies to deal with it. Modern and postmodern cultural homelessness is not abstract, even if we generalize about it. These unfolding events and their interpretations shape our lives by opening and closing possibilities for us. As the historian Oscar Handlin and others argue, we experience these phenomena spatially, in the landscapes around us. Specifically, we historically have experienced our placelessness in the density of cities, in the disorder of towns, in the distance between farms. Our American cities, for example, have their legacy of "hand-me-down housing," tenements and factories, life in the streets, and the rise of social institutions as manifestations of this cultural reality.[1]

But, to claim that displacement and the desire of many to discover or recover a new place for themselves is a serious and genuine problem is not to exaggerate it. The world is not all terrible. Not everyone is in distress, especially comfortable Americans who command an amazingly disproportionate amount of the world's resources and have wonderful power and freedom to move about socially, educationally, economically, and physically. To point out that this privileged life comes at the expense or displacement of others or that it involves its own forms of dislocation may be true, but to say so already again expands or emphasizes the theme rather than limits it.

In freeing themselves from distasteful and oppressive aspects of life, whether these arise from the "necessities" of life, or from the arbitrary power of others, or as the result of poor decisions, many Americans are happy with the way things are. The radical critique of everydayness by Heidegger, of bourgeois complacency by Scheler, of capitalism by the critical theorists, and parallel arguments by others, does not, in fact, haunt every, even most, Americans. To those who like their place as it is or as they are making it, I can say, "glad to hear it." With Thoreau,

> I do not mean to prescribe rules to . . . those who find their encouragement and inspiration in precisely the present condition of things, and cherish it with the fondness and enthusiasm of lovers. . . . I do not speak to those who are well employed in whatever circumstances, and they know whether they are well employed or not; —but mainly to the mass of men who are discontented, and idly complaining of the hardness of their lot or of the times, when they might improve them.[2]

Similarly, though in a very in a different way, with those who embrace the coming new technological world described above and who cannot wait for more systemic power and order, clearly I have substantial differences that need to be worked out intellectually and politically as we live together in a neighborly, but not always pacific, manner.

As seen from the right, mainstream empirical and quantitative researchers likely will find these investigations unscientific or too insistent on our dislocations. From the left, my radical colleagues will find the work too ordinary and too trusting that some place or strategy for belonging might be found. But, after all the thinking and writing so far, it comes as no surprise that I, and a not inconsiderable number of others, believe both that *displacement is a crucial issue* and that *some kind of homecoming*—one that stays healthily and dynamically underway all our lives—*is possible*. So, I turn to a final problem in the remaining chapters. Not the one and only problem for everyone, but an issue tough enough to warrant our attention, especially in light of the various alternatives worked through above and within the Heideggerian orientation that I follow.

EXISTENTIAL DISPLACEMENTS

The world today is the scene of substantial homelessness. The indigent sleep in doorways, under bridges, and on heating grates. Urban renewal displaces many whose needs were evoked as the cause for public concern and action in the first place. People occupying public housing not uncommonly decry well-intentioned buildings despite their newness. The growth of cities and exurban centers displaces those who lived in the small towns or who farmed the surrounding land and dramatically changes the landscape itself and the realm of other creatures living there. The rural poor and newly arrived immigrants often long for lost relationships and traditional patterns at the same time as they attempt to belong to a new rhythm and desired way of life. Displaced industrial workers seek new positions in a technological and "service" society. Countless families come and go around the country, into and out of homogeneous housing, commonly enough without establishing any focal or lasting attachment to local place or people.

Indigenous groups who managed to live in harmony with the earth have been displaced and moved about by the successive waves of conquering populations and the dominant structures of Western culture. Farmers, ranchers, and rural communities increasingly cannot economically or environmentally maintain their ways of livelihood. As it has been for centuries, the countryside frequently is a scene of isolation and hardship, either endured or fled when individuals have the opportunity, thus further draining it of resources and hope which, in turn, are fed into the cities. We are at the point of forgetting the rural areas and populations in our thoughts and plans for development. In the opposite direction, urban residents leave the cities to seek the elusive experience of a "natural and simple" way of life, perhaps finding a bit of what they want, perhaps missing the city's stimulating possibilities and rich choices.

In short, the dynamic and attraction of the city, suburb, small town, and countryside largely results from the way Americans seek to become at home—desiring and searching for a place where they can lead a meaningful existence. In the process, people sometimes succeed. They also frequently fail, never establishing a place and mode of belonging at all, or doing so only minimally, by physically occupying a decent material environment without depth of satisfaction.

Still, while this seems to be correct, the issue is much more complex. Not only is the problem pervasive, requiring thoughtful consideration of the social and economic roots of our urban life, but, in addition, *homelessness appears to characterize our age.* This is *not* to say that our era is the first or only one to have such a problem. Rather, it claims that it is *our problem now* and is deeply rooted in the character of our contemporary world, as Derrida, Foucault, Jung, Eliade, Heidegger, and many others have argued. Our homelessness, or displacement from both problematic and sustaining relationships with the natural environment, community and ethos, and the sacred, is the central theme of more than forty years of reflection by existential philosophy, humanistic social and behavioral disciplines, and cultural criticism.[3]

If homelessness is a facet of the current human condition, here and now, we need to try to deal with it. Through our daily patterns of work, play, love, and thinking, through literature and the arts, through the way we plan, design, and build, we need to try to discover ways to belong in the world and thus to become more fully ourselves.

RHYTHMS OF INDIVIDUAL DEVELOPMENT

"Individual" homelessness connotes the modern person, one who, even in crowds, is alone because of an absence of satisfying relationships to anyone in the surrounding city. But, that is old news. Here our problem is not that of the "masses" or of alienation. Rather, what concerns us is how any individual's condition is grounded in the more fundamental characteristics of what it means to be a person, that is, in *the journey each of us makes to become an autonomous, individual self.* In other words, the painful predicament we term displacement is itself unintelligible apart from the limitations and possibilities inherent in our own individual biological-psychological-cultural nature.

If we begin by considering home as the site where "I am" and perform my actions, we locate the "I" at the center of events. Other people, buildings, and things are seen in relation to my needs, wants, and prospects. The strengths and weaknesses of this assumption are obvious. We have the possibility of the autonomy of the whole self. Simultaneously, we find the danger of "egotism," where everything is evaluated from the viewpoint of the self's interests.

What, then, is the self and what are its needs? What we call the self obviously is complex. We are bodily beings and, many hold, spiritual as well as cultural. In any case, we are beginning to understand more adequately that to be human is to be an embodied consciousness.[4] Of course, we also have a rich unconscious and subconscious life in our sleeping and waking hours.

Crucially, to be embodied is to be some physical and cultural place. We necessarily are located somewhere and are within a particular set of norms and beliefs, within a received history and language. Insofar as we are living, we move; insofar as we have a spiritual dimension, we strive for meaning and value. Because of this constant movement, hopefully to different and better situations, worldwide cultural and spiritual traditions have described the condition and development of the self in terms of a quest or journey through life.

Our conscious and subconscious life establishes the self as different from the rest of what we encounter. An initial differentiation and distance between ourselves and other people, living beings, things, and events is given at the same time as is the possibility of being related to what is other. *To be an embodied self, then, means at the very foundation of our being, that we simultaneously belong to and are displaced from everything else.* Our life's quest is to overcome harmful, unhealthy, or unnecessary separations without supposing that we can achieve, or should try to, any impossible oneness or strict identity that would obliterate all fecund differences.

Individuals' growth and development include within their prospect the possibility for failure. We may be too displaced from what we need, fractured within ourselves and from the world. Yet we risk that danger in the course of life, for the alternative is to stay in the womb, or in a hermetically sealed incubator that we totally control, afraid of the task of becoming an individual. Clearly, humans grow from one stage toward another, always beginning with a familiar set of conditions and relationships and then moving through experiences of what is at first strange to us.

The biologist-psychologist Kurt Goldstein explains how our biological life consists of pulses.[5] As organisms, we need to avoid stagnation and rigidity on the one hand and chaos on the other. From a condition of stasis or balance we encounter some new element or condition which momentarily makes us "unstable." We then try to incorporate that into a new, more complex stability. This process involves a full range of activity, from our relationship with food to encountering foreign cultures. When we fail to incorporate the strange, we become sick, are threatened psychologically, or even die. When successful, we grow.

Similarly, the psychiatrist Carl Jung shows how life's task is to become an individuated self. Becoming autonomous involves consciously and responsibly understanding and acting so as to be both self-sufficient and related to a larger world. This requires a series of self-transformations, where the self is called on to integrate into its conscious and active life not only what we encounter through our usual conscious experience and perceptions, but also what lies in our subconscious and unconscious.[6]

We can see that biological growth and nurture, and cultural-spiritual development is a matter of *interaction of self and other*. The new comes to us as the natural in the form of food, biological stimulus, and the whole environment of wonder and threat; as the social, in the form of the emotional, intellectual, and volitional interaction with other selves; and, perhaps as some claim, as the sacred, where the holy would erupt into and disrupt everydayness.

In this process of growth, the self journeys into deeper and deeper relations with the other. That is why Jung describes the nature of the self as involving more than "my-self" in both our inner and outer dimensions. Just as consciousness explores the outer worlds of nature, society, and perhaps of the sacred, so too in the inner sphere we find more than just the "egotistical." Finally, even beneath and through the unconscious, we encounter the collective unconscious. Regardless of whether one accepts this particular aspect of Jung's psychological theory, the insight is important. The other appears in our lives both from the outside and as welling up from deep inside ourselves. Thus, the complex and powerful self is a goal which lies at the end of a lifelong journey to become at home in a rich and symbolic world that transcends and can nurture the individual.

The organic process of "pulse" and the stages of self-realization or individualization all show us the same thing: we grow by way of a continuous dynamic between (*a*) stability and unity and (*b*) dissonance and differentiation or complexity. In general, hopefully, we leave or transcend one condition and enter into another more complex one, only to repeat the process. Sometimes we fail. Sometimes we die.

A case in point is the normal need to establish identity and continuity of experience as a young child.[7] Later, we need to leave our childish ways and home in order to grow up. We break off being only a son or daughter to prepare for becoming fully mature ourselves. In our culture, we normally leave our family in our late teens or early twenties—later than it once occurred—to go out into the world on our own.[8] Finally, in old age, we have to find new ways to make ourselves at home in familiar surroundings newly limited by health, and often, finances; or, we may begin a new phase of identity in relocation.[9] These stages of change are the course of our entire life, which remains difficult because it is hard to give up comfortable patterns and to experience the initial dissonance and distress on the way to richer complexity, especially since there is no guarantee of success. But, as existential philosophy and psychology show, accepting responsibility for this dynamic movement is a key to a meaningful life.[10]

The very dynamic of life, then, establishes a rhythm of homelessness and homecoming: (*a*) we are at home; (*b*) we encounter the "disturbing" other outside ourselves which is different or strange, either by seeking it out or as it intrudes on us; and (*c*) we attempt to come into an appropriate relationship with it in order to become more richly ourselves, not to mention the possible benefit to the other, or change in the world that results from the new belonging together. To return to the starting point of this chapter, the obviously unhealthy and undesirable cases of homelessness need to be understood as instances of and in light of the unavoidable and essential characteristics of human nature, as an unending series of events of dislocation and attempted belonging. To become human is continually a matter of embodied placement and displacement and the attempt to arrive at or establish a new place, where we understand place as both a physical site and locus of meanings and values.

To become a self is not an abstract project, but a matter of existential encounters, choices, and actions.[11] The passage of the self, then, through continuing stages of being at home, becoming homeless, and attempting homecoming also is a passage to and through the other. We journey out of the natural world and then, transformed, back to the natural world; out of family and society, back newly to family and society.

HOMELESSNESS AND MODERN CULTURE

The modern city intensely and appropriately focuses the relationship of the self to the natural world and society because in the modern age the city itself results from two economic-technological changes or displacements in our relation to the environment and society. That is, the city is not only the site of many individuals' struggles to become at home; in addition, the story of the city is substantially the story of modern cultural homelessness and attempted belonging.[12]

For millennia the city has stood as the accomplishment and symbol of new encounters and attempts at transformation. From the earliest periods of history, people ventured from farm and field and nomadic rounds to sample the bazaar of strange peoples, foods, customs, and prospects. They still do. Some returned home, hurt or full of dreams. Many gave up or lost both nomadic and settled relations to land and ways of life to live together in the city. Still others, restless or seeking even further opportunities, moved from city to city. Some found their new life agreeable and stayed, finding a return to previous conditions unthinkable. The same basic process continues today, even increasingly, all over the world, in some cases on a mind-boggling scale, as in Mexico City with its eighteen million inhabitants.

In other words, the continuing historical growth of the city has been based on at least two intertwined sorts of displacement and attempted belonging. One is the natural pulse of the self's growth that occurs as individuals leave previous family life and customs in order to seek their own new way. Indeed, entire families come seeking the new and exciting possibilities in the rich stimulus of the city's life. Another sort of displacement, also "natural" in its way, results not so much from the self's own processes as from irresistible pressure or radically threatening disturbances: displacement because of natural disasters, environmental change, or cultural changes, such as war, economic upheaval, and the exercise of power and law.

To focus on enforced displacement, homelessness in its cultural dimension is an especially dominant feature of the modern age, and may be escalating today. That is, over and above the very old patterns of displacement, in the last four hundred years or so, the story of Western culture and the city—which means the story of America—largely is one of displacement and perhaps of daunting prospects for successful homecoming or new modes of belonging.

In the simplest sense, the city is a powerful scene where people make a place for themselves. How is a place taken up by an individual in a community? Naturally, this is a matter of social roles, of the individual's talents and needs, and general cultural, religious, political, and economic roles and customs. As Oscar Handlin argues, changes are often delicate, as is the case when a place is made through family and local structures. Or, one may leave and attempt to join an open structure somewhere else. While it may remain true that the relevant social features may be (1) chosen, when open to modifications, (2) given, in received tradition, or (3) forced on us by outside factors, a close look at the modern age shows that forced displacement, increasingly with "no one" responsible, shapes our prospects for making or finding a place.[13]

A first major shift, begun in the West and then spread throughout the world, is seen in what we label industrialization. The phenomena is now global, though the pace varies in different countries and regions, now slowing down in most of America and Western Europe. This is important, not only because of its historical impact, but because some version of the same story still is unfolding for Native Americans, for Third World immigrants to America, for rural Americans continuing the migration to the cities, for migrant farmworkers settling out.[14]

Consider a version of the archetypal story behind the movement of many people to America as wonderfully told by Handlin.[15] In the transition from peasant and other forms of rural life to the modern industrial-technological world, one of the most striking symptoms of change has been the accelerating transformation from the heterogeneous to the homogeneous. In the earlier pattern, within the unity of stable religious, cultural, and environmental forms, there was a keen sense of the uniqueness of places, where the natural world was understood as an agglomerate of specific local places and of strongly distinct individuals filling in a village's small array of roles. In the later pattern, largely the humanly made realm, homogeneity became dominant as one built environment was able to function anywhere, as individuals lost significance before industrially and technologically defined tasks and roles, as society itself became understood as a construction of our own making.[16]

To only briefly note the type of home which a village was, think of the old, original rootedness of a peasant life (recognizing that nomads, early urban peoples, and primal societies which in no way involved "peasants" had other types of stories, beyond our scope here). For each person, the meaning and understanding of one's life depended on sustained participation within a complex web of relationships. Consequently, the way to act followed from the external examples.[17] The self could be thought of as given meaning by this embracing series of expanding contexts: individual person within community; community within a distant and dimly perceived broader human realm, but more immediately, community within natural world; natural world part of a sacred cosmos. The whole was kept stable in a "cosmo-ecological" balance and, not surprisingly, involved very conservative patterns of experience.

A carefully tended belonging with the natural seasons and rhythms of the earth and heavens and with the fixed set of obligations and rights, known as the village, together provided a "place," both local and densely significant. One could not be one self just anywhere, but only in one's proper place. Just here, as related to the specifically arranged, given or fixed whole reality.

But, in contrast to local place, the outside or foreign world began to play an increasingly intrusive role. What had been an external social-political framework finally disrupted village life. The major changes in this determining "outside world" were economic pressures, changes in agricultural production and scale, consolidation of holdings and changes in who and what a landlord was, and population growth. Finally, the dramatic industrialization of the nineteenth century and the development of agriculture as the means to meet the needs of large and concentrated urban populations conclusively defined society in terms of surplus and profit. The peasant and his land were transformed into "paid labor" and "farms." Changed into a farmer, then landless, and finally become a day laborer, the peasant's old place and status were lost forever.

Naturally, there were great emigrations to cities in both Europe and America. To look at America, immigrants sought a new place for their displaced ways of life. But, it was never possible to be a peasant in America because the old enabling context of community—natural, social, and sacred cosmos, including the supporting "outside" social and economic structures of landlords, church, special artisans, marketplace, did not exist. Over and over, whether staying in cities or passing through to the interior, immigrants found themselves in a world they were not born into and where they did not belong. Somewhere-everywhere, they were displaced, homeless in the deepest sense of not being able to be fully themselves because they were not capable of the necessary relationships to their immediate families, a genuine community, or to a meaningful cosmos. While there were significant differences, the same basic story can be told of many immigrants from Asia, the Caribbean, and Central and South America, and of many who never were peasants: Native Americans, migrant farmworkers, urban residents of preindustrial societies, the "dark-skinned" who somehow were deemed not "true Americans."[18]

Where the meaning of one's life is a matter of belonging "together with" local community, landscape or site, and cosmos, the loss of such relationships is experienced as isolation and insignificance. How could one do anything significant apart from the placement where one belonged and was oneself?

The new world was of someone else's making for immigrants, unknown and foreign. One lived in strangeness while trying to adapt to new circumstances. A key to the required change was the redefinition of self and relation to others. From identity, through difference, hopefully to a new identity. In the new way of life for the last hundred and fifty years or so, the self clearly, even radically, became individual. The self became *the independent subject* who willed and acted to shape the surrounding objective world through work, that is, *who made things*. The new process involved making products in a factory, making new friends and social organizations, making a habitation within shameful buildings, making a new way of speaking and thinking, making new forms of religion, making new ways of learning and trying to continue customs, making a supporting framework for the sick, old, orphaned, and even more recently arrived—in short, making a living.

The self in the industrial age was delineated as a subject which confronted both other things and human life, including one's own, as objects before itself. Workers produced commodities to be consumed by other subjects. In turn, workers became objects supervised, controlled, or managed by more powerful subjects. Hence, the nineteenth- and twentieth-century self became extraordinarily separated from the world and even itself. The issue of overcoming the distance, the alienation, developed as a specific form of the subject-object split introduced at the beginning of the modern era.

Precisely here, the individual had no status, no special place. What counted was the labor force in general. Or, from the vantage of prospect for the modern new self, what now mattered was no longer staying in place, but the opposite: successfully moving up, through positions. Ironically, though not accidentally, where one's individual ability and achievement were insignificant, what counted was fulfilling an alien task where employment itself often was the result of chance or a passing mode.

At first this stress on individual subjects meant that each family was on its own in a way it never had been. Then, very quickly, it meant that the family was fractured as traditional responsibilities, contributions, and status of husband and wife, of parent and child broke down. Any possible homecoming required more than a new interpretation of tradition in a attempt to recover the relation to community, natural world, and if possible, sacred cosmos. Such initial attempts at reorganization yielded to an altogether new pattern to achieve some satisfactory life.

Of course, the passing of old ways also involved aspects of *liberation* from old imposed and rigid forms and from seemingly unavoidable limitations on one's life. As if released from prison, many welcomed new possibilities and still do. Thus, with loss of place many became (become) lost themselves. Simultaneously, others were (are) eager at the prospect of change, with little or no regret at what is gone. The phenomena is so pronounced, and each prospect has so many spokespersons, that it needs no further elaboration. For better or worse, modern America assumes the connection between self and the development of opportunity, where both are understood in terms of freedom and innovation.

As is obvious, the story continues through a second major displacement, even while the first continues, as industrialization is supplanted by logistical-technological culture and its attendant forms of service economies, multinational corporations, aspatial logic, and so on.[19] What were subjects and objects in the modern industrial age, become, in the postmodern, post-industrial era, facets of a system of resources. As described in the previous chapters, we now are passing from understanding ourselves, society, and environment in terms of their characteristics as subjects (as consciousness, broadly understood) and objects (what is apprehended and manipulated for subjective use, according to its physical and material properties and potentials) to interpreting everything as part of systems of standing reserve. Now, what anything is or means—including the self—appears to be a function of its readiness to "come into play" in the relational network. The network itself is made and sustained by no identifiable and responsible individual, but instead by anonymous social forces, systems specifications, and economic powers. We enter, then, a new mode of dislocation.

Obviously, to face successfully the current forms of dislocation we cannot fall back into a nostalgia for the past, nor ignore the force and character of the technological. If the human condition amounts to an "always being underway" toward a possible and desired "homecoming" as well as movement away from previous "homes," our placement today within homelessness is nothing less than the site or occasion wherein we can succeed or fail to belong appropriately, in a new manner, to the other dimensions of the world.

10

A Homecoming: Design
on Behalf of Place

Because we are embodied, we are always somewhere. In America, the vast majority of us are housed, which means we have a location and address in one or another housing unit. But, as we have seen, whether we are in a place, understood as a site for the possibility of genuine dwelling, is another matter. In place, meaning and value are made concrete, actualized in and through things as diverse as buildings, settlements, political actions, work, and poems. As Heidegger puts it: "We attain to dwelling, so it seems, only by means of building. . . . In today's housing shortage even this much is reassuring and to the good; residential buildings do indeed provide shelter; today's houses may even be well planned, easy to keep, attractively cheap, open to air, light and sun, but—do the houses in themselves hold any guarantee that *dwelling* occurs in them?"[1]

In order to dwell, we want and seek an authentic place in regard to each of the fundamental facets of reality. Recalling what we earlier saw of the self, we would need a place or site where we can become, in stages as a mortal self, the person we are potentially.[2]

We need a place where we can belong to a community, that is, a scene of being given and accepting responsibility for meaningful patterns of life which gather and hold individual selves together, as an "us." We need a specific locus on earth with a dense and fruitful relationship to the elements, to earth and water, to plant and animal life, to heavenly seasons and rhythms. We need a placement in relation to the sacred, whether that placement involves a lived experience of the sacred, an openness, even if full of doubt, to the absent or hidden sacred, or the acceptance of life altogether without the sacred. These needs show the relation of our self-identity to *genius loci*. Indeed, the nexus of identity and sense of place has become the focus of a burgeoning body of research.[3]

No doubt the necessary, inner transformation toward place and dwelling *involves more than* planning and design, because such homecoming is a matter of comprehensive understanding, description, and interpretation; of work, love, and ways of living; of language and the arts. We can not create a needed world all by ourselves, but only by appropriately responding to the rest—if it actually is given. But, fundamentally, such transformation *also does depend on* urban and regional planning, design, and architecture because they help establish and maintain the openings in which a new gathering together can occur and a new belonging of self, society, nature, and the sacred, if there is to be one.[4] The planning, design, and building would help enable the new mode of belonging to happen, just as, simultaneously, they would themselves emerge, metamorphosized, in the course of playing their proper part.

QUESTIONS FACING DESIGN ON BEHALF OF PLACE

Of course, design partially begins in reflection, perhaps in what Martin Buber calls the realistic imagination.[5] We can begin to articulate what the city designed as a place, or a site for becoming at home, would be like by focusing on *the questions* which follow from our human nature and serial dislocations, from the essence of the modern and technological epochs and the possibility of an originary alternative. Persisting in questioning does not imply that designers, planners, and architects are not already working on these issues, as we will see. Many are. The point is to resist facilely passing over the fundamental issues. Only after focally sustaining them as questions would a review of the current responses be appropriate—as part of the next step.

To remain in the question, how can we delineate the city as the site for a healthy belonging to and release of the old, as a part of our being responsibly open to new phases of growth and the possibility of a new home? Think of the self's stages in vital, normal development. For each stage of life, a city would have to be designed with homes which would provide for the needed basic stasis—unified rest—and also places where one could experience the new, unsettling, and strange without its destroying the self with chaos or inassimilable shock. The environment would include or provide physical stimulation, intellectual challenge, emotional range, and cultural diversity. Traditionally, neighborhoods and streets, markets and busy downtowns, parks and playgrounds, schools and libraries, taverns and beauty parlors, fairgrounds and sports stadiums have been the sites where experiences occurred. What will the new forms be?[6]

It is apparent that design questions developing from a concern for the growth of the self quickly involve the growth of many selves in plural relationships, that is, in community and perhaps in a coherent, yet heterogeneous society. Hence, a crucial question for design for cultural life: how would we attempt to nurture both concretely enriching differences and also a generally intelligible social identity? This is the issue of the truly particular and the still shared, an issue of many distinctive places which yet make one place.

Surely all this is not simply a matter of grand boulevards and a merely visual schematic with details left to laissez-faire. We do not need "the city beautiful" with ward bosses just a block off the main streets.[7] Nor is it a matter of lavish attention to individual but isolated buildings which are the result of the romantic cult where the architect appears as modern artist and the buildings as autonomous art objects or commodities.[8] Grandiose designs and atomic buildings will not do. Neither, however, will modern and technological planning of logistical systems which lack the power to establish place and fail to provide existential satisfaction. Of course, both modern and technological design and planning have responses to these issues—responses which still need to be taken seriously.

The shortcomings of modernity and the technological recall the deeper historical displacement of modern culture. How would we design a city that realistically deals with the industrial and technological epochs, and yet provides possibilities beyond what currently dominates?

We know that displacement involves the destruction of traditional patterns and stability, as found in the heritage of a common landscape.[9] Even leaving open the issue of whether that is avoidable or undesirable in the end, we can more modestly say that in today's homelessness people are displaced who need not be. For a variety of reasons, chiefly economic, according to those who appear to know or even champion the process, people are moved from their homes, families, and neighborhoods when they would choose not to be. We must design so residents are not displaced from the fragile physical, emotional, and intellectual-spiritual situations which nourish them. We need to try to provide for those who already have been displaced or are lost and who likely never will be replaced anywhere.

At the same time, people naturally like to move, to change. How would we design the city, and make available its housing, work, and culture, so that people can move in and begin a new life? While we want to design for coherence and stability rather than chaos, we also need openness and variety so as not to become fossilized and sterile, as happens when cultures and "places" become too closed in on themselves, too homogeneous or absolute, rejecting anyone new as an "outsider."[10]

Or, consider the *crucial transition* from the industrial to the technological era, a transformation beyond the full understanding and influence of individuals, or even whole societies, in which occur major shifts in perception, experience, and interpretation. Currently, large numbers of people are beginning to find themselves discarded as obsolete. Once part of the dynamic of the modern industrial era, now they cannot even live out their lives as producing subjects and socially compliant objects controlled by those who command capital. Increasingly, neither skilled workers nor laborers are part of the technological system of transformation of credit, energy, information, and services. Caught between eras, they have the ambivalent prospects either of finding another role as modern subjects-producers (by changing from the steel industry to housing construction or to crafting toys for tourists) or of being themselves transformed into part of the human resources of the technological era.[11]

How could we design cities so that people, buildings, and the entire city itself might endure the reigning phase of displacement and be able to move from the latest dislocation to becoming at home again? An answer is vital to individuals and to our cities, lest the latter become ghosttowns as countless sites have over time.

Instead of thinking of one city as an industrial city (a once upon a time place, now just a space to leave) and another city as a technological city (just now trying to become a place, a space to come to and transform), *what if we thought of and designed each city to be the place which is simultaneously the scene of displacement (the industrial city) and the site of a possible recovery of place (if such can be done in a technological city), or, if not, as a city of the next, originary mode.* Because the requisite designs would help us leave the one dimension behind and, at the same time, provide a means to enter the new dimension, they could be the occasion for a genuine homecoming— leaving and returning to the same place, but with its meaning somehow transformed.[12]

Planning and carrying out the integrated, self-contained transition from the industrially defined self and city is not a matter of cranking out new and attractive service modules or high-tech office parks and amenities for young professionals. It will require thinking down beneath the surface phenomena into the inner essence of technology and its components. If the technological generates the modular because the modular is the homogeneously interchangeable, that is, place independent and always in stock, how should design be related to the modular?

Should design embrace and exploit the modular since all else is fruitless nostalgia? Or, should design proceed as a form of mole warfare, in the time-honored manner of colonizing or converting sterile and hostile environments into livable cubbyholes—design by subversion and occupation?[13] Or should the modular be ignored or actively resisted, in an attempt to begin an entirely new mode of dwelling? In any case, design would have to become a path-finding which will let technology be technological, yet in a way which keeps us human, perhaps in an originary manner as Heidegger suggests and as was considered in the previous chapters.

To shift to a still larger context, we have seen that the individual self and community, in order to become fully themselves, need placement in relation to the containing natural and spiritual realms. The design issues are as profound as they are broad. How would we design in order to regain a sound relationship to the natural environment, to the rhythms of the heavens and earth? Could we learn again to harmonize with the seasons and the attendant cycles of birth, growth, and death of plants and animals by experiencing them in parks, or in yards and community gardens, or . . . ? Could we again become attuned to the sky, say at night, which now is almost totally absent from our focal experience, by somehow attending newly to the stars and moon and tides and nocturnal animal life? How could that be done with safety, in a real, dense city?

Or, what sorts of designs and buildings would aid those who seek to maintain an experience of the sacred, or those who strive to remain disposed to it, or those who find themselves better off without it? Buildings or open places; places for one, or a few, or for many; places evoking the past or somehow new, alternative sources of enrichment for our age? Would we use traditional building forms and materials or try to discover new ones?

Clearly, the possibility of our originary recovery of a profound communal, natural, and spiritual environment and life requires a new mode of architecture and planning as well as urban design. We can move to answer questions such as those just posed by reflecting on whether or how an originary beginning is underway in recent work. Figures as diverse as Louis Kahn, Alvar Aalto, Aldo van Eyck, Charles Moore, and Christopher Alexander, and movements for design as community activity often are considered promising.[14] For example, Moore's figure of the building as a geode allows an unpretentious exterior and relationship to the surrounding buildings and landscape that is interesting and yet an interior that is as creative and amazing as the most eclectic American could demand. This strategy not only is a design solution, but is a social update of the perennial democratic dilemma of how to unify the many into the one.[15]

What design strategies would be harbingers of the beginning of a solution to the technological; what actually a deepening of the technological mode? We can not expect to find our way very far unless we can begin to sort out (1) which designs and modes of building are still modern or radically "post-most" modern and, hence, substantially disinterested assemblages,[16] and (2) which may be genuinely post-technological and on the verge of originary dwelling. The project is especially important because Western intellectuals have been proclaiming the end of the modern era and the beginning of the "new age" for more than a century. The twilight of the gods is past and the new dawn is perennially at hand. Apparently, we are stuck, caught in a place where we are not able to see clearly.

DESIGN FOR PERSONAL WELL-BEING

Without any pretensions to being prophetic, much less exhaustive, to begin to articulate what design on behalf of place and dwelling would be like, recall the self's stages in healthy, normal development and the displacements we have to go through to grow. In light of these, designers and planners must discern the specific needs of young children, young adults, the middle-aged, and the elderly before it is possible to design appropriate settings.

The differences in the phases of life are too often overlooked when we think of how we attempt to dwell. Even a brief consideration of childhood, young adulthood, and old age indicates that human development in each stage has profound consequences for design of place.[17]

The needs of very young children pose special design problems. Research indicates that the condition of the home environment bears significantly on the success we have in achieving a healthy self-identity. In point, Erik Erikson contends that a coherent sense of self results from experiences of continuity, or the continuity of experience.[18] Early on, a child experiences specific sleeping arrangements in which the spatial location signals social relationships, a process contributing to recognition of similarities and differences such as those involving male and female members of the household and sexuality, and in turn, to the development of self-identity. A successful home, then, would be the site of the repeated confirmation of the same relationships which helps the young child recognize and maintain a sense of inner sameness and continuity.[19]

Similarly, cities need to be designed as places to facilitate adolescents' leaving their families by simultaneously maintaining continuity with home and also allowing movement to independence. Young people require socially acceptable places which are stimulating, where they can meet new friends in a free atmosphere. The same place would need to be both acceptably related to habits and values of home so as not to fracture the remaining connection and yet different enough to allow change and movement to independence. Further, those taking the first steps to living on their own, need employment and places to live. Of course, on a macro scale, as we saw above, the design for young and middle-aged working adults depends on the development of new and renovated cities that accommodate the larger transition from the industrial to technological epoch.

Consider a concrete domestic situation where the needs of both young children and young adults, within changing family and social patterns, require new design solutions: the residence of the single parent with young children. The prevalent American and European house form, designed for single families with two parents, one home almost all the time, certainly does not lend itself to the needs of today's children or parents. Nor do apartments in large buildings, the housing most available given the single head-of-household's typically low income, and which almost forces isolation on the occupants of the individual apartments. What is needed is a new form of communal housing, affording both privacy to the individual families and yet group support.

The reorganization of domestic space by Nina West in London in the 1960s, and the projects of Joan Forrester Sprague, Katrin Adam, and Susan Aitcheson in the United States in the 1970s are fine examples of innovative design response.[20] West began with the problem of how to take care of her young children while working to support them and went on to create a new form of housing and communal arrangement of space. In Fiona House, designed by architect Sylvester Bone in the early 1970s, "the interior corridors double as playrooms, with carpeted floors and windows from each apartment looking in, so that a parent cooking could watch a child at play. Intercoms linked apartments, enabling parents to baby-sit for each other by turning on the intercom and listening for children crying.[21] Obviously, attending to the young childrens' need for stability and continuity and to the economic limitations of the parents, who desire work in order to remain independent of social welfare, also requires new design of shared economic and spatial resources.[22]

Currently, a great deal of interest is being shown in 'Co-housing'. Here the Western values placed on privacy and ownership of individual living units is merged with the desire to escape the burdens of cooking one's own meals, especially with parents working outside the home, and to have more of a sense of community. Most co-housing designs feature some form of communal kitchen and dining area, as well as play or recreation space inside and out. Meal preparation arrangements variously provide for each person to take a turn cooking or for a hired staff to do the work. Each family unit also has its own kitchen, so residents can "stay in" if they choose. The projects provide more options that successfully seem to meet the time and energy restraints of today's urban life and to restore an open, but not forced, way to gather together with similar adults and to provide a larger, but still small-enough and known, atmosphere for children. That is, they are a place for an appropriate and balanced mode of support, safety, and convenience.[23]

Finally, in America, the elderly frequently find themselves in a state of change and relocation. Economic, health, and social changes exert substantial pressure on where and how the elderly live. After a family is raised, with retirement from a job, with the death of a spouse, or with failing health, there is no longer the same need or perhaps possibility for a large house or for living in the same location. Positive opportunities may motivate the elderly to move to a smaller place, perhaps an apartment or condominium. Free to live wherever they choose, a different city may seem more attractive. Or, negative dimensions of old age may force changes. There may not be enough money any more to live in the old large house or same neighborhood. Deteriorating health may prevent one from living at home in the same way as before, requiring a situation accommodating reduced mobility and limited independence, or, perhaps, even placement in an institution.

To cite only one major issue for design, research indicates that accommodation strategies used by the elderly, whether when remaining in the old residence or when relocating, need to be provided for in housing and community design, specifically since self-identity is maintained through contact with familiar spaces and within family and social environments.[24]

Graham D. Rowles has noted the importance of the "surveillance zone" in maintaining "a primary focus of participation in the world beyond the threshold."[25] Typically, the elderly monitor outside activities from carefully chosen vantage points by windows affording a view of neighbors' homes and, with the support of those who keep an eye on them, remain able to live at home independent of their families. It appears that within relationships of reciprocal watching, a sense of mutual obligation frequently evolves: reciprocal seeing enables the elderly to know (watch) and be known (be watched), and thus helps generate and maintain their sense of identity.[26]

Clearly, there are design implications at many levels. Cities need to be designed so that the elderly are not unnecessarily dislocated from the spaces where they have spent their lives and which sustain their memories. The location and orientation of new housing for the elderly needs to provide for zones of mutual visual surveillance, as do the elements of building design. For example, special care needs to be given to the size and location of windows, especially the inclusion of low sills, and to the outside landscaping, where even trees can block neighborly contact and isolate a person.[27] Such design needs to be intergenerationally sensitive, balancing the support the elderly need with the freedom desired by young families. In working out designs for overcoming the isolation of the old while respecting the privacy of the younger, we also will be developing strategies, which naturally develop a sense of neighborliness and thus promote a place for the dwelling of all.

DESIGN WITHOUT CULTURAL OR ENVIRONMENTAL DISPLACEMENT

As we have seen, individual life patterns and the need for place are bound together. But, local place can occur only within the context of specific, culturally developed bioregions. Finally, then, we need to consider some of the work of urban designers, community and regional planners, and architects already engaged with recovering and rebuilding our belonging to the appropriate human and natural realms.

The work in the Kreuzberg section of West Berlin, undertaken as part of the IBA (Internationale Bauausstellung in Berlin) and directed by Professor Hardt-Waltherr Hämer, is a well-known example of a large-scale effort to plan and implement urban design in a way that overcomes dreadful conditions, a long period of neglect, and the pressures of systematic, technological development. The project has kept the goal of fulfilling the spectrum of res-

FIGURE 10.1.
Hinrich and Inken Baller, Fraenkelufer-Block 70, Berlin. IBA Reconstruction as Careful Urban Renewal.

idents' needs without creating further estrangement. It is a wonderful case of, as Hämer calls it, "careful urban renewal" (an approach echoed by Roberta Graz's *The Living City,* which reports on small-scale projects that rejuvenate parts of the city's fabric and life).[28] Two aspects of the process are especially important.

First, the long-range planning and building have aimed to satisfy both the private needs of the residents and also their larger social needs. Naturally, special emphasis was placed on the individual dwelling places. In the general context of dilapidated nineteenth-century rent houses, unrepaired devastation remaining from World War II, extensive squatting in buildings by students and other tenants, and plans to clear away large corridors for a highway project, the need for decent places to live was crucial.

But, from the first, the goal was more than a certain amount of decent square footage with some access to public utilities—though even that would have been a massive accomplishment. In addition, it was insisted that the living spaces would really be places where people belonged and could live in a satisfactory set of relationships.

A central feature of planning and design was seeing the individual dwelling spaces in relation to their context, thereby enabling places to be established and cultivated. Kreuzberg had a chronic shortage of open space, which meant insufficient connection to both the natural world and the shared public sphere. One solution for enlarging access to both realms involved increasing public green space. Open green spaces provided fresh air, trees, grass, and plants and also a site for social life which was stimulated by the public atmosphere. As neighbors worked in their individual yards and in the communal areas of the courtyards, designing and maintaining them, they cultivated not only relationships to cycles of growth and life, but to each other.

Of course, emphasis on relation to earth and sky came through other avenues too, such as the intensive effort at ecological design and Green Architecture, of which, more shortly. In this regard, nature has done its share, as can be appreciated when experiencing how much more mature the landscape has become after only eight or nine years of growth. The change is especially dramatic in the interior courtyards of IBA housing. And there were other ways in which the fabric of social relationships was encouraged, such as by reclaiming the streets for play and social use and by the participation of the residents in the planning and design process.

Hence, the second major aspect of the Kreuzberg project: constant participation of the residents in the planning and design process. The intention never was for the architect to do projects *for* the area, as was the plan of the grander, avant-garde Neubau portion of IBA. In Kreuzberg, the reverse occurred. The needs, fears, and hopes of those who lived there were transformed, often through sheer tenacity, into design by the architects, who took on a role of specially trained "articulators" and, one could say, advocates, of ways of life that wanted delineation in the forms of buildings, open spaces, and community patterns.

While the IBA's individual buildings and building elements are located within a larger planned context and sphere of social participation, this is not usually the case. More often, the achievement of place is the result of the successful integration of an individual building into a pre-existing context through the work of a more independent designer or small group. Architect Jusuck Koh's design for a house appropriate to the Southwest is a good example of what is involved in designing toward "home."

Koh started with the recognition that the usual methods and forms of houses, for example, in Lubbock, Texas, are not the most appropriate for the regional climate. What of more indigenous or locally adaptive models and materials—for example, the Spanish interior courtyard house? Therein lies the rub. In the current market-place and society of West Texas, the pressure is for houses to look like the other houses already there, which can be produced with some economy, especially by large-scale builders and developers. In addition, in the automobile society and where the yard, especially the front yard, is the symbol, if not the actual site of "open" social interaction, the interior courtyard would appear as "standoffish" or "self-isolated" and thus foreign. Then there are the social and class issues of Spanish and Mexican forms in Anglo neighborhoods when the building types do not appear on the scale of mansions. In this context, the traditional interior courtyard house seems to be at odds with the social, cultural context.

Adapted to the local situation, the subsequent design accommodated the car by interiorizing the space in an integrated carport, rearranged the enclosed open space to one side of the dwelling, and "softened" the appearance of the enclosing wall by means of open, rhythmic brickwork. With such modification, Koh has worked toward a design which promises to be more appropriate to the physical and cultural environment of the Southwest and also practically mediates the needs of homeowners and builders.

As the examples clearly show, design for homecoming must be more ecologically sensitive than has been common and must enable the inhabitants to develop a more satisfactory connection to the natural world. Of course, there are old traditions of gardens and garden cities that still need to be adapted. But, a new attitude also is called for which fits people back into nature's cycles and processes, without any romantic attempt to escape back to idyllically conceived nature. Though design does not need to adapt a given ideology, examples of successful efforts at reinterpretation are found in Green Architecture, in the offshoots of the agricultural projects advocated by Britz's *The Edible City Resource Manual,* in Gary Coates' *Resettling America,* and in other projects working toward sustainable communities.[29]

The Green Architecture movement does consciously develop its background tradition of urban parkland, urban gardens, and green play areas. Yet, it is something new: the fusion of very sophisticated technology with the belief that we need plant life to live well, physically and psychologically. Though the range of solar, thermal, and wind engineering and the techniques for the use of glass, insulation, and other materials is beyond the scope of this chapter, they all contribute to the same end. Often presented in a visually stunning way, one approach is to cover over and fill in our too often bleak buildings with plants, and to open buildings and orient ourselves to the sun, wind, and weather.

The greatest number of such environments is in northern Europe at the moment, but the movement is spreading to the United States. The geomorphic designs which incorporate housing clusters into hillsides in Switzerland, Germany, and Austria are well worth emulating elsewhere, as are the many fine examples of courtyards and rooms disposed to the outside that are found in the Keuezberg project. Luckily, designs such as the Guyers' are increasingly popular and sophisticated, and thus no longer merely curiosities or "post-hippie" hangovers.[30]

As Gary Coates' remarkable book, *Resettling America*, effectively shows, we can not avoid the new post–fossil fuel age we are entering. Appropriate technology and careful attention to differentiated bioregions will be indispensable for any future way of life which will sustain a culture harmonized with physical surroundings. That is, design can not be abstractly sensitive to environment in general, but needs to concretely respond to specific places, because the earth is a "complex web of highly differentiated yet interacting assemblages of life forms and processes," that is, "bioregions." Coates points out a consequence for planning and design. Since "the bioregion sets natural limits on human intervention, . . . to be adaptive, human culture must first recognize and then attempt to enhance the inner character and potential of these bio-geographic areas. Thus, the bio-region can be viewed as a fundamental biological and social unit and the foundation for planning in the post industrial age."[31]

Of course, design adaptive to the bioregions also will be responsive to historical, cultural environments, because except in recent homogeneous, technological culture, the commonly recognized patterns of bioregions "have tended to unify the inhabitants and to differentiate them from the members of other regions."[32] Designing and building this "new symbiosis between nature and culture," to provide for "a sense of personal and regional identity," finally would require genuine regional planning. As a beginning, at least some local projects are underway, for instance at the New Alchemy Institute in New England, the Land Institute in Salina, Kansas, and Meadowcreek in Arkansas.[33]

FIGURE 10.2.
R. and E. Guyer, Hillside Housing Clusters, Effretikon, Switzerland.

FIGURE 10.3.
Terry Harkness, An East-Central Illinois Garden.

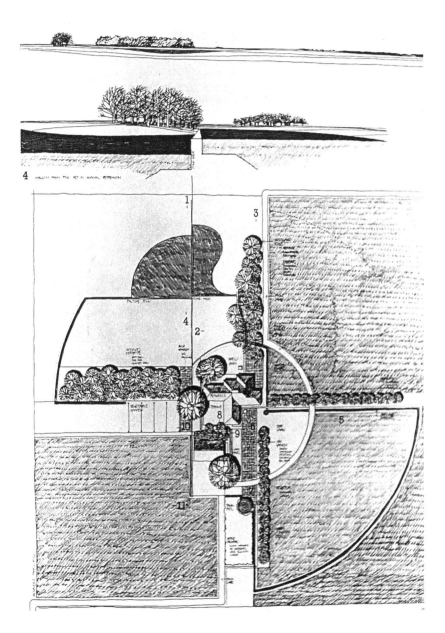

Also of interest in this regard are the sensitive designs for Midwestern gardens by Terry Harkness, carefully attuned to their natural and cultural environments. Harkness' work has its origin in a patient and keen seeing of earth, sky, and human community in the rural east-central Illinois landscape. Before he began any design, he learned the changes in light from the sky during shifts in weather and seasons; the subtle modulation of fields by frost, snow, rainwater, and crops; the modes of appropriating the landscape by geometric patterns of roads and driveways, trees, hedgerows, and fences, cropland and vegetable and flower gardens.

Based on his careful seeing, Harkness transposes the essential features of the regional landscape to his garden design: the farmstead's vernacular placement in the midst of fields, woodlands, and orchards; its entryway, yard, and garden. In treating the countryside's openness to the horizon and sky, the subtle shimmering and disappearance of evanescent water in flooded fields, the texture of soybean stubble covered with frost, he conveys the essential experience of belonging within the landscape.[34]

On the other side of the globe, Australian architect Glenn Murcutt incorporates historical, cultural interpretations as well as the natural dimensions of bioregions into the design process. A rational calculative use of local and industrial materials combined with reflection on climate and vegetation is found in his Neville Frederick House in Jamberoo (1982), the Museum and Tourist Center at Kemsey, New South Wales (1981), and the house at Bingie Point. This architecture may be the closest thing we have to a building that says both "yes" and "no" to technology, that is, that comes closest to being an example of a Heideggerian originary building, though we need to be cautious in suggesting powerful and potentially dangerous alignments. In any case, Murcutt's buildings use technology yet free us from its negative aspects in a way that positively reestablishes the human relations to earth and sky that are lost in technological systemics, as is documented by architect J. V. DeSousa in his interpretive descriptions.[35]

Built in Jamberoo in 1982, the Neville Fredericks House is one of Murcutt's best "long houses." The building is simple. A short pavilion of two bays parallels a long one of nine bays. Both pavilions are identical in section, with a steeply pitched gable roof rounded at the peak. The form recalls the primal huts of New Guinea in which the great roof shelters an open interior. Through its simple form and resonances it carries a power suitable to its site in the Australian bush.

The house is shaped by the natural environment. Located on the eastern uplands, the house faces northeast, along the coast. Except for a small kitchen window, the southwest wall is solid, blocking the cold winter winds that roll off the uplands. The northwest face is a glass wall that catches the winter sun. Actually, the wall is a composite system of wood posts infilled

FIGURE 10.4.
Glenn Murcutt, Neville Frederick House, Jamberoo

with a double-hung sash, insect mesh, and tensioned wood venetian blinds on the exterior. This system allows the wall to open and close in a variety of ways so that the interior space responds to climatic conditions. The entire house can become a veranda.

The site once was occupied by an old farmhouse in an area of farmland and rainforest gullies that often is flooded. The small plateau shelf made for the previous house more than thirty years before is maintained and the new house perches above the land with minimal disturbance. Raising the building above the earth's surfaces also allows the site to drain naturally. The house follows the Aborigine saying "one must touch this earth lightly,"[36] by showing respect for it and, at the same time, by boldly standing as different from it. As a result of this mode of placement, the house carries a substantial aura.

Clearly, for all the deference to its place, the house is a humanly made thing and a means of inserting human presence into the landscape. It is an outpost, and one that is made to endure. The simple form and cultural context are echoed in the materials: wood, glass, and corrugated iron—the latter commonly used throughout Australia for a hundred years.[37] Western red cedar sheathes the exterior, pine the interior. For all the use of vernacular materials, the manner of construction clearly is innovative: interior space is kept continuous by stopping cross walls at 2.4 meters and infilling above with mullionless glass. Free of visual obstructions, the space is unified and the dominant roof form reads through.

As noted, the ledge on which the house sits was the site of a former home. All that survived of the previous farmhouse was the fireplace, now integrated into the new house and providing the focus for the veranda or garden room. The integrated existing fireplace maintains the continuity of human occupation of the site. The fireplace also centers the new house, fixing the building in the landscape, its vertical axis mundi connecting it to earth and sky.[38]

The house establishes a place, an opening for human life in the landscape in a spare manner that sensitively gathers forms and materials together with bioregional features such as climate and previous groups' modes of habitation. The accomplishment obviously proceeds out of Pacific vernacular traditions, yet without a trace of nostalgia. The self-restraint in design and construction and the holding-back that addresses the environment in its own terms, taking care not to damage it so that it can continue to come forth, realize two-track thinking, combining tough-minded rationality with attuned meditative response.[39]

The co-housing and sustainable community movements, and the work of Hämer, Koh, Coates, and Murcutt are not isolated phenomena. Rather, they typify the emerging approaches to design for homecoming. The same attitude toward developing innovative methods of seeing, carefully discovering or recovering the essential features of bioregions, private and communal life, and building elements, forms, materials, and techniques in order to transform them into fresh designs, is found in many other projects, which for all their differences are still congruent.

An initial list of promising work would include the following: Alfred Altherr's adaptation of the cantilevered stone (*gneiss*) stem from traditional Swiss (Tessin) vernacular building; Ricardo Legorreta's sophisticated use of regional Mexican color palettes to create joyful and restful environments; Michael Benedikt's focus on "real architecture" and craftsmanship as they contribute to the existential dimensions of design and to local character; the Kansas State University design studio project participating in Meadowcreek, a learning community being created in Arkansas; and Christopher Alexander's Pattern Language as a means to specify the physical design for a community and in its applications in the production of houses.[40]

In regard to urban scale, architects Sinclair Black, Andrew Vernooy, and Simon Atkinson, originally working together but recently as two firms, have developed a number of built and unbuilt projects which exemplify the humanistic tradition in urban design. They consistently design so as to provide for a strong sense of place, mixed uses, a range of public spaces, and high-quality experiential settings by providing the physical, spatial, and economic conditions argued for by critics such as Jane Jacobs, William Whyte, Kevin Lynch, and others.

Sinclair Black has long argued for the use of inner courtyards in urban design as evocative of Austin's street and block patterns. In the Municipal Office Complex that won the competition for the City of Austin, but did not escape the byzantine political processes that leave it unbuilt, Black and Vernooy took the site on the southwest corner of the Central Business District and integrated the complex into its urban context through a gradation of building masses which connected the Colorado River with its landscaped hike and bike trails on the south, the immediately surrounding one- and two-story warehouses that are being converted into theaters, restaurants, offices, and retail establishments, and the high rises to the north and northeast. The sensitive building massings and materials contributed to the sense of place and an image of what the "compact city" might look like in an otherwise too thinly spread urban fabric. They also developed a public-private partnership plan in which retail activity and other private sector uses would pay for the project as well as stimulate part of the activity necessary for the "critical mass" which generates a successful urban life.

Simon Atkinson's approach to the design and experience of urban space and buildings is especially concerned with an enlivened, integrated yet diverse series of places. In his agenda for developing a humanistic rather than merely formalistic professional response to the city, he develops sequences of

FIGURE 10.5
Black and Vernooy, Municipal Office Complex, Austin, Texas

FIGURE 10.6.
Atkinson and Associates, Project for Sierra Alta, Monterrey, Mexico

spaces and intimate places that correspond to those advocated in the research findings of Gordon Cullen (as in *The Concise Townscape*) and Jan Gehl (as in *Life Between Buildings*). Atkinson and Associates' project for Sierra Alta in Monterrey, Mexico provides for a series of markers, each of which has a distinctive identity and is a worthwhile destination in itself. The sequence of markers thus gently orient the pedestrian as she moves about, and simultaneously promote interest in what comes next. The project provides a sense of "mystery," the safe but intriguing atmosphere that draws us through a setting, encouraging us to enjoy it and to keep exploring "just a little further." The beauty of this kind of design lies in its generosity to the ordinary person, since the designers believe that each of us should have an urban environment complex and intelligent enough to provide experiences as rich and layered as were Leopold Bloom's in the course of his day in Dublin in Joyce's *Ulysses*. Other work worth emulating is found in Anne Vernez-Moudon's and P. Laconte's ideas for the absorption of streets back into the life of the community in Seattle and San Francisco and in Charles Moore's cheerful and neighborly buildings that recall us to our better memories and prospects for satisfying experiences. In Canada, "responsive planning" of housing in a manner sensitive to client groups is being advocated by those working with native Canadians, such as K. McDowell, J. C. Simon and associates. On a larger environmental scale, the same phenomena appears in the plans by Kent Butler and his colleagues to preserve the habitat of the yellow-cheeked warbler in the grassland and marshes on Long Lake in Austin, Texas and in the surrounding Texas hillcountry.[41]

Lessons for authentic design also are found in the approaches of architects Christian Norberg-Schulz, Botond Bognar, Kimberly Dovey, Wayne Attoe, and Thomas Thiis-Evensen and planners like Francis Violich or environmental geographers such as David Seamon and Robin Doughty who develop and teach the phenomenology of seeing.

The seminal interpretations of Christian Norberg-Schulz, more than any other body of work, have brought phenomenology and Heidegger's thinking into the arena of architecture. Bognar has replaced the too common studio practice of treating design problems in solely aesthetic or scientific terms with a method which teaches students about landscape, buildings, and places in terms of experience and behavior; Dovey explores ways to use traditional forms and materials to preserve rather than violate environmental meaning. Attoe has provided a number of sensitive and realistic collaborative studies of regional architectural and urban responses to American and Mexican economic, climatic, and design problems.[42]

Thiis-Evensen is opening up an understanding of the experiences of the archetypal architectural elements of floor, wall, and roof that promises to lead to an emotionally fulfilling way to replace no-longer-dynamic architectural forms. Violich reads towns as specific environments used as frameworks for daily living, thus developing a qualitative style of inquiry for urban design. Doughty shows how the historical and perceptual transformation of natural places, including their bird and animal life, is worked out through the daily routines that enable us to make ourselves a home. Seamon's theoretical arguments and practical interpretations help explain the ordinary yet profound places and events that authentically connect us with the natural environment or the urban landscape and social human existence.[43]

Nor have we held in memory and practice all that our tradition has learned. We need to do what we already understand. This dimension begins with the retrieval and use of proven planning and design forms and strategies.

Though we each might have our favorites to recall for today's adaptation, couldn't we agree that the work of Clarence Stein, Henry Wright, and their colleagues, as built across America and published in *Toward New Towns for America*, still has an enormous potential to solve the problem of "affordable housing?" Similarly, Hugo Leipziger-Pearce has long advocated and practiced an architecture suitable to a democracy that occurs by analyzing the cultural and philosophical roots of organic architecture and the planning theories that already exist.[44]

In all these cases, the designers, architects, and planners are working toward sensitivity to local place and genuine dwelling. In each instance, the harmonious relationships of the community plan and the building design to their historical, natural, and cultural environments have the power to help establish place and an awareness that we need to adopt more modest and appropriate ways of living.

A BASIS FOR FUTURE PLANNING AND DESIGN

In the projects just considered, from regional planning to large-scale urban redesign to individual buildings, from traditional forms to ecological and feminist architecture, from the needs of children to those of young adults and the elderly, we find several constant dimensions that may provide a basis for future planning and architecture.

1. Planners and architects are thinking of people in new and changing ways, for instance, in terms of the stages of embodied human life which occur within the larger patterns of cultural modulation and rural-urban structural pressures of displacement, containment, and possibility.

2. Planners and architects are first attempting to retrieve, understand, and then sensitively enhance the relationship of inhabitants to the natural and traditional built environments, that is, to the ecological rhythms of earth and sky as they are manifest in local biocultural regions.

3. Planners and architects are responding to and carefully adapting traditional elements, preserving and yet appropriately developing them—from inside live traditions, so that the new forms, materials, and processes allow continual renewal and enrichment, as opposed to the disruption, consumption, and rejection of the past.

4. Planners and architects increasingly collaborate with inhabitants and design professionals where the latter, in the course of exercising their specialized role and skills, also are assuming a different role than they have had recently. Such designers are not doing design unto others. Instead, they are developing a process for "helping design come forward." The process moves from the roots up, as Doxiades described cultural generation, and requires dense local support networks.[45]

5. Innovative methods for interpretive seeing and, subsequently, for designing are being elaborated, though care needs be taken so that these are not mechanically systematized or inappropriately imposed. For example, Cullen's visualizations, Alexander's ''Pattern Language,'' Turner's methods for people-made housing, and phenomenology (as in Norberg-Schulz's and Thiis Evensen's holistic and historical interpretations) all are adaptable for individual local uses. By providing commonly accessible delineations, such approaches enable professional architects and planners to help local individuals and groups articulate their own worlds.[46] Thus, in the practice of their own craft, architects and planners are better able to bring forth appropriate originary designs and buildings.

These design trends and possibilities, which concretize meaning through ''creative participation'' are congruent with originary thinking and interpretation.[47] Clearly, planning, architecture, building, and originary interpretation belong together. *Planning and design are informed by* careful and caring *understanding* of human nature, of our cultural and individual displacements, and of their own role in accomplishing or hindering the building of place. Thoughtful description and *interpretation* of place and the possibilities of our building unavoidably *occur in the midst of an already given—* already built—*environment.* The promise: self-critical and originary environmental interpretation, planning, design, and building can help to open places where we may become more fully ourselves by belonging together with each other and the world.

REMAINING CRITICALLY UNDERWAY

If we believe that it is possible to discover or retrieve the essential meanings of phenomena and to adequately rethink what humans need to live as finite beings—through the historically unfolding eras of changing discourse and concealment and the phases of our lives—we do appear to have at least hints of a promising way to move forward. In fact, there is a surprising amount of good company and the path generally appears more established that we might have expected.

But, even if this is so, to lapse into a smug sense of security and comfort, confident that we know what to do, is to fall back into unthoughtfulness and the taken-for-granted, out of which all genuine thinking, and not just Heidegger's, constantly seeks to shake us. We need to persevere in radical questioning and self-critical practice, all the more so the closer we might be to really becoming attuned to a proper measure. When we think we have *an,* much less *the,* answer to issues of environmental meaning, we need to be especially sensitive to the dangers involved in being wrong and not understanding.[48]

Perhaps not surprisingly, then, the non-arbitrary basis for future planning and design that we have been considering leads us back to where we began. The movement of gathering leads not to clenching "the answer" in our fists, but to maturely opening out again, just as the gathering of grapes at the harvest is for the sake of pouring out wine in celebration and hospitality— that is, for giving. And no genuine opening is fixed or determined beforehand, but instead remains always questionable and underway. Accordingly, the path of originary and retrieving thinking and action necessarily is also the path of deconstruction, reconstruction, alterity, and same as discussed at the beginning of the book. The originary way differs not in the intensity or extent of questioning, but in the *trust* that something *may be* (not "will be," nor "is" or "has been") given to us and to which we may respond. Along the way, on the same path so much of the time, before they diverge temporarily, originary-retrieving and deconstructing-genealogical interpretation all push to unmask whatever holds us in a spell.

Thus, however valid and worth following, the best "wholesome" planning and architecture should not be blindly copied. To cite the cases from Berlin (the IBA housing reconstructions, all the green environmental projects, and Charles Moore's Tegel Library), these humane projects, theoretically grounded in sophisticated views of our private and social bodies, memories, and architecture, do not result from any sort of mechanical application of fixed ideas, forms, and materials. Each project and program, each desired cultural outcome, had to be thought and designed afresh. This does not defy tradition, but embodies our tradition's vital critical attitude.

Obviously, it is worth distinguishing and arguing about the possibility and necessity of the disassembling and gathering modes of thinking and building. And, naturally, members of the two major approaches each believe they are on the better path. But that could not be true for either side if it treated the other with disdain, for the other side is not an "other," but the other side of one and the same ultimate play. As the theoretical first part of this book and the practical second part (that follows the way of gathering and belonging) show, the difference between dissassembling and gathering matters a great deal as does the choice about which way to proceed. The difference and choice make all the difference, in fact. But, the difference is not a total difference. It is a difference about whether any disclosure might be given or not—a disclosure that might flash out of concealment, even as lightning flashes out of a dominating night storm. We neither have, nor we can expect, any certainty. There is no final security or closure in this life. We remain underway. In the end, one way apparently is an errant way. Still, we all are underway together and, with our distinctive voices, all are singing part of what, altogether, needs to be given voice. And given thought. Before we act.

In opening such theoretical and practical issues, as genuinely still-open questions, Foucault, Derrida, Eliade, and Heidegger, just as Co-op Himmelblau, Murcutt, and IBA, show us the importance of always remaining both critical and open in our thinking so that we may responsibly—probably polyvalently—plan, design, and build.

Notes

1. The argument for mobility is made, for example, by J. B. Jackson in most of his works including *Discovering the Vernacular Landscape* (New Haven: Yale University Press, 1984); by John Kouwenhoven in *The Beer Can by the Highway* (Baltimore: Johns Hopkins University Press, 1961); and by Karsten Harries in "Space, Place, and Ethos: Reflections on the Ethical Function of Architecture," *artibus et historiae* 9 (1984): 159–65. Also see the critique of Heidegger's position below in chapter six, "Using Heidegger: A Critique and Shift Toward Praxis."

2. Karsten Harries, "Comments on Four Papers, ACSA Annual Meeting, 1991," reprinted in *Environmental & Architectural Phenomenology Newsletter* 2, no. 3 (Fall 1991): 10–12.

3. My work as a Heidegger scholar and teacher in planning, urban design, architecture, and environmental research merges here with the hermeneutics discussed.

4. Because the project focuses on the American landscape, European theories, and contemporary technology, a word is in order concerning what may seem a parochial use of phrases such as "our," "our world," and "our place." The intention is neither to shut out other cultures and environments as "not ours" nor to suppose that others' problems and possibilities are identical to ours. That is one of the fundamental lessons of Heidegger: each culture, community, and person must undertake their own homecoming, must be responsive to their specific, local situation. Honestly, I can only try to move within the unfolding of my given environment. Those who share the historical American-European situation will have their own insights to add and modifications to suggest. Readers who live elsewhere hopefully will find suggestions here for interpreting and building in their own appropriate manner.

5. On the general history of hermeneutics, see Beryl Smalley, *The Study of the Bible in the Middle Ages* (Notre Dame, Ind.: University of Notre Dame Press, 1964); Henri de Lubac, *Exégèse médiévale: les quatre sens de l'Écriture*, 4 vols. (Paris: Aubier, 1955–64); Richard E. Palmer, *Hermeneutics* (Evanston, Ill.: Northwestern University Press, 1969).

6. Smalley, *The Study of the Bible in the Middle Ages*, 2ff.

7. Bonaventure, *Collationes in Hexaemeron* [1273], XIII, n.12, 390. The translation is by Angelus Gambatese in his version of Efrem Bettoni's *St. Bonaventure* (Notre Dame, Ind.: University of Notre Dame Press, 1964), p. 34. For Bonaventure, the task of hermeneutics is to help recover the meaning of the words, things, and world given meaning by God. Hence his concern with *re-ductio* "leading back" as indicated in the titles of other of his works such as "De reductione artium ad theolgiam" (Reduction of the Arts of Theology) and "Itinerarium Mentis ad Deum" (The Mind's Road to God"). This sense of positive retrieval is also found in Eliade and Heidegger (for instance, in the latter's use of "Andenken" or memorializing thinking.

8. On these aspects of meaning in scripture, see especially the useful "Supplement IV: On Medieval Exegesis" in William F. Lynch, *Christ and Apollo* (New York: New American Library, 1960), 218–54.

9. Galileo Galilei, "The Assayer" [1623] translated by Stillman Drake in *Discoveries and Opinions of Galileo* (New York: Doubleday Anchor, 1957), 237–38.

10. See Jacob Klein, *Greek Mathematical Thought and the Origin* of *Algebra*, translated by Eva Braun (Cambridge, Mass.: Harvard University Press, 1968); David Lachterman, *The Ethics of Geometry* (New York: Routledge, 1989).

11. Schopenhauer is strangely unacknowledged as a forebear of deconstruction. But, while self-consciously implicated in the unfolding of Will as World and Idea, he simultaneously is a key figure in the exposure of absolutizing, in stripping the world of the false (e.g., of reason and abstract concepts), of focusing on the unsaid, and on developing a criteria of bad art as arbitrary play without a proper end. Few besides Karsten Harries recognize Schopenhauer's importance, and his work dates from before the current rise of deconstruction. The gap shows how little has been done in regard to the tradition of deconstruction.

12. Northrop Frye, *The Anatomy of Criticism* (New York: Atheneum, 1968); Alasdair MacIntyre, *Whose Justice? Which Rationality?* (Notre Dame, Ind.: University of Notre Dame Press, 1988); Max Scheler, *Formalism in Ethics and Non-Formal Ethics of Values* [1913–1916] (Evanston, Ill.: Northwestern University Press, 1973).

13. It is not necessary to assume that a building or world is a text. What is unavoidable is that all our interpretations necessarily are in the midst of prior interpretations.

14. See my videotaped lecture "The Poststructural Sublime: From Heterotopia to Dwelling?" University of Minnesota School of Architecture and Landscape Architecture, January 1991, also presented at the University of Washington, February, 1992.

CHAPTER 2. FOUCAULT

1. On Ludwig Wittgenstein and Carl Jung as prototypes of the possibilities of, respectively, stripping away the misleading and moving deeper into mystery, see my "Jung's and Wittgenstein's Houses," forthcoming. On the relation of Wittgenstein to Nietzsche, and thus to Derrida, see Richard Rorty's works cited in the following note and Henry Staten, *Wittgenstein and Derrida* (Lincoln, Neb.: University of Nebraska Press, 1984).

2. Habermas rejects the skeptical, if not nihilistic, stance of the Poststructuralists and their resulting sociopolitical agenda in favor of a modified post-Enlightenment rationalism that is open to a universal, empirical understanding and genuine democratic consensus. Habermas also defends this modern project of "Reason" and discursive thought against Gadamer's arguments that we need to recover the older classical understanding that has been obscured in modernity. See, for example, Jürgen Habermas, *The Philosophical Discourse of Modernity* (Cambridge, Mass.: MIT Press, 1990) and Hans-Georg Gadamer, *Truth and Method* (New York: Seabury Press, 1975). Though Rorty and MacIntyre do not debate in public, they are emerging as the major spokesmen for the two alternatives in America. Rorty argues for a pragmatic anti-essentialism while MacIntyre contends that though all understanding takes place within a tradition, we are not caught in a vicious relativism since we have reasonable criteria of truth in these carefully self-refining systems and ways to understand other traditions. See Richard Rorty, *Contingency, Irony, and Solidarity* (Cambridge: Cambridge University Press, 1989) and his two volumes of *Philosophical Papers* (Cambridge: Cambridge University Press, 1991) and Alasdair MacIntyre, *Whose Justice? Which Rationality?* (Notre Dame, Ind.: University of Notre Dame Press, 1988).

Karsten Harries argues for a "non-arbitrary architecture" based on the cultural variations of basic human orientation in the world, while Eisenman argues that there is no "reality" beneath our social fictions and no way to produce anything except an arbitrary architecture. See Karsten Harries, "The Voices of Space" and Peter Eisenman, "The Authenticity of Difference: Architecture and the Crisis of Reality," both in *Buildings and Reality: Architecture in the Age of Information,* edited by Michael Benedikt. *Center,* vol. 4 (New York: Rizzoli, 1988), 34–49, and 50–57.

3. Nietzsche, *The Will To Power,* translated by Walter Kaufmann and R. J. Hollingdale (New York: Random House, 1968), passim; David B. Al-

lison, editor, *The New Nietzsche* (New York: Delta, 1977); *Thus Spoke Zarathustra*, translated by W. Kaufmann (New York: Vintage, 1966).

4. Foucault, *The Order of Things* (New York: Vintage Books, 1973), 157–58, 168, 208.

5. T. O'Conner, "Foucault and the Transgression of Limits," in A. Silverman, editor, *Philosophy and Non-Philosophy Since Merleau-Ponty* (New York: Routledge, 1988), 141.

6. Ibid., 149. For a further discussion of the objective character of Foucault's theory and method, see also R. D'Amico, *Historicism and Knowledge* (New York: Routledge, 1986), 140; Foucault, *The Order of Things*, 326; my "Post-Structuralist Planning Theory," (Austin: University of Texas Graduate Program in Community and Regional Planning Working Paper Series, 1991) 11ff.

7. Foucault, "Nietzsche, Genealogy, History," translated by D. F. Bouchard, *Language, Counter-Memory, Practice* (New York: Cornell University Press, 1977), 142.

8. Vincent Descombes, *Modern French Philosophy* (Cambridge: Cambridge University Press, 1980), 11, 115.

9. Hubert L. Dreyfus and Paul Rabinow, *Michel Foucault: Beyond Structuralism and Hermeneutics* (Chicago: University of Chicago Press, 1982), xxvi.

10. Foucault, "Nietzsche, Genealogy, History," 142.

11. Foucault, *The Archaeology of Knowledge*, translated by Alan Sheridan, (New York: Pantheon, 1972), 47; Alan Sheridan, *Michel Foucault: The Will To Truth*, (London: Tavistock Publications, 1980), 99.

12. Sheridan, *Michel Foucault*, 98.

13. Foucault, *The Order of Things* (New York: Random House, 1973), xx.

14. Foucault, "The Confession of the Flesh," in Colin Gordon, editor, *Power/Knowledge*, (New York: Pantheon Books, 1980), 194.

15. Ibid., 151–52.

16. Foucault, "Nietzsche, Freud, Marx," in *Nietzsche* (Paris: Cahiers de Royaumont, 1967), 189; Foucault, "Nietzsche, Genealogy, History," 151.

17. Dreyfus and Rabinow, *Michel Foucault*, 108–9, 117.

18. Descombes, *Modern French Philosophy*, 115.

19. Dreyfus and Rabinow, *Michel Foucault*, xxv.

20. Ibid., 135.

21. Ibid., 10.

22. Descombes, *Modern French Philosophy*, 116.

23. Dreyfus and Rabinow, *Michel Foucault*, 107.

24. Perhaps the most well-known example is Foucault's analysis of Bentham's Panopticon and the optics of surveillance found in *Discipline and Punish* (New York: Vintage, 1959), 201–2. In addition, Christine Boyer's analysis of the discourse of planning is notable for its application of Foucault's method. See M. Christine Boyer, *Dreaming the Rational City: The Myth of American City Planning* (Cambridge, Mass.: MIT Press, 1983). For an argument counter to Foucault, which emphasizes the more usual scholarly method to treat the functions of the prison in establishing stability in the Jacksonian period, see David J. Rothman, *The Discovery of the Asylum* (Boston: Little, Brown, and Company, 1971).

25. It may be that non-discursive practices now are powerful enough to operate without the need for supporting discourse, without the need for social self-justification. As to the lack of notice or discussion, for example, the recent *Handbook of Environmental Psychology*, edited by Daniel Stokols and Irwin Altman (New York: John Wiley and Sons, 1987) is instructive. The *Handbook* is the most comprehensive state-of-the-art reference to research literature in the behavioral and perceptual social sciences. "Wayfinding" has seventeen entries and "cognitive mapping" thirty-seven in the index, each with hundreds of items listed in the research bibliography; but, none of them makes any reference to the existence, much less problem of, wayfinding with the new corridor-room-numbering systems discussed here.

26. This case is based on a behavior and perception research project done by architect Stryker Sessions and Robert Mugerauer. In his report, "Bizarre Numbering Systems" (unpublished, 1989), Sessions focused on interviews with engineers, service personnel, and users (diagramatically documenting numbering sustems in use throughout the country). Mugerauer worked on the procedures articulated in manuals, standards, and codes and analyzed public and private building complexes as well as conducting further interviews with users. The interpretation by way of Foucault's methods was not contained in that earlier research.

27. Sessions, "Bizarre Numbering Systems."

28. It is little noted that Newton acknowledged and explained perceptual or relative space as a phenomenal dimension of absolute space. See Newton's *Mathematical Principles of Natural Philosophy*, translated by Andre Motte and revised by Florian Cajori (Berkeley: University of California Press, 1934).

The grid is helpfully described by J. B. Jackson, *Discovering the Vernacular Landscape* (New Haven: Yale University Press, 1984), 153; *American Space* (New York: W. W. Norton, 1972), 25–26, 44, 61–62, 67, 75, 86, 194–95; *Landscapes* (Amherst: University of Massachusetts Press, 1970), 5, 119, 135; *The Necessity for Ruins* (Amherst: University of Massachusetts Press, 198O), 116. John Kouwenhoven treats the grid's positive features and notes the German pilot Wolfgang Langewiesche's remark that the gridded landscape is "a diagram of the idea of the Social Contract," in "What's American about America?" in *The Beer Can by the Highway* (Baltimore: Johns Hopkins University Press, 1961), 37–74. Also see Hildegard B. Johnson's "Toward a National Landscape," in *The Making of the American Landscape*, edited by Michael Conzen, (London: Unwin Hyman, 1990), 127–45 and my "Chicago's Four-Layered Plan," *Crit* 17 (Winter): 17–23.

29. This spatial system also would provide a point of comparison and contrast between Foucault's approach and that of Henri Lefebvre, who treated the history of spatial constitutions and representations from a Marxist perspective. In English, see Lefebvre, *The Production of Space* (Oxford: Blackwell, 1989).

CHAPTER 3. DERRIDA

1. Derrida, *Of Grammatology*, translated by Gayatri Spivak (Baltimore: Johns Hopkins University Press, 1976), 251.

2. Derrida, *Writing and Difference*, translated by Alan Bass, (Chicago: University of Chicago Press, 1978), 278–79.

3. Derrida, *Of Grammatology*, 251.

4. Michael Ryan, *Marxism and Deconstuction* (Baltimore: Johns Hopkins University Press, 1982), 10.

5. Ibid., 7.

6. This idea clearly bears on the issue of whether it is useful or misleading to employ such methodological metaphors and techniques as "reading the city" and "interpreting the environment."

7. Derrida, *Speech and Phenomena*, translated by David Allison, (Evanston, Ill.: Northwestern University Press, 1973), 104.

8. The example is adapted from Vincent Descombes, *Modern French Philosophy*, (Cambridge: Cambridge University Press, 1980), 142–43.

9. Ibid., 143.

10. Frank Letticia, *After the New Criticism* (Chicago: University of Chicago Press, 1980), 171; cf. Derrida, *Writing and Difference*, 281.

11. Derrida, *Speech and Phenomena*, 104.

12. Derrida himself deliberately adopts the empirical fault as a strategy in order to subvert reason; see Descombes, *Modern French Philosophy*, 140ff.

13. Geoffrey H. Hartman, *Saving the Text* (Baltimore: Johns Hopkins University Press, 1981), 64.

14. Derrida, *Writing and Difference*, 280.

15. Ibid., 284.

16. Ibid., 292.

17. Descombes, *Modern French Philosophy*, 143.

18. Derrida, *Marges de la philosophie* (Paris: Editions de Minuit, 1972), 76–77; cf. Christopher Norris, *The Deconstructive Turn* (New York: Methuen, 1984), 176.

19. Derrida, *Writing and Difference*, 281.

20. Letticia, *After the New Criticism*, 161.

21. Mark Kropnick, editor, *Displacement* (Bloomington: Indiana University Press, 1983), 1, 11–12.

22. John D. Caputo, "From the Deconstruction of Hermeneutics to the Hermeneutics of Deconstruction," in John Bailiff, editor, *Proceedings: Eighteenth Heidegger Conference* (Stevens Point, Wis.: University of Wisconsin-Stevens Point, 1984), 83.

23. See Ryan, *Marxism and Deconstruction*, 32; Caputo, "Deconstruction of Hermeneutics," 81.

24. Derrida, *Writing and Difference*, 282.

25. Derrida's early writings which most explicitly took up architecture are "Interview" in *Domus* 671 (April 1986): 17–24 and "The Pit and the Pyramid: Introduction to Hegel's Semiology," in *Margins of Philosophy* (Chicago: University of Chicago Press, 1982). In addition, Peter Eisenman is the most well-known architect involved with Derrida's approach—the two of them have been involved in a collaborative project for Tschumi's Parc de la Villette. Derrida's influence is now spreading to a new generation.

26. For a more detailed deconstruction of architectural tradition, see my essay "Practicing Deconstruction: Pyramids as Posture and Strategy," forthcoming.

27. These comments draw on Bernard Tschumi, *Cinegramme Folie: Le Parc de la Villette* (Princeton: Princeton Architectural Press, 1987). The project is discussed thoughtfully in Patrick M. Condon and Lance M. Neckar, editors, *The Avant-Garde and the Landscape: Can They Be Reconciled?* (Minneapolis: Landworks Press, 1990), especially in the essays by P. Condon, R. Dagenhart, E. Meyer, and G. Strans.

28. Ibid., vii.

29. Eisenman, "The Authenticity of Difference," 50–57.

30. Interview with Charles Jencks," in Andreas C. Papadakis, editor, *Deconstruction in Architecture* (New York: St. Martin's Press, 1988), 50.

31. Eisenman speaks of "auratic" architecture, for example, in reference to the work he admires (at the conference "Philosophy, Architecture, and the City" held at DePaul University, Spring 1991). On the source of this sense, of the term see Walter Benjamin, *Passagen-Werk,* as opposed to his earlier, avant-garde *One-Way Street.* As Susan Buck Morss points out, the aesthetic and metaphysical auras are not at all the same and it is Adorno rather than Benjamin who regrets the "disintegration of the [aesthetic] aura." *Dialectics* of *Seeing: Walter Benjamin and the Arcades Project* (Cambridge, Mass. : MIT Press, 1989), 133.

32. Eisenman made these remarks at the conference cited in the previous note.

33. On Co-op Himmelblau, see Frank Werner, *Architektur ist Jetzt;* quotations are from the lecture by the same title, delivered in Frankfurt and London, November 1984 and covered in *Architecture Review* 180, no. 1074 (August 1986): 17–24.

34. See, for example, Leon Krier, "The Reconstruction of the City," in *Rational Architecture* (Brussels: Editions des Archives d'Architecture Moderne, 1988) and *Prince Charles and the Architectural Debate* (New York: St. Martin's Press, 1990).

35. *Architecture d'Aujourd'hui* 245 (June 1986): 82–89.

36. Werner, *Architektur ist Jetzt,* 17.

37. It is an interesting question to ask if there is any relation between Co-op Himmelblau's name and focal concern and the remarkable film directed by Wim Wenders (written with Peter Handke), *Der Himmel Über Berlin* (the English version is entitled *Wings Of Desire*).

38. On Ambasz's conservatory, see *Progressive Architecture* 66, no. 1 (January, 1985): 120–21 and *Domus* 667 (December 1985), 14–17.

39. See note 38 above.

CHAPTER 4. ELIADE

1. Edmund Husserl, *Philosophical Investigations* [1900–1901] (New York: Humanities Press, 1970).

2. Heidegger, *Being and Time* [1927] (New York: Harper & Row, 1962). Scheler, *Formalism in Ethics and Non-Formal Ethics of Values* [1913–1916] (Evanston, Ill.: Northwestern University Press, 1973).

3. Beyond the works cited in the previous note, on this complex position that is partially objective and partially historical and perspectival, see also, Alfons Deeken, *Process and Permanance in Ethics: Max Scheler's Moral Philosophy* (New York: Paulist Press, 1974); Robert Mugerauer, "Phenomenology and Vernacular Architecture," in Paul Oliver, editor, *Encyclopedia of World Vernacular Architecture* (Oxford: Basil Blackwell, forthcoming); Herbert Spiegelberg, *The Phenomenological Movement* (The Hague: Martinus Nijhoff, 1965).

4. John D. Caputo, *Radical Hermeneutics* (Bloomington: Indiana University Press, 1987), 95ff. My general moves are parallel to Caputo's, but differ in scope and final appraisal of Heidegger, as elaborated below.

5. Gadamer's major work relevant here is *Truth and Method* (New York: Seabury Press, 1975). See also Caputo, *Radical Hermeneutics* for more on Gadamer as on the right continuing the early Heidegger. On Eliade, see the following section of this chapter.

This account does not quite correspond to Caputo's reading, since he reads Derrida as supplementing Heidegger and thus neither quite moves to see Heidegger as achieving non-metaphysical thinking nor as failing to break through. Caputo says, "Derrida is right: the Geviert [fourfold] is the most beautiful postcard Heidegger ever sent. But I will take my Heidegger demythologized, if you please." *Radical Hermeneutics*, 185. For my analysis of Heidegger's late thinking as, at least at times, non-metaphysical, see my *Heidegger's Language and Thinking* (Atlantic Highlands, N.J.: Humanities Press, 1988) and *Heidegger and Homecoming*, unpublished Research Project, National Endowment for the Humanities, 1977.

6. It could also be argued that Habermas now is taking his place on the right with—to the right of?—Gadamer and Eliade, though this complexity can not be taken up here. Relevant to the issue are Jürgen Habermas, *The Philosophical Discourse of Modernity* (Cambridge, Mass.: MIT Press, 1990) and Richard J. Bernstein, editor, *Habermas and Modernity* (Cambridge, Mass.: MIT Press, 1985).

7. For further details on how my reading deviates from Caputo's, especially in developing this larger context of subjectivity and objectivity, see my "Post-Structuralist Planning Theory" (Austin: University of Texas Graduate Program in Community and Regional Planning Working Paper Series, 1991) and "Phenomenology: Romantic Nostalgia or New Way of Seeing?," in Gramae Hardie, editor, *New Research Paradigms* (Raleigh, S.C. South Carolina State University, 1989), 201–6.

8. Despite critics' persistently labeling the position as "nostalgic," there is no basis for such a charge in the work of Eliade or Heidegger. On the contrary, both argue against nostalgia for times gone by and against the dominant concepts of time: Eliade against linear time and progress, Heidegger against the idea of a first occurrence (he wants to substitute origin as originary). See the development below in this chapter and chapter 6.

9. Eliade's *The Sacred and the Profane* has proven especially useful in environmental interpretation. His ideas can be seen in J. B. Jackson, *Discovering the Vernacular Landscape* (New Haven: Yale University Press, 1948); Walter L. Brenneman Jr., "The Circle and the Cross: The Holy Wells of Ireland" and David G. Saile, "Many Dwellings: Views of a Pueblo World," both in David Seamon and Robert Mugerauer, editors, *Dwelling, Place, and Environment* (Dordrecht: Martinus Nijhoff, 1985); Alfonso Ortiz, "Ritual Drama and the Pueblo View," in A. Ortiz, editor, *New Perspectives on the Pueblos* (Albuquerque: School of American Research, University of New Mexico, 1972); Keith Critchlow, *Time Stands Still* (New York: St. Martin's Press, 1982). Also, see note 34 below.

10. Eliade, *Myths, Dreams, and Mysteries* (New York: Harper & Row, 1957), 239.

11. Eliade, *Myth and Reality* (New York: Harper & Row, 1963), 6.

12. Eliade, *The Sacred and The Profane,* (New York: Harper & Row, 1959), 11.

13. Eliade, *The Two and the One* (New York: Harper & Row, 1965), 201; cf. Eliade, *Cosmos and History* (New York: Harper & Row, 1959), 154–59.

14. Eliade, *Myth and Reality,* 1.

15. Ibid, 2.

16. Eliade, *Myths, Dreams, and Mysteries,* 5.

17. Eliade, *The Quest* (Chicago: University of Chicago Press, 1969), 52.

18. Eliade, *Myths, Dreams, and Mysteries,* 15.

19. Walter L. Brenneman, Jr. and Stanley O. Yarian, *The Seeing Eye* (University Park, Penn.: Pennsylvania State University Press, 1982), 61.

20. Guilford Dudley III, *Religion on Trial: Mircea Eliade and His Critics* (Philadelphia: Temple University Press, 1977), 152.

21. Eliade, *Myth and Reality*, 92; *Myths, Dreams, and Mysteries*, 11–12, 236.

22. Eliade, *Myths, Dreams, and Mysteries*, 244. Also see the analysis in Douglas Allen, *Structure and Creativity in Religion: Hermeneutics in Mircea Eliade's Phenomenology and New Directions* (The Hague: Mouton Publishers, 1978).

23. Eliade, *The Sacred and The Profane*, 29, 53.

24. Ibid., 172ff.

25. Ibid., 22.

26. Alice C. Fletcher and Francis La Flesche, *The Omaha Tribe* [Twenty-Seventh Annual Report of the Bureau of American Ethnology to the Secretary of the Smithsonian Institution, 1905–1906. Washington: Government Printing Office, 1911] (Lincoln: University of Nebraska Press, 1972), vol. I, p. 134. The example on Omaha dwelling here straightwardly uses the materials presented in this two-volume work.

27. Ibid., 135.

28. Ibid., 138.

29. Ibid., 138–95.

30. Ibid., 516–17.

31. Ibid., 223–60.

32. Ibid., 241.

33. Ibid., 137.

34. For representative studies commensurate with Eliade or explicitly using his ideas, see from the immense literature, David M. Guss on the Yekuana, *To Weave and Sing: Art, Symbol, and Narrative in the South American Rain Forest* (Berkeley: University of California Press, 1990); Suzanne

Preston Blier, *The Anatomy of Architecture: Ontology and Metaphor in Batammaliba Architectural Expression* (New York: Cambridge University Press, 1987); the treatment of the cosmic dwelling in Paul Oliver, *Dwellings: The House across the World* (Austin: University of Texas Press, 1990; many essays published by the International Association for the Study of Traditional Environments' *Traditional Dwellings and Settlements: Working Paper Series* and Jean-Paul Bourdier and Nezar Alsayyad, eds., *Dwellings, Settlements and Tradition* (New York: University Press of America, 1989); J. William Carswell and David G. Saile, eds., *Purposes in Build Form and Culture Research*, (Lawrence, Kan.: University of Kansas, 1986) and David G. Saile, ed., *Architecture in Cultural Change* (Lawrence, Kan., University of Kansas, 1986); Robert Mugerauer, "Phenomenology and Vernacular Architecture."

Eliade naturally has his critics in this area too. See, for instance, Nold Egenter, who argues that Eliade's use of the history of religion applies *a priori* concepts rather than a genuine inductive approach and thus "misinterpret[s the] factual relation between the origins and the present with his theological concept of revelation [hierophany]." Egenter, "History of Anthropology," in *Architectural Anthropology: Research Series I*, 25–35; "Architectural Anthropology: Outlines of a Constructive Human Past," Ibid., 145–71, esp. 159, 171.

35. Mike Brill has energetically developed the idea of "charged places," a very judicious phrase that avoids many of the unnecessary connotations of similar terms. He has developed the idea for some years, so it has several articulations; typical is his "The Spirit Embodied In, and Excited By Archetypes of Place," presented at the workshop on *Beliefs, Intentions, and Built Form* (Miami, October 1991). Also see Paul Wheatley, *The Pivot of the Four Quarters: A Preliminary Enquiry into the Origins and Character of the Ancient Chinese City* (Chicago: Aldine Publishing Co., 1971); Walter L. Brenneman, Jr., "The Circle and the Cross: Loric and Sacred Space in the Holy Wells of Ireland" and David G. Saile, "Many Dwellings: Views of a Pueblo World," in David Seamon and Robert Mugerauer, eds., *Dwelling, Place, and Environment* (New York: Columbia University Press, 1989).

36. Eliade has a contemporary focus in most of his work; he explicitly labels a chapter "The Myths of the Modern World," in *Myths, Dreams, and Mysteries*, and another "Survival and Camouflages of Myths," in *Myth and Reality*.

CHAPTER 5. HEIDEGGER

1. See Heidegger's comments on his earlier phase in "A Dialogue On Language," translated by Peter D. Hertz in On *The Way To Language* (New

York: Harper & Row, 1971); Robert Mugerauer, *Heidegger's Language and Thinking* (Atlantic Highlands, N.J.: Humanities Press, 1988).
Concerning Heidegger's well-known "reversal," which nonetheless is a phase of passage in a continuous and unified journey of thinking, see Heidegger, "Letter on Humanism," in David F. Krell, editor, *Martin Heidegger: Basic Writings* (New York: Harper & Row, 1977); Heidegger, "The Turning" ["Die Kehre"], in William Lovitt, editor and translator, *The Question Concerning Technology* (New York: Harper & Row, 1977); J. L. Metha, *The Philosophy of Martin Heidegger* (New York: Harper & Row, 1971).

2. Heidegger's early view that interpretation must violently wrest its subject matter away from everydayness never involved thinking "violence" in the way that modernity does, though Heidegger's position usually has been misconstrued. Actually, Heidegger's way involves a secular continuation of medieval hermeneutics which likened the literal and spiritual senses of a sacred text to the shell and nutmeat, where the outer layer needs to be considered before anything else, but also "broken through" or cracked to get at the inner meat. See Heidegger, "A Dialogue on Language," and Mugerauer, *Heidegger's Language and Thinking*, 203–43.

3. See John Caputo, *Radical Hermeneutics* (Bloomington, Ind.: Indiana University Press, 1987; Gerald Bruns, *Heidegger's Estrangements* (New Haven: Yale University Press, 1989); Mugerauer, *Heidegger's Language and Thinking* and *Heidegger and Homecoming*, unpublished Research Project, National Endowment for the Humanities, 1977.

4. *The Basic Problems of Phenomenology*, [1927] (Bloomington, Ind.: Indiana University Press, 1982), 22–23. Cf. *Being and Time*, section 6, especially pp. 43–49.

5. Heidegger believes that the early Greek thinkers, such as Heraclitus and Parmenides, were not-yet-metaphysical and that metaphysics began later with Socrates and Plato. See Heidegger, *Early Greek Thinking* (New York: Harper & Row, 1975) and *Heraclitus Seminar 1966/67* (University, Alabama: University of Alabama Press, 1970).

6. On the fourfold see Heidegger, "Building Dwelling Thinking," "The Thing," and ". . . Poetically Man Dwells," in Albert Hofstadter, translator, *Poetry, Language, Thought* (New York: Harper & Row, 1971); Vincent Vycinas, *Earth and Gods* (The Hague: Martinus Nijhoff, 1961); David A. White, *Heidegger and the Language of Poetry* (Lincoln: University of Nebraska Press, 1918), especially chapters five and six.

7. Robert Mugerauer, *Heidegger and Homecoming.*

8. See Heidegger, "Memorial Address," in *Discourse on Thinking* (New York: Harper & Row, 1966); *What Is Called Thinking?* (New York: Harper & Row, 1968); and the section of this chapter, "Originary Dwelling."

9. See Heidegger, *The Question Concerning Technology;* Robert Mugerauer, "Heidegger's Dwelling: Making and Finding a Place in Tomorrow's World," presented at the Meetings of the Society for Phenomenology and the Human Sciences, October 1981 at a special session on "Dwelling, Community, Place, and Environment."

10. See the sections on Heidegger below and Heidegger, "The Thing," and "Building Dwelling Thinking," in *Poetry, Language, Thought.* A similar attitude of people to each other and to earth and sky is explored in Ursula Le Guin's science fiction, for example, *Always Coming Home* (New York: Bantam Books, 1987).

11. On the way this occurs for architecture, see my "Architecture as Properly Useful Opening," in Charles Scott and R. Dallery, editors, *Ethics and Danger: Essays on Heidegger and Continental Thought* (Albany: SUNY Press, 1991).

12. For documents witnessing such events, see David Seamon and Christian Nordin, "Marketplace as Place Ballet," *Landscape* 24 (1980): 35–41; Wallace Stevens, "Two Letters"; Studs Terkel, *Working* (New York: Avon Books, 1975).

13. See Kimberly Dovey, "The Quest for Authenticity and the Replication of Environmental Meaning," in David Seamon and Robert Mugerauer, editors, *Dwelling, Place and Environment* (Dordrecht: Martinus Nijhoff, 1985).

14. Description and analysis of the deepening meaning of such things are found, for example, in Mihaly Csikszentmihalyi and Eugene R. Halton, *The Meaning of Things* (London: Cambridge University Press, 1981); George Ordish, *The Living American House* (New York: Morrow and Co., 1981); Jane Jacobs, *The Death and Life of Great American Cities* (New York: Vintage Books, 1961).

15. See Heidegger, "Building Dwelling Thinking," "The Thing," and ". . . Poetically Man Dwells. . . ." Thus, the opposition of Heidegger's

originary understanding of language to the scientific, representational (still metaphysical) theory of semiotics.

16. Heidegger, "The Nature of Language," in *On the Way to Language*, 108.

17. Heidegger, "A Dialogue On Language," 47ff.; Heidegger, "The Way To Language," in *On the Way to Language;* Robert Mugerauer, "Language and the Emergence of Environment," in David Seamon and Robert Mugerauer, editors, *Dwelling, Place, and Environment*.

18. On Heidegger's explanation of the originary, e.g. *Das Anfangliche Denken*, see Heidegger, *What Is Called Thinking?* and "Memorial Address," in *Discourse on Thinking;* Robert Mugerauer, *Heidegger's Language and Thinking*.

19. Martin Heidegger, "Building Dwelling Thinking" and "The Thing" in *Poetry, Language, Thought*.

20. On the nature of the fourfold see Vincent Vycinas, *Earth and Gods* (The Hague: Martinus Nijhoff, 1961); David A. White, *Heidegger and the Language of Poetry* (Lincoln: University of Nebraska Press, 1978), chapters four and five; Karsten Harries, "Heidegger's Conception of the Holy," *Personalist* 47 (1966): 169–84; James M. Demske, "Heidegger's Quadrate and Revelation of Being," *Philosophy Today* 8, (1964).

21. See my "Architecture as Properly Useful Opening" in Charles Scott and R. Dallery, editors, *Ethics and Danger: Essays on Heidegger and Continental Thought* (Albany: SUNY Press, 1992).

22. In *Being and Time*, Heidegger discusses how we are named "human" ["homo"] according to the *cura* fable in section 42.

23. Martin Heidegger, *Being and Time* (New York: Harper & Row, 1962); Otto Poggeler, "Being as Appropriation," *Philosophy Today* 19, no. 2/4 (Summer 1975). Cf. philosophical anthropology's treatment of embodiment in the final chapter below.

24. *The Uprooted* (Boston: Little, Brown and Co., 1951).

25. For a more detailed explication and analysis of Heidegger's position on interpretation, see Robert Mugerauer, "Toward Reading Heidegger's *Dis-*

course on Thinking," *Southwestern Journal of Philosophy* 8, no. 1 (February 1977): 143–56; Robert Mugerauer, *Heidegger's Language and Thinking,* chapter three, section three, "The Teaching and Learning of Thinking."

26. See especially, Heidegger, *What Is Called Thinking?,* passim.

27. There is a growing body of literature explicitly utilizing Heidegger's insights and approach in order to understand the environment. See Christian Norberg-Schulz's important works: *The Concept of Dwelling* (New York: Rizzoli, 1985), *Genius Loci* (New York: Rizzoli, 1980), and "Heidegger's Thinking on Architecture," *Perspecta* 20 (1983): 61–68; Edward Relph, *Place and Placelessness* (London: Pion Limited, 1976); Karsten Harries, "Thoughts on a Non-Arbitrary Architecture," *Perspecta* 20 (1983): 9–20 and *The Bavarian Rococo Church* (New Haven: Yale University Press, 1983); David Seamon, "Heidegger's Notion of Dwelling and One Concrete Interpretation as Indicated by Hassan Fathy's *Architecture for the Poor,"* *Geosciences and Man* 24 (1984): 54–63 and "Heideggerian Thinking and Christopher Alexander's *Pattern Language,"* presented at the Annual Meetings of the Environmental Design Research Association, New York, June 1985.

28. For the basic description of Swiss house forms and landscape, which is used directly, though obviously transformed, in this Heideggerian interpretation, see Richard Weiss, *Hauser und Landschaften der Schweitz* (Stuttgart: Eugen Rentsch Verlag, 1973). Also relevant are Walter Leemann, *Landeskunde der Schweiz* (Erlenbach-Zurich: Eugen Rentsch, 1939); Emil Egli, *Die Schweiz* (Bern: Paul Haupt, 1970); G. E. Kidder Smith, *Switzerland Builds* (New York: Albert Bonnier, 1950). As Professor Roderick J. Lawrence has helpfully pointed out to me, the best source of all is J. Hunziker's *La maison suisse d'apres ses formes rustiques et son développement historique,* six volumes (Lausanne: Payot, 1902–1913). Hunziker relates the meaning and use of a domestic architecture to careful analyses of local dialects, building layout, and construction techniques. Though I have consulted this work, and agree with Lawrence, I was not able to arrange for long enough use of the texts to completely revise the examples using Hunziker. See Lawrence's "The Interpretation of Vernacular Architecture," *Vernacular Architecture* 14 (1983): 19–28.

29. Compare Norberg-Schulz's description of romantic architecture as the eminently local, *Genius Loci,* 69ff.

30. On the former dominance of the local and the multiplicity of dialects, see George Steiner, who begins with the mind-boggling fact that hu-

mans have lived amidst up to *ten thousand* distinct tongues; *After Bable* (New York: Oxford University Press, 1975), esp. chapter two, "Language and Gnosis."

31. See Robert Mugerauer, "Language and the Emergence of the Environment."

32. The union of earth as nurturing home and human nature is named in the old German word for dialect, "Mundart," which we hear echoed in English when we acknowledge our "mother 'tongue'." For a penetrating meditation on dialect, *mundart*, see Martin Heidegger, "Sprache und Heimat," in *Hebbel-Jahrbuch*, vol. 11 (Tübigen, 1970), 17–39.

33. The way of building called vernacular is usually stereotyped and misunderstood as a rote activity. In fact, far from being a thoughtless copying, vernacular as a live tradition involves careful and thoughtful remaking each time with variations appropriate to the circumstances. The subtleties of craftsmanship, material, forms, and process are often lost on, or even hidden from, outside observers. In addition, being made over and over in the same way does not imply that things are identical. Here our expectations and analogies mislead us (we understand architecture as "creation"): vernacular buildings, as human beings, are each different, though they may seem very much alike or indistinguishable at first and from a cultural distance, like members of a family with a strong resemblance.

34. This horizontal stacking is in contrast with a dominant use experienced in the building of America and in its mythology. Though we had log cabins, the softwood tree also appears as strongly vertical pole, for example, in barbed wire fences and, joined together in the earlier prototype of protection and boundary claim that was the familiar frontier fort.

35. See, for example, Martin Heidegger, "Language," in *Poetry Language, Thought*, esp. 203–5; Richard Lang, "The Dwelling Door: Towards a Phenomenology of Transition," in Seamon and Mugerauer, editors, *Dwelling, Place, and Environment;* Val Clery, *Doors* (New York: Penguin Books, 1978), esp. 12ff.; Perla Korosec-Sefaty, "Experience and Uses of the Dwelling," in I. Altman and C. Werner, editors, *Human Behavior and the Environment*, vol. 8 (London: Plenum Press, 1985).

36. For a fuller phenomenological description of window and glass as mediating outside and inside, see Robert Mugerauer, "The Interplay of Built and Open Space," *Reflections* 4, no. 1 (Fall 1986): 35–47.

37. See, for example, Amos Rapoport, *House Form and Culture* (Englewood Cliffs, N.J.: Prentice-Hall, 1969), 54, following Weiss' original caption without comment. As an anthropological concept, "Kult," no matter whether translated as "cult" or "worship," misleads. This is a clear example of the difference between scientific, representational language and thought and originary saying and thinking.

38. The form or arrangement, in fact, varies little throughout Europe and also persists, or did until recently, in homes in the United States. For example, the same house form and interior division of space occurred in houses and family patterns in German areas of Wisconsin as late as the 1950s. A case in point is the author's grandparents' home, built in Oshkosh, Wisconsin in 1920's and used daily in the same way until 1959. It would be interesting to see if the same is true of the German hillcountry of central Texas.

39. The sole example presented here only gives a hint of how dwelling occurs in vernacular houses. *With proper differences,* a similar description could be made of vernacular Scandanavian and Japanese farmhouses. Their continuing appeal to ordinary folk and to designers alike is due, this interpretation should show, to the way they make concrete the belonging of their inhabitants to the fourfold world, that is, to their original bodying forth of dwelling—which their powerful forms continue to witness.

CHAPTER 6. USING HEIDEGGER

1. Martin Heidegger, *On Time and Being,* translated by Joan Stambaugh (New York: Harper & Row, 1972), 24.

2. On Heidegger's breakthrough, see also Mugerauer, *Heidegger's Language and Thinking* (Atlantic Highlands, N.J.: Humanities Press, 1989).

3. See John D. Caputo, "From the Deconstruction of Hermeneutics to the Hermeneutics of Deconstruction," in John Baliff, ed., *Proceedings: Eighteenth Heidegger Conference* (Stevens Point, Wis.: University of Wisconsin at Stevens Point, 1984) and "From the Primordialty of Absence to the Absence of Primordiality," in Hugh Silverman and Don Ihde, eds., *Hermeneutics and Deconstruction* (Albany: SUNY Press, 1985). Caputo brings the project to fullest fruition in *Radical Hermeneutics: Repetition, Deconstruction, and the Hermeneutical Project* (Bloomington, Ind.: Indiana University Press, 1987).
Of course, Derrida, for the most part, reads Heidegger as hopelessly mired in metaphysics. Analyzing how "Heidegger has radically decon-

structed the dominion of metaphysics by the present,'' Derrida adds, ''but the thinking of this presence can only metaphorize, by means of a profound necessity from which one cannot simply decide to escape, the language that it deconstructs.'' ''Reading Us,'' in *Margins of Philosophy* (Chicago: University of Chicago Press, 1982), 131. That is the sustained thrust of his penetrating analysis. At the same time, on a few occasions, Derrida does allow Heidegger a kind of exemption. Whether Derrida does this in order to remain consistent as the master of undecidability where nothing whatsoever is allowed to be univocal or whether he actually acknowledges a breakthrough beyond deconstruction on Heidegger's part remains undecidable. Caputo returns to stress this point repeatedly in *Radical Hermeneutics*.

4. In the course of his life, Heidegger transformed his two great themes, the question about Being and the question about truth, into what he sees and says as their deeper character. Being passes over to be thought as *Ereignis*, the primal giving, granting event; truth becomes thought as *aletheia*, the unconcealment that contains, as part of itself, concealment (*lethia* within *alethia*). For a general treatment, bibliography, and pointers to the dozens of Heidegger texts, two especially useful works are Walter Biemel, *Martin Heidegger: An Illustrated Study* (New York: Harcourt, Brace, Jovanovich, 1976) and J. L. Metha, *The Philosophy of Martin Heidegger* (New York: Harper & Row, 1966).

5. On releasement, see ''Memorial Address,'' in *Discourse on Thinking* (New York: Harper & Row, 1966).

6. See Mugerauer, ''Post-Structuralist Planning Theory'' (Austin: The University of Texas Graduate Program in Community and Regional Planning Working Paper Series, 1991).

7. David Sopher, ''The Landscape of Home,'' in D. W. Meinig, *The Interpretation of Ordinary Landscapes* (New York: Oxford University Press, 1979), 134.

8. Heidegger regularly argues that we are not yet thinking in the sense of careful meditation. See, for example, his *What is Called Thinking?* (New York: Harper & Row, 1968) and my *Heidegger's Language and Thinking*.

9. Henri Lefebvre, *The Production of Space* (Oxford: Blackwell, 1991), 120ff.

10. Also see John Pickles, *Phenomenology, Science, and Geography* (London: Cambridge University Press, 1985); A. M. Hay, ''Positivism in Human Geography,'' in R. J. Johnson and D. T. Herbert, editors, *Geography*

and the Urban Environment (New York: Wiley, 1979), vol. 2, pp. 1–26; Anne Osterrieth, "Lived Space and the Livability of Cities," in Peter Gould and Gunnar Olsson, editors, *A Search for Common Ground* (London: Pion, 1982), 58–70; Alberto Perez-Gomez, Review of Norberg-Schulz's *Concept of Dwelling,*" in *Design Book Review* 1987 (Winter): 95–97.

11. John Pickles, *Phenomenology, Science, and Geography.*

12. Denis Cosgrove, *Social Formation and the Symbolic Landscape* (Totowa, N.J.: Barnes and Noble, 1989).

13. Perez-Gomez, "Review of Norberg-Schulz's *Concept of Dwelling.*"

14. H. E. Christensen, "Geography as a Human Science," in P. Gould and G. Ollson, editors, *A Search for Common Ground,* 37–57; Derek Gregory, "Human Agency and Human Geography," *Transactions, Institute of British Geographers* 6(1981): 1–18 and "A Realist Construction of the Social," *Transactions, Institute of British Geographers* 7(1982): 254–56; J. Pickles, *Phenomenology, Science and Geography;* A. Pred, "Structuration and Place," *Journal for the Theory of Social Behavior* 13(1983): 45–68.

15. This is one of the points made by the exhibition *The West as America.* See the publication by the same title, edited by William H. Truettner (Washington, D. C.: Smithsonian Institution Press, 1991).

16. Martin Heidegger, *Being and Time* (New York: Harper & Row, 1962) and *Poetry, Language, and Thought* (New York: Harper & Row, 1971).

17. Derek Gregory, "Human Agency and Human Geography"; D. N. Livingston and R. T. Harrison, "Reflections on a Phenomenological Approach," *Journal of Environmental Psychology* 3(1983): 295–96; Mark Billinge, "The Mandarin Dialect," *Transactions of British Geography* 8(1983): 400–20.
  Or, in a derivative vein, consider the work of some recent environmental phenomenologists, work which displays the same sort of description and endorsement of "wholesome and innocent" places. To cite work close to home: I interpret "Midwestern Yards," in *Places* 2(1985) 31–38 and "Toward an Architectural Vocabulary: The Porch as Between," in David Seamon, editor, *Dwelling, Seeing, and Designing: Toward a Phenomenological Ecology* (Albany: SUNY Press, 1992); I discuss Native Americans living in the Grand Canyon in "Language and the Emergence of Environment," in David Seamon and Robert Mugerauer, editors, *Dwelling, Place and Environment*

(Dordrecht: Martinus Nijhoff, 1985), 51–70. David Seamon (with Christine Nordin) covers "Marketplace as Place Ballet," *Landscape* 24(1980): 35–41 and (with Gary Coates) Meadowcreek (a rural education retreat), a project reported on in Seamon and Coates, "Toward a Phenomenology of Place and Placemaking," *Oz* 6(1985): 6–9. Edward Relph treats *Place and Placelessness* (London: Pion, 1976). David Saile works on Zuni Pueblos, "Many Dwellings: Views of a Pueblo World"; Walter Brenneman on Irish holy wells, "The Circle and the Cross"; Fran Violich on Dalmatian villages, "Toward Revealing the Sense of Place," all three in Seamon and Mugerauer, editors, *Dwelling, Place and Environment*. Norberg-Schulz describes Khartoum and Prague in *Genius Loci* (New York: Rizzoli, 1979).

Even more to the point, home and hearth are everywhere: in my "Housing for the Full Life-Cycle," in Madas Pohak, editor, *The City in the 21st Century* (Phoenix: Arizona State University, 1988); Kim Dovey's "Home: An Ordering Principle in Space," in *Landscape* 22 no. 2 (1978): 27–30 and "Home and Homelessness," in I. Altman and C. M. Werner, editors, *Home Environments* (New York: Plenum Press, 1985), 33–64; Buttimer's "Home, Reach and Sense of Place," in A. Buttimer and D. Seamon, eds., *The Human Experience of Space and Place* (London: Croom Helm, 1980), 166–187; Seamon's "Reconciling Old and New Worlds," in Seamon and Mugerauer, editors, *Dwelling, Place and Environment*.

18. Martin Heidegger, *Discourse on Thinking; The Question Concerning Technology* (New York: Harper & Row, 1977); "Essay on Humanism" in David Krell, editor, *Basic Writings* (New York: Harper & Row, 1977), 189–242. Also see Mugerauer, *Heidegger and Homecoming*, forthcoming.

19. Martin Heidegger, *The Question Concerning Technology.*

20. Martin Heidegger, *Discourse on Thinking* and *The Question Concerning Technology.*

21. Martin Heidegger, "Poetry, Language, Thought"; "The Pathway," translated by Thomas O'Meara, *Listening* 8 (1973): 32–29.

22. Karsten Harries makes a related point when he argues for the authenticity of movement in today's environment in "Space, Place, and Ethos: Reflections on the Ethical Function of Architecture," in *artibus et historiae* 9 (1984): 159–65.

23. For example, Reiner Schurman argues that "After the 'turning,' Heidegger dismisses all root metaphors just as he dismissed the very question

of political systems. . . . Instead of tracing phenomena to their 'originary rootedness' in *Dasein*, he now says, 'The concept of "root" makes it impossible to say anything about man's relation to being.' *Vortrage und Aufsetze* 127." Schurman, *Heidegger on Being and Acting* (Bloomington, Ind.: Indiana University Press, 1987), n. 54.

24. On the possibility for the immobile, see Victor Frankl, *The Doctor and the Soul* (New York: Vintage Books, 1973); on the scholar see Thoreau, who says "A man thinking or working is always alone, let him be where he will Solitude is not measured by miles of space that intervene between a man and his fellows. A really diligent student in one of the crowded hives of Cambridge is as solitary as a dervish in the desert." *Walden* (New York: Holt, Rinehart, and Winston, 1962), 111.

25. These essays are in Eliade, *Myth and Reality* (New York: Harper & Row, 1963); *Myths, Dreams, and Mysteries* (New York: Harper & Row, 1967); *Symbolism, The Sacred, The Arts* (New York: Crossroad, 1885).

26. Martin Heidegger, *The Question Concerning Technology.*

27. To return to some of the researchers whose work was *partially* described in the critique above, but whose entire project clearly moves beyond the rustic and exotic: Seamon has focused on the nature of the city and described how the photographs of André Kertész, an emigree from political oppression, articulated the twentieth-century city. "Awareness and Relation: A Phenomenology of the Person-Environment Relationship as Portrayed in the New York Photographs of André Kertész," in *Place Images in the Media,* edited by Leo Zonn (Totowa, N.J.: Roman and Littlefield, 1990), 280–93. He has treated the city in essays such as "Different Worlds Coming Together: A Phenomenology of Relationship as Portrayed in Doris Lessing's *Diaries of Jane Somers,*" in *Dwelling, Seeing and Designing* and "Toward a Phenomenology of Citiness: Kevin Lynch's *Image of the City* and Beyond," *National Geographic Journal of India* 37 (March–June): 178–88. Norberg-Schulz produced *The Concept* of *Dwelling* and *Architecture: Meaning and Place* (New York: Rizzoli, 1988) as he shows how valued environments are existentially and ontologically set-into-work. Relph has produced books interpreting the meaning and development of the rational and modern urban landscapes: *Rational Landscapes and Humanistic Geography* (London: Croom Helm, 1981) and *The Modern Urban Landscape* (Baltimore: Johns Hopkins University Press, 1987). Dovey has refined methodology by arguing for the inclusion of critical theory in "Place, Ideology, and Post-Modernism," *Proceedings: IAPS 10* (Delft, 1988) and "Dwelling, Archetype, and Ideology," in Robert Mugerauer, ed., *Dwelling* (Austin: University of Texas Press, 1993).

28. Martin Heidegger, "The Thinker as Poet," in *Poetry, Language, Thought,* 11.

29. Mircea Eliade, *Images and Symbols* (New York: Sheed and Ward, 1969), 16–20.

30. For interesting details concerning these lectures and their publication, see Karsten Harries' excellent "Introduction" to *Martin Heidegger and National Socialism: Questions and Answers,* edited by Gunther Neske and Emil Hettering (New York: Paragon House, 1990), especially xv ff.

31. Victor Farias, *Heidegger and Nazism* (Philadelphia: Temple University Press, 1989). The book originally appeared in French in 1987 and was translated into German and English in 1989, though the story of the different translations and editions is very confused as the editors of the English translation point out in the preface (xviii–xix) and as Harries discusses in his "Introduction" to *Martin Heidegger and National Socialism* (see especially note 56). The critique of Farias's work has centered on its loose use of source material and unjustified leaps to assertion and conclusion, such as the conflation of the Sachsenhausen that was the site of concentration camp and the other Sachsenhausen that now is a Frankfurt suburb, an identification that Farias spuriously uses to make a central point in his argument. Such errors have been pointed out by many, including Hugo Ott, whose own historical work was substantially used by Farias.

32. This means to say that some of the reviews, articles, and letters were not the result of careful reading and thinking. There certainly were exceptions, such as Thomas Sheehan's first-rate review "Heidegger and the Nazis," *The New York Review of Books,* June 16, 1988, pp. 38–47.

33. Hugo Ott, *Martin Heidegger: Unterwegs Zu Seiner Biographie* (Frankfurt: Campus, 1988).

34. Karsten Harries, "Introduction" to *Martin Heidegger and National Socialism;* Thomas Sheehan, "Heidegger and the Nazis"; Michael Zimmerman, "Philosophy and Politics: The Case of Heidegger," *Philosophy Today* (Spring 1989): 3–20; Jacques Derrida, *On Spirit: Heidegger and the Question* (Chicago: University of Chicago Press, 1989); Philippe Lacoue-Labarthe, *Heidegger, Art and Politics* (Oxford: Blackwell, 1990); Jean-François Lyotard, *Heidegger and "the jews"* (Minneapolis: University of Minnesota Press, 1990); Fred Dallmayr, "Heidegger, Hölderlin, and Politics," in *Margins of Political Discourse* (Albany: SUNY Press, 1989).

35. Michael Zimmerman, *Heidegger's Confrontation with Modernity: Technology, Politics, Art* (Bloomington: Indiana University Press, 1990). Zimmerman's book also profits from Jeffrey Herf's *Reactionary Modernism: Technology, Culture, and Politics in Weimar and the Third Reich* (New York: Cambridge University Press, 1984).

36. Some of these presentations are published in Arleen B. Dallery, et al., eds., *Ethics and Danger* (Albany: SUNY Press, 1992).

37. A case in point: it has become common to criticize Heidegger for refusing to acknowledge the unspeakable horrors of the concentration camps, a fault based textually on one essay where he speaks of concentration camps while presenting a list of technological manifestations, without singling the former out as different in kind, for example, by Sheehan, Lacoue-Labarthe, and Zimmerman in the works cited above and by Levinas, "Comme un consente," *Le Nouvel Observateur*, January 22, 1988, p. 46. In fact, as should be clear to Heidegger scholars, the now notorious passage means to question and describe how things are with technology. To describe the phenomena without blinking at the dreadful confusion is *not* to *condone it*, but to hold it before us in its terrible implications and to show us the contextual fog of the concealment of meanings and differences, the blankness before the proper nature and treatment of all things that occurs at the violent heart of metaphysics, both in earlier epochs and now in the final technological era. Hanna Arendt apparently comes to the same conclusion as the result of her investigations which explore "the banality of evil." *Eichmann in Jerusalem* (New York: Harper & Row, 1971).

38. See my *Heidegger's Language and Thinking,* esp. 147–248.

39. Martin Heidegger, *On Time and Being,* 24.

40. The interested reader might look at my *Heidegger's Language and Thinking; Dwelling, Place and Environment; Heidegger and Homecoming; Post-Structuralist Planning Theory.*

41. Caputo, *Radical Hermeneutics;* and Gerald Bruins, *Heidegger's Estrangements* (New Haven: Yale University Press, 1989).

42. See Mugerauer, *Heidegger's Language and Thinking.*

43. The question is clearly put in architecture by Karsten Harries, "Thoughts on a Non-Arbitrary Architecture," *Perspecta* 19(1982): 58–69;

Michael Benedikt, *For an Architecture of Reality* (New York: Lumen Books, 1987); Thomas Thiis-Evensen, *Archetypes in Architecture* (New York: Norwegian University Press, 1987); and David Seamon's investigations into authentic life-worlds, *A Geography of the Lifeworld* (New York: St. Martin's Press, 1979); "Phenomenology and Vernacular Life-Worlds," in David Saile, editor, *Architecture in Cultural Change* (Lawrence, Kan.: University of Kansas Press, 1987), 17–24; and David Seamon and Anne Buttimer editors, *The Human Experience of Place and Space* (London: Croom Helm, 1980).

CHAPTER 7. TAKING RESPONSIBILITY FOR THE TECHNOLOGICAL LANDSCAPE

1. Martin Heidegger, *The Question Concerning Technology* (New York: Harper & Row, 1977), 12–14.

2. For the supporting analysis and argument behind the following account of the technological beyond the essays above, see Martin Heidegger, *The Question Concerning Technology;* Michael E. Zimmerman, "Beyond Humanism: Heidegger's Understanding of Technology," *Listening* 12 (Fall 1977): 74–83.

Historically, it seems to be the case that planning is a instrument of modern and technological order. See, for example, the approach positively proposed by Francis Ferguson, *Architecture, Cities and the Systems Approach* (New York: George Braziller, 1975) and the complementary critique in Michel Foucault, *Discipline and Punish: The Birth of the Prison* (New York: Pantheon, 1977) and *Madness and Civilization* (New York: Vintage, 1967); M. Christine Boyer, *Dreaming the Rational City: The Myth of American City Planning* (London: MIT Press, 1983); Alberto Perez-Gomez, *Architecture and the Crisis of Modern Science* (London: MIT Press, 1983).

3. Also see Heidegger, "Letter on Humanism," in David Krell, editor, *Basic Writings* (New York: Harper & Row, 1977); "The End of Philosophy and the Task of Thinking," in *On Time and Being* (New York: Harper & Row, 1972); "Building Dwelling Thinking" and "The Thing" in *Poetry, Language, Thought* (New York: Harper & Row, 1971).

4. *The Question Concerning Technology,* 15–17.

5. Heidegger does not say human will; he is concerned with Will in the metaphysical tradition, where it appears as another name for Being, and not merely a human faculty. But, the larger issue of Will in relation to human will is not our immediate concern here. See Nietzsche, *The Will to Power* (New York: Vintage Books, 1968); Heidegger, *Nietzsche* (New York: Harper & Row, 1979) and *The End of Philosophy* (New York: Harper & Row, 1973).

6. On technology as the systemic and modular, see below. On modular expansion of MUDs, see Kent Butler, "Growth Patterns in Texas: Missouri City, San Marcos, and McKinney," a paper presented to the Growth Forum, University of Texas at Austin, October 1985.

7. Foucault uses the pattern and logic of Heidegger's epochal historical unfolding and works out how cultures constitute themselves practically. See the essays above on Foucault and Heidegger.

8. Hence, for example, Christopher Alexander speaks of the modular as the identical in contrast to the natural and its variety. *The Timeless Way of Building* (New York: Oxford University Press, 1979), 144–46; cf. the metaphysical and epistemological foundation of the phenomena as worked out by Leibniz in his theory of the identity of indiscernables and the indiscernability of identicals.

9. From the work describing and criticizing urban renewal, see Harvey Perloff, "Common Goals and the Linking of Physical and Social Planning," *Planning* (1965); Peter Rossi and Robert A. Dentler, *The Politics of Urban Renewal* (New York: The Free Press of Glencoe, 1961); Maurice Friedman, "Urban Redevelopment and Renewal," *Government and Slum Housing* (Chicago: University of Chicago Press, 1965); Martin Anderson, *The Federal Bulldozer: A Critical Analysis of Urban Renewal 1949–1962*.

10. *One Hundred Years of Solitude* (New York: Harper & Row, 1970), 232–33. García-Márquez explores the complex ambivalence of loss and gain; the quoted passage is followed by a depiction of the disorder and the illusion of opportunity attending the "avalanche of strangers."

11. Rudolf Arnheim, *The Dynamics of Architectural Form* (Berkeley: University of California Press, 1977), 145–46.

12. There is a huge and growing place literature; it is discussed in chapter ten below and note 3 of the same.

13. See Stephen Toulmin, *Cosmopolis* (New York: Free Press, 1989).

14. On the critique of the modernist movement's failure to provide adequate housing, see Peter Blake, *Form Follows Fiasco: Why Modern Architecture Hasn't Worked* (Boston: Little, Brown, and Co, 1971); Philippe Boudon, *Lived-In Architecture: Le Corbusier's Pessac Revisited* (Cambridge, Mass.: MIT Press, 1979); James Holston, *The Modernist City: An Anthropological Critique of Brasilia* (Chicago: University of Chicago Press).

15. On the technological landscape as a ''non-visual'' ordering of space, see Mugerauer, ''The Historical Dynamic of the American Landscape,'' paper presented at the annual meeting of CELA 1985 and ''The Three Forms of Chicago,'' paper presented at AAG 1986, Minneapolis, and ''Chicago: Lessons For Bio-Regional Design,'' *CRIT* (Fall 1986).

16. See my ''The Post-Structuralist Sublime: From Heterotopia to Dwelling?,'' a videotaped lecture presented to the Department of Landscape Architecture at the University of Minnesota, January 1991.

17. On terraforming, see James Oberg, *New Earths* (New York: Meridian, 1980) and Oberg, editor, *The Terraforming Papers: Proceedings of the 1979 Houston Colloquium on Terraforming.* (Harrisburg, Penn.: Stackpole Books, 1979). Also, on the vision of spatial landscapes, see T. Heppenheimer, *Colonies in Space* (Harrisburg, Penn.: Stackpole Books, 1977). Also see Ettore Sottsass, *Ettore Sottsass Associates: 1980–1988* (New York: Rizzoli, 1988).

18. Paulo Soleri, *Arcology* (Cambridge, Mass.: MIT Press, 1969); C. A. Doxiadis, *Anthropopolis* (New York: W. W. Norton, 1964).

19. Carl Jung, *Memories, Dreams, and Reflections* (New York: Random House, 1963); Victor Frankl, *The Doctor and the Soul* (New York: Vintage Books, 1973).

20. This is not to deny that landscapes may serve important memorializing or even nostalgic functions; rather, it is to claim that as the necessary response to the technological, the inhabited public landscape needs to be much more than anything nostalgic.

21. Jellicoe calls the plan ''surrealistic'' on p. 19 of his *The Landscape of Civilization: Created for the Moody Historical Gardens, Designed and Described by Geoffrey Jellicoe* (Northiam, East Sussex: Garden Art Press Ltd., 1989). Also see E. M. Farrelly, ''The Triumph of Jellicoe,'' *Architectural Review* 1063 (Sept. 1985). Though it can not be developed here, another traditional strategy which can be adapted in regard to the technological is that of ''mole warfare.'' We may find simple and effective ways to maintain the natural in the face of the technological by cultivating the equivalents of roadways, railroad rights of way, and graveyards which have preserved the indigenous ecosystems in the modern industrial landscape.

22. Kent C. Bloomer and C. W. Moore, *Body, Memory, and Architecture* (New Haven: Yale University Press, 1977).

23. Fay Jones, "Reinvesting the Old with New Meaning," lecture delivered at the School of Architecture, University of Texas at Austin, 27 February 1992.

24. Our culture maintains traditions that enable us to come to terms with the timeless dimensions of the social and natural world. For example, Americans consistently have rejected modernism's skepticism, relativism, and disillusionment, affirming instead the common—culturally shared—view that things do have an inherent set of characteristics, potentials, and limitations which can be imaginatively modified, but which also need to be respected. See, for example, T. J. J. Lears, *No Place of Grace* (New York: Pantheon, 1981). In this regard, it may be that the postmodern indulges in modernity's escape by fostering fanciful play of the images and forms of our tradition without seeking or accepting their full import and implications.

25. From among his prolific work, especially see *Architectural Anthropology: Research Series,* volume 1: *The Present Relevance of the Primitive in Architecture* (Lausanne, Switzerland: Structura Mundi Editions, 1992) and "Architectural Anthropology—Why Do We Need a General Framework?," *Proceedings,* Second International Conference of the International Association for the Study of Traditional Environments (IASTE), October 1991, Berkeley.

26. "Architectural Anthropology: Outline of a Constructive Human Past," in *Architectural Anthropology,* 145–71.

27. "Architectural Anthropology as Inductive Theory of Architecture," in *Architectural Anthropology,* 81.

28. Ibid.

29. "The Palaeolithic Tectiforms: A Soft Prehistory?," in *Architectural Anthropology,* 143.

CHAPTER 8. FITTING PLACEMENT

1. Martin Heidegger, "Memorial Address," in *Discourse on Thinking* (New York: Harper & Row, 1966), p. 54.

2. Heidegger, "Memorial Address," 17.

3. This sets aside the question of the sense in which subatomic particles are "things" as opposed to processes or forces whose effects alone can be observed.

4. Adolf Portmann, *Animal Camouflage* (Ann Arbor: University of Michigan, 1959). Portmann's analysis of camouflage is followed closely in this section.

5. On biocultural regions as the basis for design and living, see Gary Coates, *Resettling America* (Andover, Mass.: Brick House Press, 1981); Kirkpatrick Sale, *Dwellers in the Land* (San Francisco: Sierra Club Books, 1985). Also see note number 3 on place literature in the final chapter.

6. See Kimberly Dovey, "The Quest for Authenticity and the Replication of Environmental Meaning," in David Seamon and R. Mugerauer, editors, *Dwelling, Place, and Environment* (Dordrecht: Martinus Nijhoff, 1985).

7. Crowe, *Tomorrow's Landscape* (London: The Architectural Press, 1956), 30–32, 74–75, 152ff., 161–65; Nan Fairbrother, *New Lives, New Landscapes* (New York: Knopf, 1970).

8. C. S. Stein and H. Wright, *Toward New Towns for America* (Cambridge, Mass.: MIT Press, 1957).

9. Edmund Burger, *Geomorphic Architecture* (New York: Van Nostrand Reinhold Co., 1986).

10. Doxiadis has commented on the development of built forms from the "roots upward."

11. Of course, many people complain of the monotony of dense forests, deserts, plains, the Arctic, oceans, and so on. But, arguments can be made that much of this is a function of behavioral goals, for example, to get something done somewhere else, to find a "scene," or to have an adventure, rather than the result of a deficit of inherent richness of the landscapes themselves. Indeed, the perception often changes, for example, if the place is the location where the action is to be accomplished or if a change in attitude and understanding enable a deeper seeing.

12. Interestingly, ecology has a dual nature: in one aspect it is fully scientific and adapted to the technological and thus systemic; in another, it articulates a way of living, in union with the earth's mystery, so that "deep ecology" is akin to originary thinking.

13. For an introduction to fractiles see the essay on Mandlebrot by James Gleick in his *Chaos: Making A New Science* (New York: Viking, 1987) and

Benot Mandelbrot, *The Fractile Geometry of Nature* (New York: W. H. Freeman & Co, 1983).

14. Crowe, *Tomorrow's Landscape*, 14–15, 28, 30–33, 66, 73, 92–93, 151ff., 184; Fairbrother, *New Lives*, 132, 218, 224–29.

15. Crowe, *Tomorrow's Landscape*, 15, 151ff; Fairbrother, *New Lives*, 311ff.

16. The DFW Airport has been both praised and criticized. For coverage that describes its systemic design, see Edward G. Blankenship, *The Airport: Architecture, Urban Integration, and Ecological Problems* (New York: Praeger Publishers, 1974).

17. C. D. Johnson and P. Marcias, "Report on Orientation and Site Visit," on 8 July 1969 (document number 20679), p. 2.

18. For the striking Japanese images, see Hideyuki Oka, *How to Wrap Five Eggs: Japanese Design and Traditional Packaging*, photography by Michikazu Sakai (New York: Harper & Row, 1967). From the large literature on Kahn, see especially Heitz Ronner et al., *Louis I. Kahn: The Complete Works 1935–1974* (New York: Birkhouser, 1987); John Lobell, *Between Silence and Light: Architecture of Louis I. Kahn* (Boulder: Shambhala, 1979); Alexandra Tyng, *Louis I. Kahn's Philosophy of Architecture* (New York: Wiley, 1984); my "Architecture as Properly Useful Opening."

19. On figural unity, see Louis Mackey, *Kierkegaard: A Kind of Poet* (Philadelphia: University of Pennsylvania Press, 1971), 259ff.; Erich Auerbach, "Figura," in *Scenes from the Drama of European Literature* (New York: Meridian Books, 1959), 11–76. The use of "figura" here is *not* the same as in C. Norberg-Schulz' *The Concept Of Dwelling: On the Way to a Figurative Architecture*.

20. David Seamon treats the topic in "Towards a Phenomenology of Environmental Meaning: The Example of Flowforms," in *The National Geographical Journal of India* 34, pt. 1 (March 1988): 66–74. And see J. Wilkes, "Flowforms: An Innovative Approach to the Rhythmic Properties and Uses of Water," *Planned Innovation* 3: 97–103.

21. See Nadar Ardalan, *Nuran: The City of Illumination* (Isfahan, Tehran, Iran: Mandala Collaborative, 1978); Cf. Nadar Ardalan and Laleh Bakhtiar, *The Sense of Unity: The Sufi Tradition in Persian Architecture*

(Chicago: University of Chicago Press, 1979); Hans Asplund, "Twotown," *Ekistics* 306 (May/June 1984): 267–78.

22. Martin Heidegger holds that "use" does not merely mean utilization or exploiting, but more fundamentally, a fitting response to the essential nature of a thing. *What Is Called Thinking* (New York: Harper & Row, 1968), 186ff. See my *Heidegger's Language and Thought*, 97, 99, 132–33, 233–34.

23. Soleri, *Arcology*, passim.

24. This does not take up the issue of sexist language. At the nonliteral archetypal level, the archetype itself indicates the need and result of the union of naturally given fecundity (e.g., Mother Earth) and human cultivation (e.g. husbanding).

25. See Martin Heidegger on sparing and preserving as the basic features of dwelling, "Building, Dwelling, Thinking," in *Poetry, Language, Thought* (New York: Harper & Row, 1971).

26. Crowe, *Tomorrow's Landscape*. And note the affinities in tone and approach in phenomenology, Zen, and the work of Christopher Alexander and Ian McHarg. (For example, see, respectively, David Seamon and Robert Mugerauer, eds., *Dwelling, Place, and Environment;* Shin'ichi Hisamatsu, *Zen and the Fine Arts* (New York: Kodansha International, 1971); *The Timeless Way of Building* (New York: Oxford University Press, 1979; *Design With Nature* (New York: Doubleday, 1971).

27. On attunement (*Gestimmtheit* and *Stimmung*) in Heidegger, see William J. Richardson, *Heidegger: Through Phenomenology to Thought* (The Hague: Martinus Nijhoff, 1963).

CHAPTER 9. HOMELESSNESS AND THE HUMAN CONDITION

1. Oscar Handlin, *The Uprooted* (Boston: Little, Brown, & Co., 1973), 129ff. Cf. Heidegger's and Foucault's analysis in the essays above in part one; Edward Relph, *Place and Placelessness* (London: Pion, 1976); Michael Hough, *Out of Place: Restoring Identity to the Regional Landscape* (New Haven: Yale University Press, 1990).

2. Thoreau, *Walden* (New York: Holt, Reinhart, and Winston, 1962), 11–12.

3. From the large literature, see especially Robert Bellah, *Habits of the Heart* (Berkeley: University of California Press, 1985); Peter Berger, B. Berger, and H. Kellner, *The Homeless Mind* (New York: Vintage, 1974);

Marshall Berman, *All That Is Solid Melts into Air* (New York: Simon and Schuster, 1982); Martin Buber, "What is Man?" in *Between Man and Man* (New York: Macmillan, 1972), 118–205; Oscar Handlin, *The Uprooted* (Boston: Little, Brown and Co., 1973); Martin Heidegger, *Being and Time* (New York: Harper & Row, 1962); Joshua Meyrowitz, *No Sense of Place* (New York: Oxford University Press, 1985); Edward Relph, *Place and Placelessness;* Michael Hough, *Out of Place.*

4. Erwin Straus, *Phenomenological Psychology* (New York: Basic Books, 1966) and Richard Zaner, *The Problem of Embodiment* (The Hague: Martinus Nijhoff, 1971).

5. *Human Nature* (New York: Schocken, 1963).

6. Carl Jung, *Symbols of Transformation* (Princeton: Princeton University Press, 1967).

7. Eric Erikson, "Identity and the Life Cycle" *Psychological Issues,* 1, no.1: 89.

8. Oscar Handlin, *The Uprooted;* and with Mary F. Handlin, *Facing Life* (Boston: Little, Brown and Co., 1971).

9. Graham Rowles, "Between Worlds: A Relocation Dilemma for the Appalachian Elderly," *International Journal of Aging* 17:4.

10. Victor Frankl, *The Doctor and the Soul* (New York: Vintage Books, 1973); and Carl Jung, *Modern Man in Search of a Soul* (New York: Harcourt, Brace, Jovanovich, 1955).

11. On the importance of action, see Robert Inchausti, *The Ignorant Perfection of Ordinary People* (Albany: SUNY Press, 1991).

12. Of course, to understand the whole phenomenon, we would need the complementary description of attempts to become at home in rural and wilderness settings. See, for example, my "American Nature as Paradise," forthcoming, and Robin Doughty, *At Home in Texas: Early Views of the Land* (College Station, Tex.: Texas A & M University Press, 1987).

13. Michel Foucault, *Madness and Civilization* (New York: Random House, 1965) and *Discipline and Punish* (New York: Vintage, 1979).

14. Because there is an enormous variety and detail behind the genuinely common pattern of experience and event, for the sake of a coherent and brief presentation, much of the following discussion closely follows the thread presented by Handlin in *The Uprooted;* see also Peter Berger et al., *The Homeless Mind;* Gideon Sjoberg, *The Preindustrial City: Past and Present* (New York: Macmillan, 1960); Lyn H. Lofland, *A World of Strangers* (New York: Basic Books, 1973).

15. The following section is a synopsis of Handlin's *The Uprooted.*

16. It is an important task, though beyond the scope of this book, to trace the phenomena of seeing the world as the product of a human making back to its earliest stages, for example, in the Greek and Roman *ethos.* See, Martin Heidegger, "Letter on Humanism," in David Krell, ed. *Basic Writings* (New York: Harper & Row, 1977), 189–242.

17. Mircea Eliade, *Myth and Reality* (New York: Harper & Row, 1963) and *Myths, Dreams, and Mysteries* (New York: Harper & Row, 1960); Oscar Handlin, *The Uprooted.*

18. From the large literature on the topic of attitudes toward and treatment of the "dark-skinned," see Richard Drinnon, *Facing West: The Metaphysics of Indian Hating and Empire Building* (Minneapolis: University of Minnesota Press, 1980); Paul Jacobs and Saul Landau with Eve Pell, *To Serve the Devil* (New York: Vintage Books, 1971); Dale Van Every, *Disinherited* (New York: Avon Books, 1966).

19. Martin Heidegger, *The Question Concerning Technology* (New York: Harper & Row, 1977) and "Letter on Humanism"; Manuel Castells, *The Space Question* (Oxford: Basil Blackwell, 1990).

CHAPTER 10. A HOMECOMING: DESIGN OF BEHALF OF PLACE

1. Martin Heidegger, "Building Dwelling, Thinking," in *Poetry Language, Thought* (New York: Harper & Row, 1971), 71.

2. These points result especially from the analyses above, "Technology and Originary Dwelling" and "Taking Responsibility for the Technological Landscape."

3. There has been such a boom in place studies and literature in the last several years that any listing can only hint at the literature and inevitably will

leave out a large number of worthy works and approaches. The now venerable classics include Yi-Fu Tuan, *Space and Place* (Minneapolis: University of Minnesota Press, 1977) and *Topophilia* (Englewood Cliffs, N.J.: Prentice Hall, 1974); Edward Relph, *Place and Placelessness* (London: Pion, 1976); Christian Norberg-Schulz, *Genius Loci* (New York: Rizzoli, 1979); Kevin Lynch, *The Image of the City* (Cambridge, Mass.: MIT Press, 1960); J. B. Jackson's many works, such as *Discovering the Vernacular Landscape* (New Haven: Yale University Press, 1984).

More recent interesting works are Christopher Day, *Places of the Soul* (Northamptonshire: Aquarian Press, 1990); Robin Doughty, *At Home in Texas;* Tony Hiss, *The Experience of Place* (New York: Knopf, 1990); Michael Hough, *Out of Place;* Belden Lane, *Landscapes of the Sacred* (New York: Paulist Press, 1988); Joshua Meyrowitz, *No Sense of Place* (New York: Oxford University Press, 1985); Ray Oldenburg, *The Great Good Place* (New York: Paragon, 1989); John F. Sears, *Sacred Places: American Tourist Attractions of the Nineteenth Century* (New York: Oxford University Press, 1989); Dell Upton and John Vlach, editors, *Common Places: Readings in American Vernacular Architecture* (Athens: University of Georgia Press, 1986); E. V. Walter, *Placeways: A Theory of the Human Environment* (Chapel Hill: University of North Carolina Press, 1988). Also part of the phenomena is the success of *Places: A Quarterly Journal of Environmental Design.* In addition, a series of interesting Ph.D. dissertations are appearing on the topic, such as those in Geography and American Studies at the University of Texas at Austin: Barbara Parmenter, "The Northern Lakes of Egypt: Encounters with a Wetland Environment" (1991); and, in progress, Tim Davis, "Snowbirds: An Ethnographic and Photographic Investigation of Retirement in the American Southwest"; John Morris, "El Llano Estacado: Early Environmental Perception and Deception on the Great Staked Plain" (1992); Janet Valenza, "Creation and Dissolution of Place: Taking the Waters in Texas" (1993).

4. "Architecture as Properly Useful Opening," in Charles Scott and R. Dallery, editors, *Ethics and Danger: Essays on Heidegger and Continental Thought* (Albany: SUNY Press, 1992).

5. On Buber and the "realistic imagination," see Martin Buber, *Between Man and Man* (New York: Macmillan, 1972) and my "Buildings, Imagination, and Reality," forthcoming in ACSA *Proceedings.*

6. Ray Oldenburg, *The Great Good Place;* Jane Jacobs, *The Death and Life of Great American Cities* (New York: Random House); William Whyte, *Social Life in Small Urban Spaces* (Washington, D.C.: The Conservation Foundation, 1980); Oscar Handlin, *The Uprooted.*

7. See Mario Manieri-Elia, "Toward an 'Imperial City': Daniel H. Burnham and the City Beautiful Movement," in Manfredo Tafuri et al., *The American City: From the Civil War to the New Deal* (Cambridge, Mass.: MIT Press, 1973), section on the laissez-faire city, 1ff.

8. See, for example, Jusuch Koh, "Survival Kits For Architects through Cultural Changes into the Post Industrial Age: An American Perspective," in *Proceedings*, (EDRA 16, New York: July, 1985).

9. See J. B. Jackson, *Discovering the Vernacular Landscape* (New Haven: Yale University Press, 1984) and *The Necessity for Ruins* (Amherst: University of Massachusetts Press, 1980); John R. Stilgoe, *Common Landscape of America: 1580 to 1845* (New Haven: Yale University Press, 1982).

10. Scholarship shows that such closure and "stability," though certainly real, has not prevailed to the extent that the stereotype would have it. See Oscar Handlin's analytical and concluding remarks on the peasant village, *The Uprooted* (Boston: Little, Brown and Company, 1973), 308ff.; Max Beloff, "The Uprooted," *Encounter 1* (December 1954): 78ff.

11. On the transformations of people in the technological systems, see Manuel Castells, *The Spatial Question.*

12. This is the lesson of Hölderlin's experience and poetry. See Heidegger's famous interpretation of Hölderlin's elegy "Homecoming": "Remembrance of the Poet," translated by Douglas Scott, in Werner Brock, editor, *Existence and Being* (Chicago: Henry Regnery, 1967).

13. See Michael Thompson's paper on occupation of space in inner London, "Your Place or Mine?," delivered at IAPS 8, Berlin, July 1984.

14. On the figures noted, see Heitz Renner et al., *Louis I. Kahn Complete Works, 1935–74;* M. Quantrill, *Alvar Aalto: A Critical Study* (New York: New Amsterdam, 1989); Herman Herzberger et al., *Aldo van Eyck* (Amsterdam: Stichting Wonen, 1982); Johnson, *Charles Moore: Buildings and Projects* (New York: Rizzoli, 1986); Christopher Alexander) *Pattern Language.* On the movement of community design, see Gary Coates, *Resettling America* (Andover, Mass.: Brick House, 1981), passim.

The figure most obviously missing from this list is Hassan Fathy. In earlier drafts, I had elaborated his contribution, but now do not include it because of the evidence that the projects do not finally work economically and politically and because of the vexing questions about the authenticity of his "invented" vernacular forms and artificial behavior patterns. There is no doubt, however, about his importance as an inspiration and explorer of what can be done. His groundbreaking efforts to incorporate historical and cultural interpretations of bioregions into the design process in projects for the rural community in Gournia on the upper Nile begin to work out the problems faced by an effort in today's technological world to rejuvenate traditional building techniques and materials, which, in turn, might establish a pattern of belonging to the local earth and climate, cultural and religious-cosmic forms. The question substantially is how to memorialize systems of value and also unfold future possibilities.

See Hasam Fathy, *Architecture for the Poor* (Chicago: University of Chicago Press, 1988) and *Natural Energy and Vernacular Architecture* (Chicago: University of Chicago Press, 1986); James Steele, *Hassan Fathy* (New York: St. Martin's Press, 1988).

15. See Charles Moore, Gerald Allen, Donlyn Lyndon, *The Place of Houses* (New York: Holt, Rinehart, and Winston, 1974).

16. As noted above in chapter three, postmodern architecture needs to be deconstructed, since the postmodern is itself a deconstruction of tradition.

17. On psychological ideas about persons, see Robert Moore and Douglas Gillette, *King, Warrior, Magician, Lover: Rediscovering the Archetypes of the Mature Masculine* (San Francisco: Harper Collins, 1990) and the corresponding feminist works, many of which also focus on space.

18. Erik Erikson, *Childhood and Society* (New York: W. W. Norton, 1963), 237, and "Identity and the Life Cycle," *Psychological Issues* 1, no. 1:89.

19. Erikson, himself an immigrant, considers the issue of personal identity and childhood within the context of the dynamic polarity of stability and movement, especially characteristic of America, and in spatial terms. Too often, he believes, in American society and much of the Western world, "communities are so heterogeneous, disorganized, and rapidly changing that they can not provide their children with the consistency of support and recognition necessary for the development of a viable identity." See Don Browning, "Erikson and the Search for a Normative Image of Man," in Peter Homans, editor, *Childhood and Selfhood: Essays on Erikson* (London: Associated University Presses, 1978), 271ff.

The topic is helpfully researched by Robert Coles, who has demonstrated that the relationships within the family initially determine the ease with which we accept and express emotion, the degree we think of ourselves as individuals and as members of groups, the extent to which we move freely in the built and natural environments, and our later isolation or integration to outside society and institutions. See *Children of Crisis* (Boston: Little, Brown and Company, 1977), five volumes and *The Migrant Farmer* (Birmingham: Southern Regional Council, 1965).

Importantly, both Erikson and Coles hold that the placement which leads to healthy self-identity is *first in all a placement in human relationships and only secondly a spatial location.* For example, migrant farmworker children have a strong sense of self-confidence, emotional closeness, and belonging in the realm of their large, extended families and an estrangement from, and guarded attitude toward, "outside" institutions. The lesson here is that we need to more fully distinguish and analyze (1) the differences and connections between stable or mobile spatial location and social relationships, and also (2) our cultural attitudes and assumptions about the supposed "non-belonging" of migrants, nomads, and "drifters," before we can adequately "design" to encourage being at home. At the very least, we need to stay alert to the dangers of the careless application of middle-class *prejudices and assumptions* regarding the connection (taken, uncritically, to be the identity) of (1) "stable" relationships with others to (2) "stable" residence—an attitude which too often *unthoughtfully* identifies "being at home" with "staying in one spatial location." Also see Robert Mugerauer, "Migrant Farm Worker Children: Self-Identity and Attitudes toward Place," *Proceedings* of the Educational Commission of the States, San Antonio, 1984.

20. Dolores Hayden, *Redesigning the American Dream* (New York: W. W. Norton, 1984), 167ff.

21. Ibid., 166–67.

22. "Bridge over Troubled Water," *Architect's Journal* (Sept. 27, 1972): 680–84.

23. Karen A. Frank and Sherry Ahrentzen, *New Households, New Housing* (New York: Van Nostrand Reinhold, 1989); K. McCamant and C. Durrett, *Cohousing: A Contemporary Approach to Housing Ourselves* (Berkeley: Habitat Press, 1988).

24. Graham Rowles, "Between Worlds: A Relocation Dilemma for the Appalachian Elderly," *International Journal of Aging* 17, no. 4.

25. Graham Rowles, "The Surveillance Zone as Meaningful Space for the Aged," *Gerontologist* 21, no. 3: 305, 309.

26. Ibid., 308.

27. Ibid.

28. H.-W. Hämer and Stan Krätke, "Urban Renewal without Displacement," *Architecture in Progress: Internationale Bauausstellung Berlin 1984,* edited by Frank Russell (New York: St. Martin's Press, 1983), 27–30 and H.-W. Hämer, "The Center City as a Place to Live," *Urban Design International* 2, no. 6 (Sept./Oct. 1981): 18–19; Dennis Domer, "Building among Builders in Berlin: The IBA," *Proceedings: 1984 Southwest Regional ACSA Meeting* (Austin: University of Texas Press, 1984), *International Building Exhibition Berlin 1987* (Tokyo: ATU Publishing Co., 1987). Hämer's idea of "careful urban renewal" is close to Roberta Graz's "urban husbandry," in *The Living City* (New York: Simon & Schuster, 1989).

29. Britz, *The Edible City Resource Manual* (Los Angeles: William Kaufman, 1981); Gary Coates, *Resettling America;* also see Sim van der Ryn and Peter Calthorp, *Sustainable Communities* (San Francisco: Sierra Club Books, 1986).

30. See, for example, Michael Andrizky and Klaus Spitzer, editors, *Grun in der Stadt* (Hamburg: Rowohlt, 1981); and documentation at IAPS 8 in West Berlin, July 1984.

31. Coates, *Resettling America,* 401.

32. Ibid., 402.

33. Ibid., 401–2, 475–515.

34. Terry Harkness, "Landscape Designs," in *Places* 3, no. 3 (1986); 6–9.

35. This example is drawn directly from Robert Mugerauer and J. V. DeSousa, "Murcutt, Heidegger, and a No-Longer-Technological Architecture," presented at the Third Conference on Built Form and Culture, held at Arizona State University, Fall 1989. The analysis of the Neville Fredericks House is by J. V. DeSousa from this presentation and is based on his experience while staying with the architect in Australia and on the architect's Project Description Sheet. Also utilized are J. V. DeSousa, "Realist Architecture in the Australian Idiom: The Work of Glenn Murcutt," in *Center: Buildings and Reality* (New York: Rizzoli, 1988), volume 4, 90–99; Philip

Drew, *Leaves of Iron* (Sydney: Law Book Co., 1985); Jennifer Taylor, "Revision of a Corrugated Iron Tradition," in *Architecture and Urbanism*, 11, no. 146 (November 1982); 113–18.

36. Cited in Drew, *Leaves of Iron*, 55.

37. Taylor, "Revision of a Corrugated Iron Tradition," 113–18.

38. Drew, *Leaves of Iron*, 123.

39. The claim is that Murcutt's work exemplifies a Heideggerian attitude toward design, not that Murcutt knows or uses Heidegger's thinking. In fact, when asked, the architect responded that he remains innocent of influence from the philosopher.

40. G. E. Kidder Smith, *Switzerland Builds* (New York: Albert Bonnier, 1950), 79, 120; *The Architecture of Ricardo Legorreta*, edited by Wayne Attoe and Brisken (Austin: University of Texas Press, 1990); Michael Benedikt, *For An Architecture of Reality* (New York: Lumen Books, 1987) and "Craftsmanship," *Texas Architect* 30, no. 5 (Sept./Oct. 1980); 26–37; Gary Coates and David Seamon, "Promoting a Foundational Ecology Practically through Christopher Alexander's Pattern Language: The Example of Meadowcreek," in Seamon, ed., *Dwelling, Seeing and Designing*; Christopher Alexander, *Pattern Language* (New York: Oxford University Press, 1971) and Christopher Alexander with Howard Davis, Julio Martinez, and Donald Conner, *The Production of Houses* (New York: Oxford University Press, 1985).

41. Sinclair Black, "Keeping Austin Austin," *Urban Design International*, no. 2:44; Gordon Cullen, *Townscape* (London: Architectural Press, 1961). Anne Vernez-Moudon and P. Laconte, *Streets as Public Property* (Seattle: University of Washington Press, 1984); Charles Moore et al., *The Place of Houses*. Kenneth McDowell, "Housing and Culture for Native Groups in Canada," in Setha M. Low and Erve Chambers, editors, *Housing, Culture and Design* (Philadelphia: University of Pennsylvania Press, 1989) uses a protocol of J. C. Simon, R. R. Forster, T. Alcose, E. A. Braber, and F. Ndubisi from "A Culturally Sensitive Approach to Planning and Design with Native Canadians" (Ottawa: Canadian Mortgage Housing Corp., 1984). Kent Butler et al., *Management Options for Austin's Nature Preserves* (Austin: City of Austin, 1984) and Butler and the EHA Team, *Balcones Canyonlands Conservation Plan* (City of Austin: Environmental and Conservation Service Department, 1992).

42. Christian Norberg-Schulz, *Genius Loci* and *The Concept of Dwelling*; Botond Bognar, "A Phenomenological Approach to Architecture and Its

Teaching in the Design Studio," in D. Seamon and R. Mugerauer, *Dwelling, Place, and Environment* (Dordrecht: Martinus Nijhoff, 1985) and Botond Bognar, *The Challenge of Japanese Architecture* (New York: Van Nostrand Reinhold, 1984); Kimberly Dovey, "The Quest for Authenticity and the Replication of Environmental Meaning," in Seamon and Mugerauer, *Dwelling, Place and Environment,* "The Creation of a Sense of Place: The Case of Preshil," *Places* 1, no. 2 (Winter 1984): 32–40, and "Dwelling, Archetype, and Ideology," in *Dwelling,* edited by R. Mugerauer (Austin: University of Texas Press, 1993); Wayne Attoe, editor, The *Architecture of Ricardo Legorreta* and (with Don Logan) *American Urban Architecture: Catalysts in the Design of Cities.*

43. Thomas Thiis-Evensen, *Archetypes in Architecture* (New York: Norwegian University Press, 1987); Francis Violich, " 'Urban' Reading and the Design of Small Urban Places: The Village of Sutivan," *Town Planning Review* 54 (1983): 41–62 and "Towards Revealing the Sense of Place: An Intuitive 'Reading' of Four Dalmatian Towns," in Seamon and Mugerauer, *Dwelling, Place, and Environment;* Robin Doughty, *Wildlife and Man in Texas: Environmental Change and Change* (College Station, Tex.: Texas A&M University Press, 1983) and *At Home in Texas: Early Views of the Land* (College Station, Tex.: Texas A&M Press, 1987); David Seamon, *A Geography of the Lifeworld* (New York: St. Martin's Press, 1979), "Phenomenology and Vernacular Life-Worlds," in David Saile, ed., *Architecture in Cultural Change* (Lawrence, Kan.: University of Kansas Press, 1987), 17–24, and (co-edited with Anne Buttimer) *The Human Experience of Place and Space* (London: Croom Helm, 1980), and his edited *Dwelling, Seeing and Designing* (Albany: SUNY Press, 1993).

44. Clarence Stein and Henry Wright, *Toward New Towns for America* (Cambridge, Mass.: MIT Press, 1957); Hugo Leipziger-Pearce, "The Roots and Directions of Organic Architecture," *The Texas Quarterly,* 1 (Spring 1962) and *The Architectonic City in the Americas 8 Significant Forms, Origins and Prospects* (Austin: University of Texas Press, 1944.)

45. J. F. C. Turner, *Housing by People* (New York: Pantheon Books, 1977).

46. Helping people in their own articulation of the world is akin to the goal of educator Paulo Freire; see Freire's *Pedagogy of the Oppressed* (New York: The Seabury Press, 1970) and *Education for Critical Consciousness* (New York: The Seabury Press, 1973). Also, Jürgen Habermas, *Theory of Communicative Action* (Boston: Beacon Press, 1984 and 1987), 2 volumes.

47. On "creative participation," see Norberg-Schulz, *Genius Loci* (New York: Rizzoli, 1980), 182ff. Norberg-Schulz's phrase does not refer to "user design"; rather, also following Heidegger, it indicates the historical and existential unfolding of meaning and value necessary for a person's inner and outer dimensions. The idea, as Norberg-Schulz uses it, is essentially the same as that worked out above (using philosophical anthropology and Heidegger), which delineates the self's need for *internal* coherence and value and also for significant *external* relations to society, nature, and the sacred. Also, see Owen Barfield's development of "original and final participation" in *Saving the Appearances* (New York: Harcourt, Brace and World, 1965).

48. Many places around the world testify to our memories and present moral dilemmas, even when we effeciently suppress or erase all physical traces. This topic is treated, especially for the United States, by Kenneth Foote in his research on "landscapes of violence," particularly those sites where we elimate or refuse commemorative markers of violent events. See his "Stigmata of National Identity: Exploring the Cosmography of America's Civil Religion," in Shue T. Wong, editor, *Person, Place, and Thing: Interpretive and Empirical Essays in Cultural Geography, Geosciences and Man* (Baton Rouge, La.: Department of Geography and Anthropology, 1992), 379–402; "To Remember and Forget: Archival Memory and Culture," *American Archivist* 53 (1990): 378–92.

INDEX